Rugby

FOR

DUMMIES®

3RD EDITION

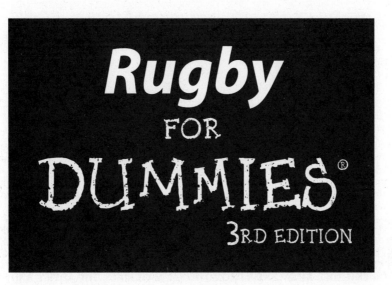

Rugby
FOR
DUMMIES®
3RD EDITION

by Mathew Brown
Patrick Guthrie
Greg Growden

WILEY

John Wiley & Sons Canada, Ltd.

Rugby For Dummies®, 3rd Edition

Published by
John Wiley & Sons Canada, Ltd.
6045 Freemont Boulevard
Mississauga, ON L5R 4J3
www.wiley.com

For general information on John Wiley & Sons Canada, Ltd., including all books published by Wiley Publishing Inc., please call our warehouse, Tel. 1-800-567-4797. For reseller information, including discounts and premium sales, please call our sales department, Tel. 416-646-7992. For press review copies, author interviews, or other publicity information, please contact our publicity department, Tel. 416-646-4582, Fax 416-236-4448.

For authorization to photocopy items for corporate, personal, or educational use, please contact in writing The Canadian Copyright Licensing Agency (Access Copyright). For an Access Copyright license, visit www.accesscopyright.ca or call toll free 1-800-893-5777.

Brown, Mathew (Mathew Timothy)

    Rugby for dummies / by Mathew Brown, Patrick Guthrie, Greg Growden. — 3rd ed.

Includes index

ISBN 978-1-118-04332-5

    1. Rugby football. I. Growden, Greg II. Guthrie, Patrick, 1962– III. Title.

GV945.B76 2011   796.333   C2011-904294-0

Printed in the United States

 5 BRR 16

WILEY

About the Authors

Mathew Brown is America's foremost rugby writer. From 1999 to 2004 he wrote about rugby for Fox Sports.com and, was a producer and host of *Championship Rugby,* the Fox Sports World *Rugby Report,* and *The Rugby Club.* From 2005 to 2009 he was the rugby producer for MediaZone Rugby and wrote the Best of the Weekend and Weekend Preview columns. Since 2010 he has been the producer and host of Rugby World on Fox Soccer Plus. Brown began his rugby career at Occidental College, has been a member of various clubs from Missoula to Riga, played international rugby for Latvia, and has coached at the collegiate and club level.

Patrick Guthrie pioneered the delivery of rugby programming to North Americans. He produced more than 700 rugby television shows including *Championship Rugby* and *The Rugby Club* for the International Channel, FOX Sports International, ESPN, ESPNU, and Versus from 1995 to 2011. Mr. Guthrie was Executive Producer of the USA Sevens from 2003-2007 and the Churchill Cup in 2006. He launched and ran the MediaZone Rugby worldwide broadband service from 2005-2009. Since 2009, he's served as the Director of Broadcast and Sports Development for the City of Glendale, CO. A former member of the USA Rugby Board of Directors from 2003 to 2006, he currently serves on the USA Rugby Congress. Guthrie is head coach of the Oxy Olde Boys, and assists the Occidental College men's and women's rugby teams, the Blackshirts. When he's not getting rucked-over by his twin sons Royal and Vaughn, he referees local matches.

Greg Growden is one of Australia's best-known sports writers. He began writing about rugby union in 1981, and since 1987 has been the chief rugby writer for the *Sydney Morning Herald.* He is also a regular on New Zealand television rugby shows.

Greg's other books include *A Wayward Genius: The Fleetwood Smith Story* and *Gold, Mud 'N Guts, The Incredible Tom Richards: Footballer, War Hero, Olympian.*

Dedication

This book is dedicated to rugby and all who have ever played, watched, or enjoyed it. The sport has been the driving force in both our lives and we're hopeful that this attempt to enlighten the uninitiated will bring a greater audience to this fascinating and wonderful game.

— Mathew Brown and Patrick Guthrie

Authors' Acknowledgments

Thanks to Wiley for hanging in there through three editions and to all of the teammates I've ever played with from the Blackshirts, Oxy Olde Boys, Powell River, All-Maggots, Miesnieks, Exiles, Vail, Flies, Tsunami, and many more over the years. I fully appreciate the support you've given me and the enduring camaraderie you've created.

— Mathew Brown

Thanks to Smurf for your wisdom and support. Kudos to Kirsten and our twins Royal and Vaughn for renewing the child in me. Special thanks to all the rugby men and women around the world who've treated me like family over the years. But most of all, thanks to the Oxy Olde Boys, Kev, Yauch, and Brownie in particular for introducing me to my life's great passion.

— Patrick Guthrie

Publisher's Acknowledgments

We're proud of this book; please send us your comments through our online registration form located at www.dummies.com/register/. For other comments, please contact our Customer Care Department within the U.S. at 877-762-2974, outside the U.S. at 317-572-3993, or fax 317-572-4002.

Some of the people who helped bring this book to market include the following:

Acquisitions, Editorial, and Media Development

Editor: Robert Hickey

Copy Editor: Andrea Douglas

Production Editor: Lindsay Humphreys

Editorial Assistant: Katie Wolsley

Technical Editor: Ken Hodge

Cover photo: © Gary Coldwells (rugbyphoto.com)

Cartoons: Rich Tennant (www.the5thwave.com)

Photo Credits:

Figs 2-2, 3-2, 7-2, 7-3 and 8-2: Patrick Guthrie; Fig 9-2: City of Glendale; Fig 9-3: Patrick Guthrie; Figs 10-3 and 10-6: USA Rugby; Fig 10-8: Patrick Guthrie; Figs 10-10, 15-2, 15-3, 15-4: USA Rugby; Fig 16-1: Rugby Canada; SB16-1: City of Glendale; Fig 17-1: USA Rugby; SB 17: City of Glendale; SB 18: Rugby Canada; Fig 22-1: Sport the Library; Fig 23-1: Doug Crosse; Fig 23-2: Kevin Roberts; Fig 24-1: Dave Stephenson (www.luminaphoto.com); Fig 24-2: Rugby Canada

Composition Services

Senior Project Coordinator: Kristie Rees

Layout and Graphics: Corrie Socolovitch, Lavonne Roberts, Kim Tabor

Proofreaders: Laura Albert, Leeann Harney

Indexer: Claudia Bourbeau

John Wiley & Sons Canada, Ltd.

Deborah Barton, Vice-President and Director of Operations

Jennifer Smith, Vice-President and Publisher, Professional & Trade Division

Alison Maclean, Managing Editor, Professional & Trade Division

Publishing and Editorial for Consumer Dummies

Diane Graves Steele, Vice-President and Publisher, Consumer Dummies

Kristin Ferguson-Wagstaffe, Product Development Director, Consumer Dummies

Ensley Eikenburg, Associate Publisher, Travel

Kelly Regan, Editorial Director, Travel

Composition Services

Debbie Stailey, Director of Composition Services

Contents at a Glance

Table of Contents

Introduction

Welcome to *Rugby For Dummies*, 3rd Edition. This book is your introduction to a sport that has attracted a passionate following around the world for more than a century, but is just now exploding in popularity in the United States and Canada. As rugby devotees ourselves, we understand the natural appeal of the sport and why you feel the need to find out more about it.

Rugby is the world's third-most popular team sport and is played in more than a hundred countries. The nonstop action is breathtaking as the athletes confront each other over 80 minutes of gut-wrenching competition.

Although it was first introduced here more than 137 years ago, up until very recently rugby was a mystery to most North Americans. In the last two decades rugby has made the transition from being a totally amateur game to a fully professional sport. This revolutionary development has increased the fitness of the players, sped up the game, and created a vastly more entertaining, television-friendly product that is growing by leaps and bounds all across North America.

This book is intended to help parents, players, coaches, and their families get acquainted with the basic elements of this fantastic game. We hope this book lifts the veil of mystery that has shrouded the sport and enables you to appreciate both the excitement on the field and the camaraderie off it that makes rugby truly unique.

About This Book

Rugby For Dummies includes all the information you need to get started in the sport, whether you want to be a player, coach, or spectator. It's the first comprehensive guide to all things rugby and was written specifically for a North American audience. Plenty of foreign books talk about rugby, but to our knowledge, this is the only one that explains the game in terms that Americans and Canadians can easily understand.

We've made ease of access and cross-referencing a priority at all times, so you can use this book to quickly locate a specific topic, find the information you're looking for, and get on with your life.

Conventions Used in This Book

Rugby has its own language, so to help you understand what we're talking about we've made a point of putting rugby jargon in *italics* and then defining those terms right away. If we missed one here or there, however, and you encounter a term you're not familiar with, check the Glossary.

Why You Need This Book

If you tried to figure out rugby on your own, it would take you at least a decade of constantly watching, playing, asking questions, and absorbing the atmosphere for you to get a good feel for the game. We know, because that's how we did it. Until we wrote this book there was no easy way to access and assimilate all the information needed to gain a solid understanding of the game — other than personal experience through trial and error.

Whatever your reasons for reading this book — whether you're barely acquainted with the game or possess a wealth of knowledge about it — *Rugby For Dummies* answers your questions and increases your understanding of the sport.

How This Book Is Organized

This book is organized into six parts. Each of the parts covers a major aspect of the game.

Part 1: Rugby: Roots, Boots, and All

The first chapter tells why rugby is a unique sport and gives you a preview of all the information that's contained throughout the book. Then we cover the basics of the field, explain the scoring system, and take a quick look at all the positions. To prevent you from showing up unprepared, we also list all the gear you need to play.

Part 11: Getting Down and Dirty

The second course is the meat-and-potatoes portion of this book. First, we explain the various responsibilities and skills needed to play all 15 positions. Second, we introduce the laws of the game and the match officials, which leads to an explanation of the object of the game, what happens after a tackle, and the concepts of offside and foul play. Then we discuss the differences among tackles, rucks, and mauls. Next, we analyze scrums and line-outs. We then shift gears to address the individual skills of running, passing, kicking, and tackling, and finish off with a look at tactics and training for rugby.

Part III: Welcome to the Oval Planet

This part spans the globe to survey the annual calendar of provincial, inter-provincial, and international competitions. We move next to the Rugby World Cup and the International Rugby Board's (IRB) stable of events. Then we move back closer to home with a look at the USA National Team — the Eagles, followed by a look at the pride of Rugby Canada — the Canadian National Team. We conclude with a tour of the heart and soul of North American rugby — the club game.

Part IV: Coaching and Refereeing

Part IV covers the full spectrum of coaching — from kids to adults — and explains how you can become a certified coach. The refereeing section reviews the responsibility of the ref and what you need to do to become one so that we can address the current shortage of whistle-blowers.

Part V: Following the Game: The Informed Fan

The fifth part brings joy to your household, as we lay out when and where you can watch rugby on TV and follow the game on the Internet. We survey the various channels and Web sites and tell you what's on tap so you can watch rugby across North America. Next, we tell you how you can find a local match to attend. In order to satisfy your thirst for more knowledge, we also detail all the rugby-related media that's available to access rugby information.

Part VI: The Part of Tens

In the sixth part we offer three top ten lists. The first provides our ten best male North American players and the second covers the best female ruggers. The third covers the ten best rugby moments of all time.

The Glossary

Finally, we've included a handy glossary of rugby terms for your edification. The Glossary will help you understand rugby's unique vernacular.

Icons Used in This Book

To help you navigate your way through this book, seven icons appear in the margins. The icons point you to a particular type of information, depending on your needs. The icons mean the following:

This icon indicates useful information for players looking to improve their skills. Even if you're not a player, they'll help you understand what players are trying to accomplish and elevate your knowledge and enjoyment.

This symbol is used when we offer advice to coaches. All of these suggestions have worked for us in our coaching experience, so we hope you'll find them useful and we encourage you to give us feedback.

Whenever we use a word or phrase that is unique to rugby speak, we employ this icon to identify the term and then define it.

This icon indicates a technical discussion is underway. You can skip this information if you want to, because it isn't necessary for an understanding of the basics. If you do read it, though, your rugby expertise goes up a few notches.

Whenever safety is an issue, we use this symbol to alert you of the potential risk and then explain how to minimize or avoid harm.

When you see this icon, get buckled in for an entertaining tale from your author's vast reservoir of rugby exploits, recounted from his unique rugby-centric perspective of the universe.

When you find this icon, remember that your author has been at the forefront of bringing rugby to the North American audience for almost two decades and has, by necessity, become a self-educated expert in everything related to the game.

Where to Go from Here

So now you're ready to start your incredible journey into the world's most amazing game. Where you go from here depends on your experience and the type of information you're looking for. If you've got no clue at all, start at the beginning and enjoy the ride. If you have a question about a particular phase of play, head directly to that chapter and get the answers you need.

Regardless of where you begin, we're confident that by the time you reach the end of your trip through these pages, you'll see the light and share our love for the game they play in heaven. Welcome to the rugby family!

Part I

Rugby: Roots, Boots, and All

The 5th Wave   By Rich Tennant

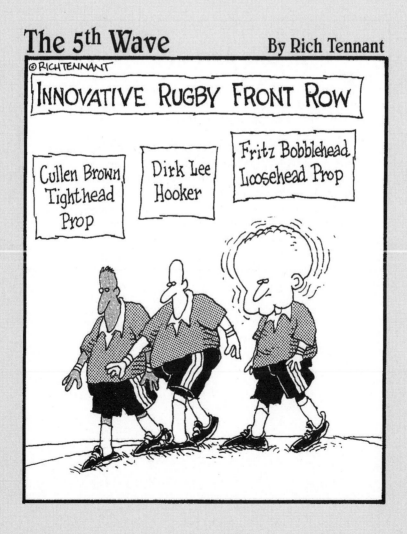

In this part . . .

To make you feel comfortable about everything rugby, this part provides an introduction to the game and lays out the basic parameters of the sport.

To start, we tell you why rugby is so awesome and one of the most widely played sports around the world. We explain what's required to win, describe how the scoring system works, show the field on which the game is played, and spell out what goes on during a match. Finally, we tell you what gear you'll need to have when you show up for that first training session.

Chapter 1

Rugby's Beginnings, Allure, and a Basic Overview

In This Chapter

▶ Exploring rugby's illustrious past

▶ Understanding how the game is played

▶ Boning up on rugby's laws

▶ Going around the world with rugby

▶ Calling the shots with coaches and referees

▶ Staying in touch with the rugby world

*W*hy do millions of fans around the globe watch 30 players chase an oval ball on a field of grass as if the world would end if they missed one pass, kick, or tackle? Because they're hooked on rugby — a game of passion that's full of action, excitement, and beauty, as well as unpredictable moments and dramatic resolutions on the field, and unique camaraderie off the field. When played by the best exponents of the game, rugby satisfies the soul like nothing else.

Rugby's Roots — the Birth of the Game

The game gets its name from Rugby, a town in England's Midlands, where it was first played at Rugby School. The legend goes that in 1823 a schoolboy by the name of William Webb Ellis first picked up the ball in the middle of a soccer game and ran with it, thereby breaking the old rules and setting the stage for an entirely new game (see the following section for the creation of this myth).

What is true is that the game was popularized and the rules codified at Rugby School. The school's alumni spread the game throughout Britain to other schools and universities, like Oxford and Cambridge, and eventually to the far reaches of the British Empire.

The mythical pick-up of William Webb Ellis

William Webb Ellis was indeed a student at Rugby School from 1816 to 1825, and then he went on to study at Oxford before joining the clergy. He died in 1872 and is buried in Menton, in the South of France. But his being a student at Rugby School in 1823 is about as much historical fact as can be determined about him regarding his invention of the game of rugby. In reality, four years after his death the myth was created for a specific purpose — so that the upper classes in England could justify their control of the game. Around the time the story was concocted, rugby was in the throes of a great battle between amateurism and professionalism that would eventually split the sport into two different codes.

Ellis's posthumous anointment as father of the game was a significant event in that battle, and his name lives on today as the embodiment of the sport's crowning achievement, the William Webb Ellis Cup, which is awarded to the winner of the quadrennial World Cup (see Chapter 13 for more about the World Cup).

A century of amateurism

From its beginnings at English public schools, rugby was definitely an elitist pursuit that actively discouraged and prohibited the payment of players. In 1895, after the Rugby Football Union (RFU) refused to allow clubs to compensate players for missing work to play the game, 22 clubs broke away from the union to form the Northern Football Union. This forerunner of professional rugby league (a similar game but with only 13 players) eventually adopted its own set of rules and began paying players — something rugby union wouldn't do for another century.

Up until the 1990s, rugby union was a strictly amateur sport. While there were obviously numerous cases of cushy jobs, special treatment, and under-the-table payments, rugby administrators in both hemispheres diligently ferreted out cases of direct pay-for-play offers and banned those who were caught. Making the jump to rugby league meant no further involvement in rugby union at any level.

The fact that this prohibition against remuneration outlasted even the Olympic movement's similar rule is a testament to the amount of control the game's conservative governors exerted over a worldwide sport. By 1995, the pressures of money and television had become too great and, under threat of losing the best players to league or upstart union competitions, the powers that be capitulated and the sport entered a new era of professionalism.

Reasons why rugby is so awesome

We've been collectively around the game from club to international level for almost 40 years, and have observed the following truths about the game. Here are the reasons we think rugby is the best sport in the world:

- **Anyone can play rugby.** The game does not discriminate — rich or poor, male or female, young or old, every person can enjoy this fantastic game.

- **There's a position for everyone.** Whether you are 7 feet tall or 5 feet tall, 100 pounds or 300 pounds, fleet as a cheetah or slow as an ox, an appropriate position exists for every body type.

- **Everyone participates fully.** Although there are 15 different positions, each player uses a skill set that includes running with the ball, passing, tackling, rucking, mauling, and kicking.

- **Rugby tests athleticism and courage.** Fast running, towering kicking, and fearless tackling are all elements of the game that challenge players to reach their athletic potential in the face of danger.

- **Rugby players share a global bond.** The game is played in more than 100 countries, but its devotees nevertheless belong to a select group. No rugby player is ever without a friend as long as another rugby player is nearby.

- **Rugby has a unique ethos on the field.** Rugby is a hard, aggressive game that attracts fierce competitors. Regardless of the intensity, however, honorable conduct is expected of all participants, and you won't find the sort of trash-talking that pollutes most other professional sports in North America.

- **Rugby has a unique ethos off the field.** The same players who do their best to legally smash each other for 80 minutes during a match will always shake hands and share a beverage and a chat afterward. Whether at a club game or the highest international level, socializing with the opposition is mandatory.

- **Rugby is easy to follow.** Although it looks chaotic at first, rugby is easy to understand and appreciate when you become familiar with a few simple principles of play.

- **Rugby people are cool.** Rugby brings together a gregarious, intelligent, diverse group of characters who are fun to be around.

- **Rugby has a proud history.** While it is new to many North Americans, rugby has a long and storied tradition of competitive excellence, fair play, and sporting spirit that transcends the game itself.

How the Game Is Played

At first glance, rugby can look very complicated. The rugby field is covered in a myriad of lines and populated by 30 players running around and performing seemingly disjointed actions while wearing a variety of accoutrements. Don't fear, though — a little bit of explanation will clear up exactly where they are, what they're doing, and what they're wearing.

The field

Rugby is played on a grass field measuring 100 meters long by no more than 70 meters wide (109.4 yards long by 76.5 yards wide). At each end of the field there are goalposts on the goal line and an in-goal area that varies by venue but is usually between 10 and 22 meters long (10.9 yards to 24.1 yards). (All measurements in this book and in rugby are given in meters.)

Lots of lines are marked on a rugby field. The most important ones are the following:

- **Goal lines:** Players have to reach these lines in order to score.
- **22-meter lines:** These lines are vital, because they influence where play restarts after the ball is kicked out from behind them.
- **Halfway line:** This is where play starts after every score.

We talk more about the field — and all its other lines — in Chapter 2.

The scoring

The aim of rugby is to score more points than the opposition. This is done in four different ways:

- **Try:** The most valuable play is to score a *try,* which means touching the ball down in the opponent's in-goal area or on their goal line. Doing so is worth five points and earns that team the right to attempt a conversion kick.
- **Conversion kick:** This kick is worth an additional two points. The conversion kick is taken from a spot in line with where the ball was originally grounded, so scoring as close to the posts as possible is best.
- **Penalty kick:** Penalties for various infractions can be used to take a kick at goal, which is worth three points.
- **Dropped goal:** A *dropped goal,* which occurs when the player drops the ball on the ground and then kicks it just as it bounces, is worth three points if it goes through the uprights.

We cover scoring in greater detail in Chapter 2.

The gear

In the old days, rugby players wore boots, socks, jerseys, and maybe a bit of tape. The laws have changed over the years to allow much more safety gear to be worn. In the modern era, seeing players wearing padded headgear, compression shorts, light padding under their jerseys to protect shoulders and ribs, and, of course, mouth guards is common. Chapter 3 lets you know what's legal to wear and what's not.

Understanding the Essentials of the Game

Like most sports that didn't originate in North America, rugby can be difficult to comprehend at first glance because of the large number of players involved, the seemingly random calls of the referee, and the wide variety of strategies employed by different teams to score points and get wins. To help you begin your journey toward a complete understanding of the game, in the following sections we outline who all the players are, explain what the referee is generally looking for during the match, and spell out the basic skills required to be successful on the pitch.

Puzzling out the positions

A rugby team has 15 positions. Each one wears a specific number and has individual responsibilities:

- 1 and 3 are the props
- 2 is the hooker
- 4 and 5 are the locks
- 6 and 7 are the flankers
- 8 is, conveniently enough, the eightman

This group is collectively referred to as the *pack* or the *forwards*.

A rugby team has another group as well — the *backs* or *back line:*

- 9 is the scrumhalf
- 10 is the flyhalf
- 11 and 14 are the wings
- 12 and 13 are the inside and outside centers
- 15 is the fullback

To get a feel for what each player is charged with doing on the rugby pitch, see Chapter 4.

Grasping the laws of the game

Rugby is governed by laws, not rules. The laws of the game are designed to produce an entertaining and free-flowing contest for possession in an attempt to score the most points. Twenty-two laws cover all aspects of the field, the players, and the match officials. The referee, helped by two touch judges, is the sole judge of fact and law during a match.

The laws are constantly evolving and are the same all over the world, wherever the game is played. Chapter 5 details where the laws come from and also shows pictures of all the different referee signals to help you figure out what's going on the very first time you watch a match.

In general the laws governing play are straightforward about what's allowed, but three crucial parts can be somewhat confusing: the tackle situation, advantage, and offsides:

- In a nutshell, when a tackle is made in rugby the requirements are that the tackler releases the tackled player, who then releases the ball so that players who are on their feet can use it.

- Advantage simply means that when one team makes an error the other team can try to capitalize on it, instead of the referee immediately stopping the action. If the players can't capitalize on the error, play restarts where the original mistake took place.

- Specific offsides laws exist for different phases of play, but essentially players can't be involved if they're in front of a teammate who last played the ball or are behind the ball when the opposition has it.

Chapter 6 explicates all the intricacies of the game and will have you understanding like an expert in no time.

Scoping out skills, tactics, and training

The four basic skills necessary for any rugby player to excel at the game are running, passing, kicking, and tackling. In Chapter 10 we explain how to execute each skill, including doing the goose step with ball in hand, throwing the cut-out pass, making a grubber kick, and pulling off a ball-and-all tackle. (And while these names may seem slightly humorous to you now, when they're explained within the context of play they'll make perfect sense.)

Plenty of rugby teams are filled with great athletes who never get to hoist trophies in triumph, either because they don't have the right game plan or they aren't employing the correct tactics in accordance with their abilities. Rugby coaches have lots of options open to them as far as strategy is concerned, but the most important thing for them to do if they want to win is to select an over-all structure that fits their players' strengths. Either that or go out and get players who can play the type of game the coach envisions! Chapter 11 looks at the various ways to attack and defend in order to create a winning team.

Rugby has always been a physical game, but since the advent of the professional era the strength and speed of the participants have grown by leaps and bounds. That growth has been achieved not just through more time in the weight room and on the track but also by adhering to better diets and mental preparation regimes. Chapter 12 features all the necessary elements to get ready to play the game, including warming up, stretching, developing a rugby fitness program, and managing the intake of food and fluids.

Rugby's a Worldwide Game

Rugby is played all over the planet by everyone from little kids to millionaire athletes. What binds them together in one collective embrace is passion for the game. More than any other sport, rugby is about tradition, lifestyle, and a noble ethos. Whether you're interested in watching the professional game abroad or playing for your local third-division club, rugby offers an entertaining spectacle or years of athletic enjoyment that can't be matched.

An international affair

The Rugby World Cup is a relatively new tournament, having made its debut in 1987. Now, the tournament is by far the most important event in the minds of fans — and of national unions, who go all out to win it every four years. So far, only New Zealand, Australia (twice), South Africa (twice), and England have managed to lift the William Webb Ellis trophy. Chapter 13 delves deeply into the origins and history of the World Cup (including sections on the U.S.'s and Canada's participation), plus gives loads of info on all the other International Rugby Board (IRB) World Cup competitions, from Women's to Sevens.

The World Cup may be a newcomer on the global sporting scene, but rugby's international tradition goes back to 1871, when England and Scotland squared off in the first test match (which is when the national teams of two countries play an official game). The international calendar is chock-full of exciting action from both hemispheres, with the Six Nations Championship and Tri Nations Series supplemented by the top countries taking annual tours to play on each other's home turf. The interprovincial and provincial scenes are every bit as entertaining, with Super Rugby, Heineken Cup, Magners League, Aviva Premiership, Top 14, ITM Cup, and ABSA Currie Cup providing nearly year-round action. Chapter 14 gives an overview of all these international, interprovincial, and provincial tournaments.

North America gets into the action

North Americans are relative newcomers to the sport of rugby, but both Canada and the United States are passionate about the game. In Chapter 15 we provide the lowdown on their respective histories and detail how the national governing bodies are organized on both sides of the border.

Before you can earn your international call-up, you need to play some club rugby. In Chapter 16, we survey the amateur club game across North America. Over the past 15 years, the most encouraging development in North American rugby has been the rapid growth of the sport at the youth, high school, and collegiate levels, a trend we examine in Chapter 17.

Coaching and Refereeing

Other than the players themselves, the two next most important jobs in rugby are the referee and the coach. Neither is an easy assignment, nor one to be taken lightly. In our experience, coaching can be one of the most satisfying (and sometimes frustrating) things you can do.

Nothing compares to the feeling of watching your charges artfully deploy your brilliant game plan with devastating effect, complete with the knowledge that you were the one who devised and implemented the whole plan of attack! When that happens, the unavoidable pains of being a coach seem a distant memory — at least until the next training session.

Chapter 18 talks about what it takes to be a good coach and outlines the various other support roles available to those who want to be involved in the sport. Chapter 19 details the different procedures to become a coach in the U.S. and Canada, and provides some background about what doing so at various levels of the game entails.

The most important person at any rugby match is the referee — without their presence, the game would evolve into a giant wrestling match and tempers would certainly flare out of control. Although the referee is always respected by the players on the field (and if not, he's got the power to effect change), the job is still a tough one. The laws of the game don't protect him from criticism by spectators or, at higher levels, from media scrutiny. In other words, refereeing isn't for everyone, but it is for a select knowledgeable and confident few who dearly love the game as much as, if not more than, the players they adjudicate. Chapter 20 provides the pathway to taking up the whistle in Canada and the United States.

Keeping Informed about the Game

Rugby used to be a purely local affair, but in today's globally interconnected, media-driven world watching the sport wherever you are — whether you live in a rugby-mad country or not — is possible. Chapter 21 takes all the guesswork out of the process for you with a handy guide to watching rugby on TV. Chapter 22 delves into the Internet and provides a plethora of Web sites to keep you up to date on your favorite country, competition, team, or player. Plus, we list our favorite books and magazines that will give you the real flavor of the sport. We also give you advice about how to actually go see a rugby match in person, where you'll be able to soak up the positive atmosphere that makes rugby such a unique endeavor.

Chapter 2

The Basics

*L*ike most things in life, you need to understand the basics before you can really appreciate rugby. Whether you're a complete newcomer, have had some exposure to the sport, or are a full-fledged expert, the material we cover in this chapter helps you get that much more familiar with the ins and outs of the game.

In this chapter, we describe the playing field, outline how points are scored, explain timekeeping, and describe the positions of the players.

Figuring Out the Field

Rugby is primarily played on a grass field, although sand, clay, dirt, and artificial surfaces are permitted as long as they're not dangerous. Using a permanently hard surface, such as asphalt or cement, is prohibited. The place where rugby is played is variously referred to as the field of play, the playing field, the ground, and the pitch, but they all refer to the same place, which is shown in Figure 2-1.

Dimensions of the playing area

Rugby players do battle on the playing area. The playing area comprises the field of play and two in-goal areas.

- **The field of play:** The area where the bulk of the action takes place is referred to as the *field of play*. It measures no more than 100 meters long by no more than 70 meters wide (109.4 yards long by 76.5 yards wide). The field of play does not include the touchlines or the in-goal areas at either end of the ground (see Figure 2-1).

- **The in-goal areas:** At each end of the playing area are the *in-goal areas,* which must be between 10 and 22 meters long and 70 meters wide (10.9 yards to 24.1 yards long and 76.5 yards wide). The in-goal areas include the goal lines, but not the touch-in-goal or dead-ball lines.

- **The playing area:** This includes both the *field of play* and the two *in-goal* areas. The touchlines, touch-in-goal lines, and dead-ball lines are not part of the playing area.

What all those lines mean

Like most newcomers, we saw the field markings as an indecipherable mystery of seemingly random chalk marks when we began playing rugby. The rugby pitch has numerous lines marked on it — confusing at first, but after you know what all the lines mean and comprehend their strategic importance your overall understanding of the game will be significantly enhanced. Keep reading, and you'll understand in five minutes what it took us five years to figure out! Here's a rundown of the lines and what they signify (see Figure 2-1):

- **Halfway line:** The *halfway line* is a solid line that marks the center of the field, and is where the game starts. Play is also restarted at the halfway line after successful tries, drop goals, or penalty goals. One of the objectives in rugby is to spend as much time as possible in the opponent's half of the field.

- **10-meter line:** Two broken *10-meter lines* are placed 10 meters on either side of the halfway line. When a team kicks off, the ball must reach this line for the kick to be legal.

- **22-meter line:** Two solid *22-meter lines* are located 22 meters out from each goal line. Drop-outs, a specific kind of restart (which are discussed in more detail in Chapter 7), are taken from behind the 22-meter line. The 22-meter line is also crucial in positional play (see Chapter 9 to find out how the 22-meter line affects the kicking game).

- **Goal line:** The *goal line,* also called the *tryline,* is a solid line that delineates the beginning of an in-goal area. There are two goal lines, one at either end of the field of play, which players must reach to successfully score a try.

✔ **Dead-ball line:** The line beyond the in-goal area at each end of the pitch is the *dead-ball line.* When the ball touches or goes over this line, the ball is considered "dead," or out of play.

✔ **Touchline:** The two solid lines that run from goal line to goal line are the *touchlines* — just like the sidelines in football, but called touchlines because when the ball contacts the line or the ground beyond the line it's considered to be *in touch,* which means out of bounds (see Chapter 9 for more on the touchlines).

✔ **Touch-in-goal line:** The *touch-in-goal line* is the continuation of the touchline between the goal line and the dead-ball line.

Grasping the meaning of the principal lines described in the preceding list allows newcomers to follow the flow of play. However, some other broken lines and dash lines in Figure 2-1 remain unaccounted for.

✔ **5-meter line:** The *5-meter line* is a broken line that runs from one tryline to the other, parallel to the touchlines. It marks the front of the lineout and the minimum distance a lineout throw must travel (see Chapter 9 for more lineout particulars).

✔ **15-meter line:** The *15-meter line* is a broken line located 15 meters in from and parallel to each touchline. The broken lines intersect the goal lines, the 22-meter lines, the 10-meter lines, and the halfway line. They define the back of the lineout, and also where scrums and penalties are taken after lineout infringements (see Chapter 8 for more on scrums and Chapter 9 for more on lineouts).

✔ **Dash lines:** Three different lengths of dash lines provide reference points for both referees and players:

• **5-meter dash line:** Six 1-meter long dash lines are positioned 5 meters in front of and parallel to each tryline. They are placed in from each touchline at 5 and 15 meters, and one in front of each goalpost. The dashes mark the minimum distance from the defending team's tryline, where a scrum or lineout can be set or a penalty can be taken.

• **Halfway dash line:** This is a half-meter-long dash that intersects the halfway line at midfield. It's the spot where kickoffs and restarts are supposed to originate — even though most kickers will cheat a meter or two sideways in either direction.

• **Goal line dash line:** Two 5-meter-long dash lines start at each goal line and end at the 5-meter dash lines 15 meters in from each of the touchlines.

Basic rugby terminology

A *scrum* is used to restart play after certain minor infractions. The scrum is a contest for the ball involving eight players who bind together and push against the other team's assembled eight for possession of the ball (see Chapter 8 for a full description). A *lineout* is used to restart play after the ball, or a player carrying it, has gone out of bounds (check out Chapter 9 for all the details). The lineout looks somewhat like a jump ball in basketball, with both teams lining up opposite each other and one team throwing the ball down the middle of the tunnel.

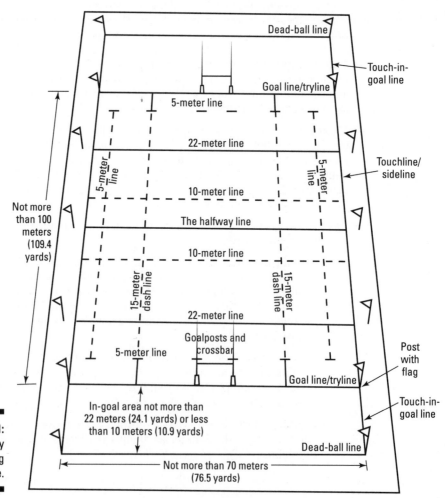

Figure 2-1:
The rugby playing enclosure.

Goalposts and flags

Old-time football fans will immediately recognize the H-shaped structures at either end of the pitch — the goalposts situated at each end of the field of play, directly on the trylines. The uprights must be 5.6 meters (6.12 yards) apart with a *crossbar* (the horizontal beam between the goalposts) measuring 3 meters (3.28 yards) above the ground. The minimum height of the goalposts is 3.4 meters (3.71 yards) above the crossbar. As a safety precaution, the goalposts have to be covered with padding to prevent injury if players crash into them. The pads also provide great advertising opportunities for sponsors!

The rugby pitch has 14 flags on it. Four of the flags mark the intersections of the dead-ball and touch-in-goal lines. Another four flags mark the three-way intersection of the goal lines, touchlines, and touch-in-goal lines. These eight flags used to be considered out of bounds, but because of a recent law change players may now contact them without being considered in touch or in touch in goal as long as they are otherwise in the playing area. Although it may seem self-evident, the game of rugby is meant to be played within the boundaries, with limited exceptions (see Chapter 9 for the times when you're allowed to play from out-of-bounds areas).

The remaining six flags are outside the playing area, positioned 2 meters (2.2 yards) beyond the touchline, at the 22-meter and halfway lines.

Understanding the Scoring System

Football developed from rugby, so if you understand touchdowns, extra points, and field goals, getting a handle on rugby's scoring system is a breeze. How points are accumulated in rugby has evolved over the last hundred years, with the addition of awarding points for tries and conversions. Long ago, scoring a try didn't result in points — it just earned the right to attempt a kick at goal. The modern system encourages teams to score tries over simply kicking penalties.

Points are tallied in five ways in rugby. The ease or difficulty of achieving each of them plays a crucial role in strategic decision making by players and coaches. When you understand what the five ways are, your enjoyment of the game really takes off as you come to appreciate what the players are doing at crucial moments on the field.

Scoring a try

Scoring a try is the quickest way to amass the most points in rugby. A try is the *pièce de résistance* of rugby, similar to scoring a touchdown in football. In fact, rugby is where the term "touchdown" came from, because the ball must actually be touched down for a try to be awarded. A try is scored when the ball is grounded by an offensive player in the in-goal area, on the tryline itself, or on rare occasions against the goalpost padding.

To signal a try, the referee raises an arm and blows the whistle at the spot where the ball came into contact with the turf (see Chapter 5 for a complete list of all the referee signals). The exact place is important because it determines where the conversion kick can be taken from (see "Converting a try" later in this chapter).

A try is worth five points, which is the highest number of points a rugby team can score at one time.

Awarding a penalty try

The awarding of a penalty try is one of the most contentious and misunderstood aspects of rugby, usually because of when and why it occurs. A *penalty try* must be awarded if the referee believes the defending team committed a penalty that prevented the attacking team from scoring a try that otherwise probably would have been scored. This gives the referee plenty of latitude to negate cynical or desperate acts of cheating by awarding points to override what happened on the field. This unique license to rectify the impact of unsportsmanlike conduct is in keeping with the honorable ethos of the game.

When a penalty try is awarded, the referee runs beneath the crossbar in the center of the goalposts, raises an arm, and blows the whistle.

Just like a normal try, the attacking team receives five points, but also gets to attempt the conversion as if the try had been scored in the most advantageous position under the posts.

Converting a try

After a try or penalty try is awarded, the attacking team has the chance to add a further two points to the scoreboard by kicking a *conversion*. The referee marks the place where the try was scored, and then the *goal kicker* can tee up the ball anywhere along a line parallel to the touchline, out from where the ball was grounded. In other words, if the try was scored 5 meters (5.46 yards) from the sideline, then the conversion must be taken 5 meters (5.46 yards) from the sideline. (Figure 2-1 shows the sideline.)

Usually the goal kicker takes the ball back as far as she needs to get a better angle in order to improve her chances of making the kick.

Another reason for taking the kick from farther away is that on a conversion, the opposition may charge the kicker and block her attempt. The defending team must stand on or behind the goal line until the kicker begins to approach the ball — then they're allowed to rush the kicker.

The goal kicker places the ball on either a specially constructed kicking tee or a mound of hand-sculpted sand. A *kicking tee* is a small plastic device that's placed on the ground and holds the rugby ball upright. Making a sand castle is the old-fashioned way, but unfortunately for silica aficionados, it's rarely seen anymore. Andre Pretorius, who plays in South Africa, is the last big-name kicker to use sand.

Goal kickers have their own unique routines for kicking goals, including how many steps they take, where they aim, and how they position the rest of their body (see Figure 2-2). Setting up for a kick used to be a long and drawn-out process that interrupted the flow of the game and wasted time. To speed up play, after the 1999 Rugby World Cup the International Rugby Board (IRB) imposed a one-minute time limit for conversions and penalties, which begins when the kicker receives the tee from the sidelines. Gone are the days when a game consisted of a never-ending series of interminable stoppages for penalties and conversions, punctuated by short bursts of actual rugby.

If the conversion kick flies through the uprights, the touch judges (also known as assistant referees) raise their flags and the referee blows the whistle. (See Chapter 5 for more on touch judges, the match officials who use signal flags to assist the referee.)

Conversion kicks are worth two points. Thus, a "converted" try is worth seven points in total: five for the try plus two for the conversion. If the goal kicker misses, the team gets only the five points for the try.

Figure 2-2:
Preparing
to take a
conversion
kick.

Kicking a penalty goal

If the referee determines that a team has broken one of the laws of the game, a penalty can be awarded to the other side. The non-offending team can choose among several options of how best to use the resulting possession. One of those choices is to kick a penalty goal.

The referee signals a penalty by blowing the whistle and raising an arm in the direction of the team to whom the penalty has been awarded (there's a diagram of all the penalty signals in Chapter 5). Next, that team's captain has to make a decision. If the captain chooses to kick at goal, the kicker places the ball on the spot where the penalty occurred, or anywhere on a direct line behind it, just like a conversion. Unlike a conversion, however, the defending team is not allowed to rush the kicker at any time while a penalty kick is being attempted.

A successful penalty goal is worth three points.

Drop kicking a goal

A *dropped goal* (also called a *drop goal, drop kick,* or *droppie*) is different than a conversion or penalty kick because it takes place while the ball is in play. A drop goal involves a player dropping the ball and trying to kick it between the poles just after it hits the ground, as shown in Figure 2-3. (We discuss the finer points of the drop kick in Chapter 10.)

Figure 2-3: Scoring a drop goal with a drop kick requires a lot of skill and excellent timing.

Slotting a drop goal is a clever maneuver that most teams don't use. Drop kicks are rare because they require perfect timing and lots of practice to properly execute.

If the ball passes between the goalposts and above the crossbar, the team earns three points.

Timekeeping on the Field

Play is divided into two halves. Each half is 40 minutes, with a 10-minute halftime in between. The referee has the power to extend play to make up for time lost because of injuries or delays. This is called *injury time* and is entirely up to the referee's discretion. Unlike most other clock-governed sports, the referee is the official timekeeper. When the referee determines that all time has expired, he blows the whistle to signal the end of the match, which is called *fulltime*.

When the clock runs and when it stops

The 40 minutes in each half is running time, not elapsed time. In rugby the clock counts up rather than down, beginning at the kickoff. Running time stops for injured players to be quickly treated or removed from the pitch, occasionally for water when it's really hot out, for players' clothing to be replaced, and for times when the referee wants to speak with the respective captains, the individual players, the touch judges, or the television match official (TMO).

When someone's injured

Stopping the clock for injury or continuing to play is another decision made by the referee. If a player can be quickly treated, most refs will allow a slight delay in the game. Special dispensation and a little extra recovery time are afforded front-row players if a scrum or lineout is required to restart play (see Chapters 8 and 9 for more on scrums and lineouts). The referee also has the option of letting the match continue while a player receives treatment, if the player isn't in the way. For serious injuries, time stops until medical personnel can remove the player from the pitch.

When the TMO is looking at play

The TMO is the equivalent of instant replay in football. In selected leagues and international competitions, if the match is produced for television the referee has the option of checking with a fellow official who can review various angles the referee didn't see (see Chapter 5 for the TMO's scope and responsibilities). When the referee and the TMO are communicating, running time is off.

When the hooter sounds

The *hooter* — or *horn* or *siren* — is a relatively new addition to most professional rugby stadiums. By keeping track of when the referee's time is running and when it isn't, the stadium timekeeper sounds the hooter when 40 minutes of running time has expired in each half. The hooter does not mean the end of the match, and play can continue after it sounds. It's more like a signal to players and fans that time is almost up. In many cases, the next time the ball goes dead, the referee will blow the whistle to signal fulltime (the end of the match).

Introducing the Players

Rugby is one of the few sports that caters to all sorts of body shapes and sizes. A photograph of a rugby team often looks as if one specimen of every human body type has been assembled at the same spot, at the same time, to provide an illustration for an anthropological study.

A quick scan of any team out at training is proof that anyone can play the game. Within every team, the tall, the small, the fat, the skinny, and everyone in between can find a position that suits them.

Taking up position

Each *squad* or *side* — the group of players who make up a rugby team — comprises 22 players. This includes the 15 who start the match plus the 7 reserves. The starting 15 take the pitch at the beginning of the match, and the 7 reserves sit on the sideline in case of injury or tactical substitutions.

Although most of the positions involve specialized skills, that doesn't mean players are stuck in the same position for the rest of their rugby lives. Players often move around throughout their careers, especially if their body shapes change with age. In this section, we give you a brief overview of the positions on a rugby team. We discuss the positions in more detail in Chapter 4.

The 15 players who start the game are divided into 8 forwards (also referred to as the *pack*) and 7 backs (commonly called the *back line*). The forwards are primarily responsible for winning the ball, and the backs are charged with doing something positive when they get it. An old oval adage says the forwards decide who wins a match and the backs decide by how much.

Regardless of position, however, every rugby player must possess a basic set of skills. Each player must be able to tackle opposition ball-carriers, catch the ball, run with it, and competently pass it.

Positions by the numbers

The 15 starters on a rugby side all wear specific numbers on their jerseys to designate their positions. Even among English speakers, some of the names of the individual positions vary depending on where you are in the world (we cover these name variations in detail in Chapter 4), but the following terms are the most generally recognized:

- ✔ **Loose-head prop (jersey number 1):** A big, strong player who is responsible for scrumming in the front row and lifting the jumpers in the lineout.

- ✔ **Hooker (jersey number 2):** This front-rower actually hooks the ball with her foot at scrumtime, hence the name; plus, she usually does the throwing at lineouts.

- ✔ **Tight-head prop (jersey number 3):** The rock upon which the scrum is built, he has to be the strongest and most technically proficient player in the pack.

- ✔ **Locks (jersey numbers 4 and 5):** Locks form the second row in the scrum and are normally used as lineout jumpers and restart takers because of their superior height and reliable hands. Some teams number their locks according to left or right, others by seniority, or others simply by the players' preferences for a specific number.

- ✔ **Blindside flanker (jersey number 6):** This player must be powerful and make an impact in contact on offense and defense. She must have excellent ball-handling skills.

- ✔ **Openside flanker (jersey number 7):** This is usually the most dynamic and best defensive player on the team, responsible for making critical tackles, creating turnovers, and ranging all over the pitch.

- ✔ **Number 8 (jersey number 8):** The number 8 (or eightman) plays a crucial role on the team. This player directs and controls the scrum from the rear and is often a pivotal link between the forwards and the backs.

- ✔ **Scrumhalf (jersey number 9):** Also known as the halfback, this player must be compact and quick, with excellent passing skills and the ability to operate in tight quarters.

- ✔ **Flyhalf (jersey number 10):** This is the player who runs the show on offense by running, passing, or kicking the ball.

- ✔ **Wings (jersey numbers 11 and 14):** Two of the fastest players on the pitch, the wings must be able to kick and play good positional defense. Which side the two wings play on is usually decided by kicking ability and side-stepping preference.

- ✔ **Inside center (jersey number 12):** This is a physical player with quickness and power when running the ball and no fear when tackling.

- ✔ **Outside center (jersey number 13):** The outside center is a creative runner and ball-handler with very good speed and solid defensive skills.

- ✔ **Fullback (jersey number 15):** This is the back-line general. This player must possess excellent tactical knowledge, have a strong leg for kicking, be an attack-oriented runner, and be the last line of defense.

The reserves

Players who don't start the match but come on as replacements or substitutes are called *reserves*. The reserves sit near the field of play ready to go on at any time. Coaches can replace players who are injured, make tactical changes to combat a threat posed by the opposition, or simply remove a player who is tiring or having a poor game. Each reserve has the same basic designated role as the player he or she replaces. The seven reserves wear jersey numbers 16 to 22, which are usually, but not always, assigned as follows:

- ✔ **Reserve hooker (jersey number 16):** The hooker replacement has to be able to come off the bench and hit the lineout jumpers with minimal warm-up.

- ✔ **Reserve prop (jersey number 17):** This player needs to be able to cover for both the tight-head prop and loose-head prop.

- ✔ **Reserve forward (jersey number 18):** This player can be used to cover either lock position.

- ✔ **Reserve forward (jersey number 19):** This player can provide backup for all three back-row forward positions (the flankers or the number 8).

- ✔ **Reserve scrumhalf (jersey number 20):** This reserve is a specialized scrumhalf replacement.

✔ **Reserve back (jersey number 21):** This player can usually replace either the inside or outside center.

✔ **Reserve back (jersey number 22):** The second reserve back is used to provide backup for the wings or the fullback.

Of the seven backup players who sit on the *reserve bench* (the name given to the place the replacement players sit), three are specialist positions: the hooker, the prop, and the scrumhalf. For a scrum, an injured prop or hooker must be replaced by another suitably trained prop or hooker, not by just any player filling in, because of the particular technique, strength, and experience required to safely compete in the front row.

Officials are deeply concerned about the risk of serious injury to front-rowers if a scrum is incorrectly set, or to someone who doesn't have the ability to withstand the pressure coming through from the opposition. Safety on all levels has improved in recent years, with a greater emphasis on injury prevention (player safety is discussed further in Chapter 18).

Clever use of the reserve bench can often mean the difference between winning and losing a match, particularly if it's going right down to the wire. With the faster and fitter game of rugby being played these days, the reserve bench has become a vital part of every coach's arsenal.

Bringing on players from the reserve bench for tactical reasons is now a well established practice in the professional game. It has changed the way coaches select their 22-person squad and plan their strategy throughout. Fresh players are brought on as impact players, usually in the second half, to try to take advantage of a tiring opposition. This doesn't mean a team gets an unfair advantage — the opposition also has the chance to use fresh legs whenever required.

Being a reserve is a tough assignment in rugby, especially if the conditions are foul. Sitting on the sidelines while your teammates do battle is never easy, and is even more difficult when you have to be ready to join the fray at any moment.

Each player on the reserve bench is there for a specific reason. Whenever you're in the reserves, you have to stay focused on how the game is unfolding. Watch the players you're likely to replace, and see what's working and what's not against the opposition. The key is to be mentally switched on and ready to get stuck in right away if the need arises.

Chapter 3

Grab Your Rugby Gear

In This Chapter

▶ Putting your kit bag together

▶ Looking like a rugby player

▶ Protecting yourself from injury

People often refer to rugby as football without pads. Of course that's not true, but it does highlight one of the main advantages of rugby — that you don't need to break the bank buying all those expensive football pads, helmets, and uniforms to outfit your team or yourself for action. All you need is a jersey, some shorts, a mouth guard, a pair of cleats, and a ball, and you're on your way to playing the game.

In this chapter, we describe the necessary items to pack into your bag, as well as some extra stuff you may consider worthwhile — in rugby circles, your gear is collectively referred to as your kit, which you lug around in your kit bag. Next, we discuss the important issue of personal safety while playing rugby and the precautions you can take to protect yourself on the pitch.

Getting It Together: The Essentials of the Kit Bag

A strong, yet lightweight sports bag is essential to carry your rugby kit around in. The bag should be big enough to hold a rugby jersey, socks, shorts, boots, rugby ball, and towel, plus a change of clothing. Bag sizes vary, but look for one that's larger than a normal gym bag — you'll soon have it stuffed to capacity. Try to find a bag that has a separate pocket for your valuables and has a waterproof compartment, either on the outside or the inside, where you can stuff your muddy socks, shorts, and boots.

Before you rush out and purchase a kit bag, inquire whether your team has bags for sale. Many clubs periodically order personalized team bags, sometimes to commemorate tours or championship seasons — it's the ultimate in sophisticated rugby luggage!

Having a ball

A rugby ball is oval, not round. It can be made of leather or a strong synthetic material and consists of four panels. Some balls are designed to be easier to grip when playing in muddy or wet conditions. The ball used in youth rugby is slightly smaller than the one for adults. Whatever your age, though, training with the same size ball you play with in a game is important.

A rugby ball is the first item any aspiring rugby player buys. Even though rugby clubs usually have an abundance of balls, having one to practice with on your own is still a smart idea. Coaches recommend you get a ball in your hands as often as possible so you can practice your kicking, passing, catching, and handling skills.

Although you can now purchase a good variety of rugby balls at Sports Authority stores across the United States, finding a rugby ball in any other sporting goods store in North America is more serendipity than certainty. Your best bet is to order a ball online from one of the many online rugby stores.

The dimensions of a rugby ball are as follows:

- ✔ **Length:** 280–300 millimeters (11–12 inches)
- ✔ **Circumference (end to end):** 760–790 millimeters (30–31 inches)
- ✔ **Circumference (width):** 580–620 millimeters (23–24 inches)
- ✔ **Weight:** 400–440 grams (14.5–15.5 ounces)
- ✔ **Air pressure:** 0.67–0.70 kilograms per square centimeter, or 9.5–10 pounds per square inch

Maintaining the proper air pressure is important. Make sure your ball has enough give in it for you to push your fingers in slightly at one end. A softer ball is easier to catch, handle, and pass, and is therefore better suited for training purposes.

You'll find two categories of rugby balls:

- ✔ A *match ball* is a top-of-the-line rugby ball. Match balls are well balanced to pass, kick, and punt consistently. You'll pay $50 U.S. or more for a match-quality ball. Don't bother buying a match ball to kick around the neighborhood.

✔ A *training ball* is virtually the same as a match ball but is less expensive and should be used for practicing. Although a training ball isn't as good as a match ball, it's perfectly fine for your needs and is much more affordable. The average training ball costs about $30 U.S.

Kicking in with a kicking tee

Over the last few years, the introduction of kicking tees has made life a lot easier for goal kickers. This small plastic apparatus is placed on the ground and holds the ball upright, as shown in Figure 3-1. A kicking tee holds a rugby ball in the same way as a golf tee holds a golf ball when a golfer prepares to hit a drive. In rugby, a tee is used when a team attempts to kick a conversion or a penalty goal (the scoring system is explained in Chapter 2).

Figure 3-1:
Placing the ball at the correct angle on the kicking tee.

Kicking tees are quicker and less messy than the old method of kicking off a hand-sculpted mound of sand or dirt: Players used to have to wait for a ball boy to run onto the pitch with a sand bucket, wait for the goal kicker to build a sandcastle, wait for the goal kicker to be satisfied with his work, and then wait for the kicker to place the ball on top of his castle, check the wind, gauge the distance one last time, and finally kick the ball.

Using a kicking tee isn't compulsory, because some players still prefer sand. Try both to see what's most comfortable for you.

Different goal kickers like to place the ball on the kicking tee at different angles, depending on their kicking style — the kicking tee caters to all the different variations.

Not every player on the team has to own a kicking tee, especially if you have no interest in goal kicking. However, if you want to kick for goal, a kicking tee is a must-have on your shopping list. You won't use your own tee in a game, because clubs have plenty of them, but you'll need a kicking tee to practice with. Your club may even let you have one of their spares, particularly if you start kicking match-winning penalties or conversions.

Kicking tees are a one-time purchase, usually costing between $10 and $20 U.S., and can be found online and in selected sports shops.

Miscellaneous kit items

If you're lucky, your club will sell team bags, hats, T-shirts, jackets, and warm-up outfits. Nothing's quite like showing up for a match with the whole squad decked out in matching outfits. Even if you get thumped by 100 points, you'll look good, improve team morale, and make a much-needed contribution to the club's treasury.

To heighten your experience, consider a few more handy items to toss into your kit bag for use on match day. To supplement the team's medical kit, bring some plastic bandages and antibiotic ointment to treat the minor cuts and scrapes that are inevitable if you've played hard enough. Bring a roll of white cloth athletic tape to keep your ears fully attached to your head and for other running repairs. Invest in a pair of good sunglasses, a wide-brimmed hat, and sandals to wear after the match, while you root your second-side teammates to victory from the sideline.

Getting the Gear

The International Rugby Board (IRB) in Dublin, Ireland, sets the standards for rugby regulations. The IRB allows for pads made of soft, thin material to be incorporated into an undergarment or jersey, provided the pads cover the shoulder and collarbone only. No part of the pads can be thicker than 1 centimeter (0.4 inches) when uncompressed, or have a density of more than 45 kilograms per cubic meter (2.8 pounds per cubic foot).

Rugby jerseys

Rugby jerseys can be short- or long-sleeved, and they have traditionally featured a full collar. They're made of thick cotton, or synthetic fibers, which tend to breathe more than other materials. Because rugby involves tackling and binding onto one another, wearing a jersey that won't be easily destroyed by the constant aggression is important.

BROWNIE SAYS

Jerseys then and now

When I first started playing rugby in 1986, jerseys were generally made of a cotton/polyester blend. They were comfortable at first, but they'd get very heavy at the end of a draining match or in wet weather. Because the jerseys had a collar and long sleeves, they also doubled as smart casual wear that made the statement wherever I went that I was a rugby player. Back then, the jerseys for the props (numbers 1, 3, and 17) were usually the biggest ones in the set and were sufficiently large enough to fit over my extra-extra-large frame.

With the advent of form-fitting jerseys designed for more aerodynamic performance and made of synthetic materials capable of wicking moisture away from the body, the era of wearing a rugby jersey out and about as well as in a game or at training came to an end. Why? Because now jerseys are collarless, short sleeved, and almost all about the same size. And though the new jerseys are great to play in, they tend to look more like sausage casings than shirts — definitely not a good look for an aging front-rower!

Game-day rugby jerseys are usually supplied by the club, but you'll need your own to wear at practice. You can purchase a proper rugby jersey for about $40 U.S., which should get you through your first season of play.

TIP

Your jersey needs to be sturdy enough to withstand some punishment, so don't make the mistake of buying a department store knockoff. Designer-label rugby jerseys may look cool, but they aren't designed for the rigors of practice on the pitch.

Rugby shorts

Like jerseys, rugby shorts must be able to withstand punishment. Most rugby shorts have pockets, but you can find some varieties without them. Generally, you want a pair of shorts that are thick enough to last (and provide some protection to sensitive areas) and don't give your opponents too much to hold on to.

New players usually have to obtain their own shorts. The color and style are determined by the club you play for. There may even be two different colors, for games at home and away. Different brands fit differently — over the years we've found that Canterbury (New Zealand) and Barbarian (Canada) shorts are the most durable and comfortable available.

Make sure the shorts you buy are comfortable and not too tight or too loose. If anything, go bigger rather than smaller. We also recommend you buy shorts with a drawstring in the waistband to ensure they remain snugly in place around your waist. Tackling an opponent is hard enough without your efforts being impeded by a pair of shorts heading south. Moreover, if you're a lineout jumper (see Chapter 9 to see if you'll soon be launched to new heights), you'll be lifted by your shorts — so they'd better be fastened well, or you'll get a serious wedgie.

Rugby shorts are usually priced between $20 and $35 U.S. They can be purchased online, in Canterbury clothing shops, or at specialty sporting goods stores.

Booting up

Of all your rugby equipment, footwear is probably the most important. A perfectly good rugby game can be ruined by the discomfort caused by a pair of ill-fitting boots. If your feet aren't happy, brace yourself for an uncomfortable afternoon on the pitch.

Rugby boots (or cleats) are similar to soccer shoes or football cleats, but the studs need to be circular and otherwise meet IRB specifications. You can wear football cleats for rugby, but you'll need to remove the front center toe studs (if your boots have them) for them to be legal.

Forwards' boots are generally mid- to high-cut with different stud patterns designed for the rigors of scrummaging, rucking, and mauling. Backs' boots are more often low-cut — built for speed and easy direction change. However, whether you're a forward or a back, buying the boots that are most comfortable on your feet is most important.

The first rule of *boot law* is to make certain that your boots fit snugly around your feet, side to side and heel to toe, to prevent blisters caused by friction. Boots should be comfortable and have the required traction on the pitch.

The best place to buy boots is online or, if you're one of the geographically fortunate few, at a rugby shop in your area. Also keep in mind that at most large rugby tournaments you'll find vendors offering their wares. Take the opportunity to try on a variety of makes and models to find the boots that are just right for your feet. When you've found the right fit, you'll have more confidence ordering online.

When you buy a new pair of boots, walk around in them for a while to get comfortable before practice — and never use a brand-new pair for a match! At your first training session with new boots, apply a little petroleum jelly inside the boot along the back of the heel and above your toes to prevent blisters.

Although rugby boots range widely in price, you'll find good reliable brands that start at $50 U.S. Although a lot of rugby gear is available at fairly low prices, please don't economize in the boot department — cheap can be very painful and take all the fun out of the game.

When heading off to the game, always remember to check your kit bag to ensure that your boots are included. If you forget your socks, jersey, or even your shorts, usually someone on the team can lend you his or hers — but if you leave your boots behind and wear a teammate's pair that doesn't fit, you'll be cursing your forgetfulness with every step. When it comes to rugby players and boots, when you find a pair that fits right you'll do just about anything to keep them in action.

Socking it to you

Rugby socks are similar to soccer socks and are worn to the knee. Soccer socks from any sporting goods store will get you started until you can purchase your game socks from your club — just make sure they stretch up slightly above your knee, enabling you to roll the top over to just below the knee.

Make certain each sock has an elasticized band near the top so it stays up during the match. Socks dangling around your ankles are not a recommended fashion statement. If your socks have a propensity to sink to half-mast, get a couple of short lengths of shoelace and tie a piece around each sock just below the knee and then fold the top of the sock over. Don't tie it too tightly, or you'll impede the flow of blood to your legs, which may give you cramps or cause your lower legs to turn blue, wither, and eventually fall off. Old-style rugby socks used to be secured in this way before the advent of elastic (and some of us old-timers still prefer to keep ours up the old-fashioned way).

Depending on the club you play with, you may be supplied with rugby socks to ensure you're wearing the right club colors. If not, the club can tell you where to buy the right pair. Socks are not expensive, and the type for players at club level are available at sports shops starting at about $4 U.S. a pair.

Finding gear in North America

In North America, you can get gear in three ways. If you happen to live near a Sports Authority store, or one of the few rugby supply houses, consider yourself lucky. For the vast majority of rugby players, your best options are to buy online (or by mail order) or attend one of the many annual tournaments where rugby retailers set up mobile stores to display their wares. Sports Authority now carries rugby balls, mouth guards, shoulder pads, headgear, and a limited selection of rugby cleats. Other than mouth guards, don't expect to find proper rugby gear at your local sporting goods store — and, whatever you do, don't try to adapt football, hockey, or other sports' pads for use in rugby.

One of the best places to start outfitting yourself online is at WorldRugbyShop.com (www.worldrugbyshop.com). Your local sports shop may have two or three models of football or soccer cleats that can work okay for rugby, but WorldRugbyShop.com has a dazzling array of real rugby boots. They have four separate categories of boots designed for soft or firm grass fields, turf fields, plus women's boots. They offer 39 soft-ground choices and an incredible inventory of 90 firm-ground models, along with 39 models specially designed for women to choose from. They also carry a comprehensive selection of jerseys, balls, bags, technical videos, and official team jerseys for virtually every national team and most of the overseas professional teams. You can also find protective gear of every shape and size (see "Protecting Your Assets" in this chapter).

Protecting Your Assets

After you experience the joy of playing rugby, you're likely to regard the myriad bumps and bruises as badges of courage and come to enjoy the horrified reactions of family, friends, and co-workers who cringe at the sight of your occasional black eyes and minor facial stitches. Despite temporary trivial cosmetic alterations to your visage, rugby is actually very safe, considering the fact it is a full-contact sport.

In Chapter 18, we address safety and the truth about injuries in rugby. Here, we detail the variety of protective clothing available to lessen your chances of getting hurt.

Choosing protective equipment

In recent years, the increased emphasis on safety has led the IRB to approve the use of more and more articles of protective gear. Responding to the challenge and commercial opportunity, manufacturers have improved existing devices to protect teeth and have developed new products to lessen the impact of collisions. Following is a list of the most widely used safety items.

Before you buy headgear or shoulder padding, make sure they comply with IRB specifications. The IRB has strict standards for rugby gear, and manufacturers must have their products approved by an IRB testing house. When an item is approved, it's given an approval number and the garment label is marked with the IRB logo and the words "Approved Clothing." Don't get too intimidated by all this IRB stuff. When buying protective gear, check the packaging to see if the product is approved for use (to see a full listing of all IRB-approved shoulder padding, breast padding, and headgear, go to www.irb.com, click on Laws and Regulations, and then click on Equipment Approval).

- **Mouth guards:** Almost all professional players wear mouth guards to protect their teeth from wayward fists, boots, or bodies. A mouth guard is an essential piece of protective gear, and anyone who takes the pitch at any level should always wear one. Most sporting goods stores stock mouth guards for football, and they can be molded at home to fit your teeth by following the directions that are included. The Shock Doctor Gel Max and Gel Nano are two of the best off-the-shelf mouth guards on the market now. The new gel-filled guards cost a bit more, but do offer some additional cushioning or dampening functionality, which may help reduce the severity of concussions. Compared to the cost of dental reconstruction, a guard is a worthwhile investment priced at $3 to $25 U.S.

- **Headgear:** Regardless of whether you're a forward or a back, if you feel more comfortable or confident wearing padded headgear don't hesitate to use it. Headgear must be made of soft and thin material, and the IRB has set standards for what is legal. Look for the IRB logo to be sure that your headgear is approved for use. Good, comfortable, reputable brands can be purchased for between $50 and $100 U.S.

- **Shoulder padding and vests**: Shoulder padding and padded vests, as shown in Figure 3-2, provide rugby players with shoulder, collarbone, and chest protection. Those made with Lycra allow more air circulation and dry more quickly. They also come in various sizes, so you can choose the amount of padding you're comfortable with. Some are short, covering mainly the upper chest and shoulders. Others are long and will protect the entire torso as well as the biceps. Female rugby players should look for vests that are designed for women. These vests are longer and have more padding for chest protection. The IRB states that these chest pads can be made of soft, thin material, as long as no part of the pad is thicker than 1 centimeter (0.4 inches) when uncompressed. Keep in mind that shoulder protection alone won't prevent injury — you need to use good technique at all times during contact sports. Vests are generally priced from $60 to $70 U.S., but can be more expensive if they have special features.

Figure 3-2:
Protective
shoulder
padding.

✔ **Sports bras:** Most female rugby players also wear sports bras to reduce breast pain and limit movement. No specific bra is designed for rugby players (yet), but finding one that provides good support and protection is important. Sports bras help to protect women as long as they fit properly. If you've never purchased a sports bra before, getting measured by an expert so you can get the right one is a good idea. A good sports bra will cost around $30 U.S.

✔ **Compression shorts**: These are worn under your rugby shorts to provide extra protection and support. They also help prevent hamstring and groin injuries. The shorts are usually made of thick Lycra or cotton, allowing for maximum airflow. Prices vary, but a good pair shouldn't cost more than $25 U.S.

✔ **Jock straps:** As an alternative to compression shorts, jock straps provide support for men who prefer the more traditional method of protection. These can be found at any sporting goods store and cost about $10 U.S.

Preventing serious injury

Although mouth guards, headgear, and shoulder padding offer some protection if you're hit in a certain spot, they don't guarantee a totally pain-free experience.

The best way to prevent serious injury is to play hard and at full throttle every minute you're on the pitch: "The half-hearted are the first to get hurt" is an old adage. Your club will teach you how to take other precautions, such as tackling safely and falling properly.

Rugby administrators are on the side of the player, instituting numerous laws to protect those on the pitch from serious injury. The referee is also required to stop any play that he or she determines to be dangerous and where a player may get hurt.

Don't hesitate to use any form of protection allowed by the IRB. Ignore any nonsense about forwards who wear shoulder vests and headgear being cowards — try telling that to All Blacks captain Richie McCaw or Springbok player Victor Matfield, who both wear protective gear. Like so many other professional players, they choose to wear protection — and if you've ever stood next to either one of them, you know that whatever they want to wear is A-okay with us.

Knowing what's barred on the pitch

You need to take note of things that aren't allowed on the rugby pitch. For safety reasons, players can't wear or take these items onto the pitch:

- ✔ Anything contaminated with blood
- ✔ Anything sharp or abrasive
- ✔ Anything containing buckles, clips, rings, hinges, zippers, screws, or bolts
- ✔ Jewelry, such as rings or earrings
- ✔ Communication devices, such as two-way radios tucked into rugby boots
- ✔ Shorts with padding sewn into them

In addition, players aren't allowed to have any toe cleats on the soles of their boots, nor are players allowed to wear gloves onto the pitch, other than the fingerless variety. If you wear a knee brace that's reinforced with metal parts, you'll need to pick up a soft brace to play rugby.

Referees are required to examine both teams before the game to ensure players aren't equipped with anything that may be dangerous. Part of this inspection is the boot check — when the referee looks at both teams' boots for worn-down studs or other prohibited items.

Part II
Getting Down and Dirty

In this part . . .

1 t's time to get serious and find out exactly what's required to play the game. In this part, we start off by listing the various positions and outlining the skills you need to be a star. We then explain the laws of the game so you know what's legal and what's not. We also detail the object of the game and then demystify the scrum, rugby's signature formation that's used to restart play. Then we cover the lineout, and finish this part with a chat about training smart to win.

Chapter 4

Location, Location, Location: Positions on the Pitch

● ●

In This Chapter

▶ Defining the role of each player

▶ Playing by numbers

▶ Scrapping in the scrum

▶ Playing in the back line

● ●

*T*hirty strapping rugby players all taking the field at once is a rush of beef to rival the greatest cattle stampede. To the rugby-watching novice, it can look like total confusion. But don't despair. Rugby has a major advantage over a lot of other sports — the number on each player's back actually determines the exact position he or she plays.

In this chapter, we help you sort out which number goes with which player and what the person is trying to do in the game.

A Place for Everyone

Rugby is an equal-opportunity game. Whether you're 5 feet tall or 7 feet tall, 100 pounds, 300 pounds, or anywhere in between, you have a place on a rugby team. If you want to play rugby, deciding which position best suits you is easier when you understand the typical characteristics and role on the team of each player.

A *side* is made up of 15 players — 8 forwards and 7 backs. The forwards (known collectively as the *pack*) have the primary role of winning the ball, while the backs are responsible for doing something productive with it. Generally, the bigger you are, the more likely you'll become a forward; the faster you are, the more likely you'll become a back.

Regardless of position, every rugby player needs a basic set of skills. Everyone on the team plays both offense and defense throughout the match. This means that the shortest player and the tallest, the lightest and the heaviest, all must be able to perform various duties such as tackling, catching, carrying the ball, and passing it when necessary.

Playing the Numbers Game

Unlike American football, where the players' numbers are individually selected within a certain range for each position, and baseball, where numbers are essentially random, rugby uses specific jersey numbers to identify each position on the field. In this regard, rugby is spectator-friendly. On the field, the players who start the game are numbered from 1 to 15, and the reserves are numbered from 16 to 22 (refer to Chapter 2 for more about reserves).

Jersey numbers indicate the position each player occupies on the team. Numbers also let spectators, players, and coaches know who to cheer for when something wonderful happens. At the same time, everyone, including the referees and touch judges, can identify who is to blame if something goes wrong. When you're clear about the designated role and responsibilities of the player in each position, you'll be able to pick the stars from the slugs.

Figure 4-1 shows the forwards and backs in typical scrum attacking formation. Referring to this figure often while you're reading about each of the positions may be helpful.

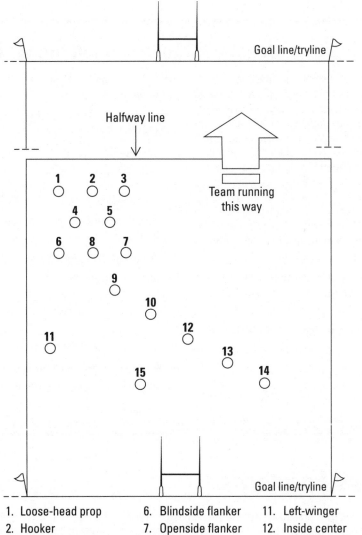

Figure 4-1: The forwards and backs getting ready to attack.

1. Loose-head prop	6. Blindside flanker	11. Left-winger
2. Hooker	7. Openside flanker	12. Inside center
3. Tight-head prop	8. Number 8	13. Outside center
4. Lock (second row)	9. Scrumhalf	14. Right-winger
5. Lock (second row)	10. Flyhalf	15. Fullback

What's in a name: Positions around the world

Rugby originated in England in the early to mid-1800s and has spread throughout the world during the last couple of centuries. As such, the game has developed on similar but somewhat divergent paths, depending upon where you are in the world. One of the by-products of these unique threads of evolution is reflected in the proliferation of different position names. Although most of the positions on the rugby pitch have standardized names all over the English-speaking world, a few regional variations that can be confusing crop up in certain countries.

Terms that are interchangeable with the standard nomenclature and are not specific to any country or region include the following:

✔ Scrumhalf — halfback, inside half

✔ Flyhalf — pivot, first receiver, outside half

✔ Lock — second-rower

✔ Flanker — wing forward, breakaway, break

✔ Flankers and the number 8 — loose forwards, loosies

Names that are a product of regional variation include the following:

New Zealand:

✔ Flyhalf — halfback, first five-eighth

✔ Inside center — second five-eighth

✔ Outside center — center, center three-quarter

✔ Wing — wing three-quarter

United Kingdom and Ireland:

✔ Flyhalf — standoff, outhalf

South Africa:

✔ Flankers — jersey numbers are reversed

✔ Openside — wears jersey number 6

✔ Blindside — wears jersey number 7

✔ Eightman — eighthman

Fearless Forwards

Eight players make up the forwards (or pack) of a rugby team — two props, the hooker, two locks, two flankers, and the number 8. This group's main goal is to win possession of the ball. These players are usually the heavyweights of the team, using their bulk and strength to try to overpower their opponents. Forwards can be broken up into three groups: front-rowers, second-rowers, and back-rowers.

A quick word on rucking and mauling

Here's a quick primer on rucks and mauls. A *ruck* usually forms after a tackle is made when two or more players who are on their feet come into contact over the ball on the ground. The goal is to compete for possession by driving over the ball and using their feet to move it back to their team's side. A *maul,* in contrast, requires a minimum of three players. It occurs when a player carrying the ball in hand, off the ground, is held by one or more opponents and one or more of her teammates bind onto her. In a maul, everyone must be on their feet.

Getting in tight with the tight five

The *tight five* is the group of players who wear the jerseys numbered 1 to 5. This group consists of the three front-row players (tight-head prop, hooker, and loose-head prop — or front-rowers, collectively) and the two second-row players (two locks, or second-rowers, collectively) who line up behind them. The tight five forms the core of the pack. The group's main function is to keep the scrum steady and productive in the hope that when the ball is placed in the scrum it ends up in their team's possession. After a minor infringement occurs, the three front-rowers bind together and are joined by the two second-rowers (plus the three back-rowers) to compete for possession of the ball in a *scrum.*

A *scrum* is the term used for the interlocking formation of the team where the forwards' arms are around each others' shoulders, their knees are bent, and their heads are up. As shown in Figure 4-2, all eight players bind together and face their opponents. Both units then come together on the referee's call (four parts — crouch, touch, pause, engage), creating a tunnel in the middle. The ball is put in this tunnel by the scrumhalf, and both teams' hookers attempt to channel it back to the rear of their own scrum with their feet. This is one of the signature elements of rugby and is used to restart play after a minor infraction. A scrum is over when the ball has been released from the web of players and is in play (see Chapter 8 for more details on the scrum).

Picture those wildlife documentaries where two huge rams slam together and head-butt each other for supremacy of the herd, and you've got some idea of what goes on when a scrum is engaged. Brute force and strength are only half the battle. Proper, usually hard-learned technique will invariably prevail over simple bulk in the tight five. Understanding play is a little bit easier if you take the tight five positions one by one. In the next section, we explain the function of the three front-rowers (tight-head prop, hooker, and loose-head prop), and follow that by talking about the two second-rowers (the locks).

Facing off in the front row

The front row is easy to pick out: the loose-head prop wears the number 1 jersey, the hooker wears number 2, and the tight-head prop wears number 3. Don't panic — we explain these unusual names in the next few paragraphs. (Remember, the location of these players is outlined in Figure 4-1.)

The front-rowers form the platform upon which the whole team is built. These three players must be uncompromising, technically sound, and committed to doing whatever it takes to win the battle up front. If the front-rowers are weak or off their game, the team is at risk of collapsing.

Front-rowers take enormous pride in their scrummaging technique and revel in the fact that it's literally the only head-to-head confrontation in the game. Other rugby players may make jokes about props' less-than-svelte physiques, but the ribbing also involves a huge amount of respect because everyone loves playing behind a solid front row.

You won't find many flashy or cocky front-rowers, but they believe they're the three most important rugby players on the field, and in many respects, they're right.

Propping up: Tight-heads and loose-heads

The *props* are the players who wear numbers 1 and 3. They can be found on either side of the hooker in the front row. Because props take most of the physical impact in the scrum, they must possess superior upper and lower body strength.

The term "prop" comes from the fact that these two players "prop up" the hooker when the scrumhalf (more about this position later in the chapter) puts the ball into the scrum. Figure 4-3 shows the scrumhalf putting the ball in at the scrum and the hooker being supported by his loose-head and tight-head props.

Figure 4-3:
The scrum-half putting the ball in at the scrum.

The words "loose" and "tight" simply describe how the props are positioned in the actual formation of the scrum. Because of the alignment of the scrum, the loose-head prop has his head outside the scrum and can see what the others are doing. The tight-head prop, however, positions his head between the opposition's hooker and loose-head prop. In other words, the loose-head has no other head to his left, whereas the tight-head's noggin is sandwiched between two opposing players' heads (we talk more specifically about scrums in Chapter 8).

Don't be discouraged if it takes some time to tell the difference between a tight-head and a loose-head prop. The best way to remember exactly who is who is to picture the loose-head on the left-hand side of the scrum and the tight-head on the right-hand side of the scrum. The way to remember this is that "tight" rhymes with "right."

Tight-head props and loose-head props have exactly the same aim, though their techniques are different. The tight-head is the anchor of the scrum, requiring enormous strength to keep the scrum straight and intact. The loose-head is more of a technician, using different tricks to give his team an advantage in winning the ball.

Props are crucial performers at the *lineout* (a lineout is how play is restarted when the ball has been taken out over the sideline or kicked into touch; we discuss lineouts in detail in Chapter 9) because they're required to lift their teammates at exactly the right time and place. This takes excellent footwork, timing, quickness, and strength. They're also prized defenders who take on other hard-charging forwards in tight quarters. In an attack, one of a prop's main tasks is to drive defenders back a few yards whenever they carry the ball; the occasional long run is a bonus, not a requirement.

Highlighting the hooker

In between the two props is the *hooker,* who wears the number 2 jersey. This is the most versatile of the three front-row positions. The hooker is seen around the field more often because this position has a wider range of responsibility. The hooker needs to have superior hand-eye and foot-eye coordination, flexibility, agility, upper body strength, and quickness. Powerful legs are also an asset.

At the scrum, the hooker is supported by his two props, enabling him to hang suspended over the scrum opening. When the scrumhalf puts the ball into the tunnel between the feet of the opposing front rows, the hooker is required to "strike" at the ball with his foot, guiding it back toward the feet of the players in the second and back rows so that his team gets possession.

The hooker must also be right on his game at every lineout, because he has the tough task of throwing the ball in and making sure that it's on target to one of the lineout jumpers. Because lineouts are used to initiate play more than any other restart, a hooker's ability to accurately hit his jumpers on a consistent basis is imperative.

Hookers can make or break their reputations based on their ability as lineout throwers. The ranks of former internationals are littered with hookers who were great in every other aspect of the game but couldn't regularly maintain possession at the lineout with their throws. If throwing isn't one of your strengths, then this probably isn't the position for you.

BROWNIE SAYS

Technique beats athleticism

Years ago, a beautiful annual rugby tournament was held on the polo grounds at Pebble Beach in Monterey, California. A few years after I took up the game, my team, the Oxy Olde Boys, was scheduled to play a side from Sacramento that was made up mostly of Pacific Islander players. As we watched them warm up in their sweats prior to kickoff, we focused on one particular athlete who was about 6'2", 225 pounds, incredibly fast, and looked menacing in his athleticism and obvious strength. A long ponytail and a glowering countenance completed the effect. Somebody eventually muttered what everyone was thinking: "Who is going to have to play directly against that guy?" As the other team took off their jackets just before kickoff, I saw the number 3 on his back, indicating that he was a tight-head and would be opposite me, a loose-head, in the scrum.

As luck would have it, that must have been his very first outing in the front row, because I had my way with him, relentlessly bending him every which way, lifting him off the ground (that was before it was made illegal for safety reasons), driving him mercilessly backward at each scrum, and generally making his life miserable to the point where he eventually took to trying to punch me as a means of self-preservation. The thumping he took in the scrums totally negated his effectiveness in the rest of play as well. At the time I was still a relatively inexperienced prop, but I had the basics down and was therefore miles ahead of this newcomer — and it showed on the pitch. Rugby is a game where physical attributes are important but technical proficiency is even more significant, and nowhere is that more true than in the front row.

The hooker is often expected to function as an extra loose forward, so he must be a courageous tackler and able to provide a link between forwards and backs in support play.

The second row: Exerting in the engine room

The second row of the tight five is made up by the two *locks,* who wear numbers 4 and 5. This pair is referred to as the *engine room* because this is where the power is generated in a scrum. While the front row sets the platform, the locks drive it forward — or keep it from being driven backward.

Locks are typically tall, athletic players with strong backs and powerful legs. These two (who often look like they got lost on the way to an NBA game) are the players who are lifted high in the air to catch the ball tossed in by the hooker in a lineout. Because of their height, they're also usually the two key ball-takers on kickoffs. Simply being tall isn't enough — locks also need to have good hands, balance, and coordination in the air. The ideal lock will have legs like springs and hands like glue.

Most locks either have athletic tape wrapped around their heads or wear protective headgear. This is done to prevent their ears from chafing when they pack down in the scrum.

Locks are the workhorses of the pack. They bind to each other and the props in front of them to attain the cohesion required to ensure that the scrum stays stable and doesn't collapse. This position generally requires someone tall and sturdy enough to not snap in two when pressure is applied in the scrum.

A truly great second-rower is almost superhuman. Although a second-rower may have a physique that at first sight doesn't look as if it belongs on a rugby field, she needs to be an outstanding ball-carrier, have tremendous agility, and be an enforcer on defense.

The back-row forwards: Breaking loose with the loosies

The back row consists of the players in jersey numbers 6, 7, and 8 (blindside flanker, openside flanker, and the number 8). Collectively, these players are referred to as the "loose forwards" (or loosies), because they're the first players to break away from the formation when the scrum ends. An excellent back-row combination is vital for a successful team because the three players are involved in so much of the game, creating numerous opportunities and thwarting many of the opposition's tactics.

These three players must be strong, quick off the mark, agile, and fearless in order to effectively tackle, carry the ball, and compete for possession.

Foraging with the flankers

The primary role of the two *flankers* is to tackle everything that moves and to steal the ball whenever possible. Flankers are built like football linebackers, with excellent quickness, agility, strength, and courage. These players are willing to sacrifice their bodies in a mission to gain possession of the ball and prevent their opponents from doing so.

The terms "openside" and "blindside" refer to which side of the scrum the flankers line up on. A scrum is usually set up on either side of the field, with the open (or larger amount) field on one side and the sideline on the other. The openside flanker joins the scrum beside the open field. The blindside flanker joins the side of the scrum closest to the sideline. The flankers bind to the locks' bodies on the "flanks" of the scrum, switching from one side of the scrum to the other depending on field position.

Toughing it on the blindside

The *blindside flanker* (number 6) has to be industrious. Along with the number 8, he is usually the second or third player to arrive at the breakdown. He must be an outstanding defender, particularly as many opposing teams attempt to attack down the blindside from a scrum. The blindside flanker has to always be mindful of this and be ready to cut off this option immediately with a devastating tackle. Usually, he is also required to be the third major lineout jumper. And, like the number 8, the blindside flanker must also be one of the real hard men in the team, and take on the enforcer's role if need be.

Discipline is a critical component of this flanker's makeup, because if he can't regulate his emotions and behavior, his actions will often get him in trouble. A flanker's mantra should be controlled aggression in search of and mainte-nance of possession. Flankers also need superior handling skills to support other ball-carriers and must be ready to transfer the ball in any situation.

Patrolling the openside

The *openside flanker* is usually the smaller and speedier of the two because she patrols a greater amount of field. Her prime aim is to be the first to the ball wherever it is on the pitch. She has to be quick to arrive at the scene after a tackle has occurred so she can wrestle the ball away from the opposi-tion on defense before others get there and the ruck forms (see Chapter 7 for more on the intricacies of the ruck). For offensive support, the openside must reach the breakdown first to make sure that possession is maintained if her teammate is stopped by a defender.

The good and not-so-good things that openside flankers do are often obscured by the heaps of bodies on the ground where they put in a substan-tial amount of their work. They fight and tussle for the ball whenever there's a chance to take it away, but must also know when to give up the struggle for possession to avoid a penalty. If they're good enough to pilfer the ball with-out upsetting the referee, they're worth their weight in gold. A good openside must have a perfect knowledge of rugby law and be able to adapt to different referees' interpretations and commands.

Piloting the pack at the number 8

The pack leader is the *number 8,* who, not surprisingly, wears the number 8 jersey. The ideal number 8 is shorter than the locks and taller than the flank-ers, with a bit more bulk to smash through opposing defensive lines. This position usually goes to the most skillful and savvy forward because so much of the match happens around him; he is often the first to receive the ball from scrums, lineouts, and in open play. He has responsibilities all over the field, so he has to make his presence felt from sideline to sideline.

The best in the business — Richie McCaw

New Zealand's Richie McCaw exemplifies all the skills, athleticism, and rugby IQ needed to excel on the openside. He's big and strong at 6'2" and 231 pounds, and has tremendous quickness and agility, plus the stamina to maintain a high work rate for the entire 80 minutes. His greatest asset, however, is his command of the subtleties of the breakdown. He's the best in the world at contesting for possession after a tackle occurs. The 29-year-old has been named the IRB Player of the Year three times, in 2006, 2009, and 2010. He has earned 92 caps and has been the longtime captain of both the All Blacks and the Crusaders. He draws a couple of penalties every game because he always plays right on the edge of the law, but he more than makes up for his infractions by regularly producing multiple turnovers. As teams get better at maintaining continuity on offense through multiple phases, having a player on your team who can create turnovers in general play each game is a huge advantage. One of the main reasons why New Zealand is the number-one ranked team in the world is because they have Richie McCaw wearing number 7.

From any scrum, the number 8, working in tandem with the scrumhalf and flyhalf (we explain the roles of these players later in this chapter), decides how the team initiates the attack or structures its defense. If the team is attacking, the number 8 must decide, as the ball arrives at his feet, whether to run with it, pass it to the scrumhalf, or protect the scrumhalf while he plays the ball.

A good number 8 always knows exactly what the opposition is up to and seizes any opportunity to take the ball forward himself if he believes he can expose a defensive weakness by making a quick run from the base of the scrum. He basically has to be anywhere and everywhere, always thinking and anticipating the flow of the game to stay near the ball, especially when there is a breakdown in play.

Get to the Back of the Line

The seven remaining players, who wear jersey numbers 9 to 15, are often referred to collectively as the *back line* (not to be confused with the back row of the forwards).

Like in football, where the linemen do all the dirty work in the trenches and the quarterback, running backs, and receivers get all the glory, in rugby an old oval adage says, "The forwards win the ball, and the backs win the game." A team with great backs and mediocre forwards will find itself starved of ball to work with. The opposite will produce plenty of possession but few chances to attack and score. To play winning rugby, you need 15 players totally committed to their roles and each other.

Passing and pestering for profit: The scrumhalf

The *scrumhalf* wears number 9, and is the border collie of the team. This is the team's organizer, who commands the forwards, directing their movements at ruck and maul time. Scrumhalves are usually the smallest players on the field and must have exceptional balance, be lightning-quick, and have superior passing skills. The very best scrumhalves are considered part of the pack by admiring forwards.

The scrumhalf's main aim is to be the team distributor. Because she is supposed to be one step away from everything that's happening, she is the one who usually distributes the ball from the scrums, lineouts, rucks and mauls, and whenever there is any form of breakdown in play. (We discuss the scrumhalf's passing skills in Chapter 10.)

The scrumhalf must be agile, intensely courageous, and the best passer on the team. The scrumhalf upholds communication between the forwards and the backs, and constantly urges the scrum on to greater heights, directing the rolling maul and calling for runners to take it up hard off of rucks. The scrumhalf usually works in tandem with the flyhalf, and the pair decides on the best attack and defensive options (for more about game tactics, see Chapter 11). When you see the scrumhalf and flyhalf making weird hand signals, or cupping their hands around the mouth so that they won't be heard by the opposition, it means they're calling plays for the next phase of attack and something interesting is about to occur.

A scrumhalf has to be able to make a variety of kicks to both relieve and impose pressure. On defense, a scrumhalf has to repeatedly tackle much bigger players, so her technique must be exemplary.

Feeling footloose and fancy-free: The flyhalf

The *flyhalf* wears number 10 and is the chief playmaker on the team, making the big decisions that often determine whether a team wins or loses. He is usually the player with the best combination of tactical acumen, kicking ability, and distribution skills.

The flyhalf is sometimes called the *pivot* because so much turns on what the player does. The flyhalf dictates the flow and style of the team's game plan, determining whether the team adopts a running game, relies instead on midfield kicking, or uses forward power to grind out a victory. (Chapter 11 discusses the flyhalf's role in devising winning tactics.) The rest of the back line has to be on the same wavelength as the flyhalf. He generally calls the various moves and plays, and chooses who will be chasing his variety of kicks downfield. In this sense, he is very much like a quarterback in football, deciding where the ball is going and to whom. On most teams, the flyhalf is also the first-choice goal kicker, but not always.

A flyhalf of any note must have a very cool demeanor and an ability to think clearly under pressure. A flyhalf also needs to possess good all-around skills, because every one of those skills is usually put to the test. Flyhalf is a very demanding position, but it's also one of the most rewarding in the game.

Mastering the midfield: Centers

Although both are called *centers*, the players wearing numbers 12 (inside center) and 13 (outside center) fulfill slightly different roles. The aim remains the same: trying to elude their opponents so that they can set up tries. Typically, centers have excellent kicking, passing, and handling skills, and can deliver a mean tackle.

Attacking from the inside out

Number 12 is the *inside center,* the player who stands closest in attack to the flyhalf (number 10) and who often acts as a back-up flyhalf, being the second midfield organizer of the attack. In simple terms, the main goal of the inside center is to keep attacks in some sort of formation by providing the link between the flyhalf and the outer backs.

A good inside center must be dependable, able to straighten the attack when required, and fearless in all facets of play. Few players touch the ball more often than the inside center, so she needs to have exceptional ball-handling skills and a tough hide to know when exactly to pass, when to run, or when to try to mix it up a bit with a chip kick (we explain kicking skills in Chapter 10). Most important, she cannot drop the ball, especially as she is invariably play-ing in a confined area with opponents hovering all around her. She has to be the coolest of customers with great hands. Centers are more likely to be drawn into rucks than other backs, so they should have more highly devel-oped skills in this area.

Like the flyhalf, the inside center often has to decide whether to straighten the attack by running directly upfield with the ball, or to push the attack wider by passing to either the outside center or the fullback. She often plays a "battering ram" role in running the ball hard into the opposition's defensive line, plowing into defenders, and challenging them to tackle her. Ideally, she's strong enough to maintain the appropriate body position in the tackle so that her teammates have a better chance to recycle the ball — the quicker the better! (We talk about running with the ball and tackling in Chapter 10.)

The best in the business — Daniel Carter

New Zealand All Black and Crusader Daniel Carter is the world's best flyhalf. Since his international debut in 2003 at the age of 21, Carter has amassed more points than any other player in the history of the game. He currently holds both the all-time records for points scored in test matches and for Super Rugby. He's the highest paid player in New Zealand, collecting $750,000 N.Z. (about $600,000 U.S.) a year.

Carter's greatest asset is his unique combination of physical gifts and tactical command of the game. From the pivot, he's the best in the world at controlling a match. He glides through gaps effortlessly when the opening is there, yet instinctively knows just when and where to pass or kick, relying on his uncanny ability to read the flow of a match. He's also a solid defender. Carter's importance to the All Blacks is undeniable; whenever he's not in the lineup because he's injured or unavailable, they suffer.

On the defensive side of the ball, the inside center's job is to stop her opposite number from breaking through the line. Missed head-up tackles by inside centers are anathema to any coach's defensive stratagem. This means taking on a speedy, aggressive runner, built like herself, over and over during the course of 80 minutes.

Attacking from the outside in

Number 13 is the *outside center,* who is generally the faster of the two centers and, along with the wings, is among the team's more important attacking players. The prime aim of the outside center is to set up teammates playing outside him, in particular the fullback and wings. This usually involves luring the opposition's defense into pursuing him and, thus, creating enough room to throw what must be a perfectly timed pass, putting a teammate through the opposition's defensive line. But he must also have the attacking instinct to know when to attack the line himself — and have faith in his own speed to get him through. The outside center is the player who tries to ruin the opposition's defensive pattern by providing an unpredictable attacking spark.

The outside center usually has more space to work with than the inside center. Many tries have been achieved after a number 13 has broken his way through the opposition's defense and then put his wing or fullback over the goal line with a precise kick into the corner of the field, well behind the opposition's defense. (Shown in Figure 4-1, the goal line is the line on or over which the attacking team must ground the ball in order to score a try.)

Just as important, the outside center must also be one of the best defenders, especially because a fast-running fullback is usually charging at him with ball in hand. This is no position for the fainthearted.

To be successful, the two centers must work together. Good chemistry between this pair is an important element of a rugby team's dynamics. Centers who work well together are able to read each other's intentions without giving them away — like bridge partners or old married couples.

Running wild out wide: The wings

Each team has two *wings*. Number 11 is the left wing, and number 14 is the right wing. When facing the defenders, the left wing is on the left-hand side of the team, and the right wing is on the right-hand side.

Wings have to be the fastest players on the team, possessing extraordinary acceleration and the ability to beat their opponents and then out-sprint them to the tryline. Wings need to be fast in attack and able to work well in a limited amount of space; they also need to be furious in defense, especially when the attack is focused on the outer reaches of the field.

The demands of playing on the left and right wing are basically the same. However, who plays on which wing is usually determined by which foot a player prefers to kick with, or if he has a better left- or right-footed *side-step* (side-stepping is where you dart off in a different direction than that anticipated by the opposition; we discuss it further in Chapter 10).

Wings are regarded as the "glory boys" of the team, whose primary function is to finish off attacking moves and score heaps of tries. On any team, they should be the most prolific tryscorers, because their teammates devote so much of their energies into putting them in a perfect position to get over the opposition's tryline.

Roaming the range: The fullback

The *fullback* wears the number 15 jersey and has more freedom to roam than any other player on the pitch. The fullback's prime responsibility is to be the last line of defense to prevent tries. Fullbacks are generally well-rounded rugby players. They must be able to catch the opposition's high kicks during attacks, or become the extra player in an attack.

The fullback has to have a kicking leg on her equal to that of the flyhalf because she will invariably be forced to clear the ball from deep in her own territory. Accuracy in kicking is paramount, because if her kick doesn't find touch, she has to chase it down and put her teammates onside before they can participate again (we cover the complexities of the offside law in Chapter 6).

A good fullback is like a chess player who uses intuition to anticipate what's going to happen a few moves ahead and then gets herself into the right place to deal with it. The best fullbacks also use their skills to predict their opponents' next move and then counter before the other side can react.

When the opposition has the ball, the fullback has to know where and when to join in the team's defensive line, to ensure that the correct number of players are in the right spots to stop the opposition from scoring. This can mean joining the defensive line between the centers, or among the forwards, to fill any gaps that may occur. Or it can mean placing herself in a strategic position behind the defensive line so she is in the right spot to catch a clearing kick from the opposition, or even a chip kick, which is aimed at turning around and disorienting her side.

Forwards and the midfield attackers have relatively defined areas of ground to work in and cover. However, the fullback, as the team's gatekeeper, has a lot of territory to patrol.

A fullback's normal position on the pitch is standing several meters behind her attacking line. This means she usually has half the pitch to cover, and even more when her own side is close to the opposition's tryline. So knowing how to cover that area is important. No other player on the pitch is on her own so often without the support of a teammate. It's a demanding position, which explains why a good fullback is so vital to a team's prospects of winning. It also explains why this is probably the most stressful position on the field — the fullback is the last tackler, so if she misses her entire team is let down plus the other side gets five points!

Surprising the enemy

A fullback can really make her mark on attack. Because she's relatively free to move about the field, the fullback should be used as the surprise attack weapon — she can pop up anywhere and everywhere on the pitch. A running fullback radically improves the attacking prowess of any back line, particularly if she is able to read a play, knowing when it's time to hit the line at pace or to join the line to act as an extra attacker.

The aim of most rugby attacks is to create an overlap where the attacking team has more players than the defensive line in front of them. The fullback can create that overlap if she chooses to enter the back line either near the centers or wings at an opportune moment.

Defusing bombs

In addition to being a sure tackler and intuitive attacker, the fullback needs to be cool under pressure. To break up their attacking patterns, or to take advantage of wet or windy conditions, teams often kick high balls to test the fullback. A *high ball* (or an *up and under*) is a kick from the opposition that's aimed downfield, traveling high in the air, usually 20 to 30 meters (22 to 33 yards) above the heads of the players. The number 15 must have great intestinal fortitude to maintain total concentration when fielding the ball, all the while knowing that tacklers are bearing down on her. The ball usually swirls in the air and is often tricky to catch, making it a fullback's nightmare.

The fullback is usually the first opposing player a team tests. If she's not up to the task of fielding the high ball, you can be sure her opponents will target her and keep applying pressure. If the fullback mishandles the ball, the opposition usually gains serious ground, if not a try.

Chapter 5

Laying Down the Laws

. . . .

. . . .

*R*ugby is a game governed by laws rather than rules — rules are imposed to regulate behavior, but laws are implemented to achieve a desired result. In the case of rugby, the IRB designs the laws to produce a free-flowing game during which two teams score as many points as possible, with the team that scores more being declared the winner.

Arguing about interpretations and discussing the laws of the game is a noble pastime that takes place in pubs, clubhouses, and rugby grounds all over the world. In this chapter, we introduce you to the laws by telling you where they come from and how they've evolved. We explain how you can get a copy of the coveted law book, and we detail the responsibilities of the people who are charged with running the game on the pitch from start to finish.

The Laws of the Game

Twenty-two laws cover every aspect of how the game is played on the field. From how the pitch is laid out and marked to what happens in the in-goal area, the laws of the game encompass all the information necessary to allow the game to be played. (A separate set of regulations involves how the sport itself is governed.) Although regional variations may develop in terms of style and technique in playing the game, the laws at the senior level are exactly the same whether the match is the World Cup Final or a third-division match in a less-developed country. (Laws for younger rugby players are age-appropriate for safety reasons; see Chapter 17.) Rugby is a centrally administered sport, which means that the International Rugby Board (IRB) decides on the laws and controls when and if they are to be changed.

The International Rugby Board (IRB)

The IRB, founded in 1886, is the world-governing and law-making body for the game of rugby. The Executive Council meets twice a year and consists of the eight founding nations — Scotland, Ireland, Wales, England, Australia, New Zealand, South Africa, and France. Each founding nation has two seats. Argentina, Canada, Italy, and Japan each have one seat on the Council, as does FIRA-AER (the International Amateur Rugby Federation – European Rugby Association). The day-to-day business of the Board is conducted by a professional staff of more than 50, the majority of whom are based in Dublin. Rugby is played by men and women and boys and girls in more than 100 countries across 5 continents. The IRB has 97 member Unions, 19 Associates, and 6 Regional Associations.

The IRB writes the law

Until the 21st century, 28 laws existed, many of which overlapped in a mish-mash of repetitive jargon. Fortunately, the IRB saw the detrimental effect this was having on the development of the game, and simplified the jumble quite a bit by consolidating the essential knowledge into 22 laws with far less repetition and a lot more clarity. Although still seemingly daunting to the rugby novice, the newer version of the laws has been instrumental in producing some of the finest examples of rugby matches ever played in just the last few years.

The IRB doesn't make lighthearted changes for the sake of seeing bigger numbers on the scoreboard, but instead has a detailed process for updating the law book. According to the organization's bylaws, a Laws Committee considers changes proposed by the individual unions that make up the IRB, recommends changes and amendments to those submissions, and clarifies real-life situations that occur during the course of each year. In this way, the IRB can respond to trends in the game happening around the world and also prevent harmful alterations that detract from the overall spirit of the laws. From time to time, the IRB authorizes the application of experimental law variations (ELVs) in prescribed competitions to test whether they may benefit the sport. The most recent ELV trials occurred in 2008 and resulted in the adoption of ten law variations. The IRB also continually amends the language of the law book to clarify points of confusion without making material changes.

The laws are dynamic and ever-changing

If you were to pick up a law book from the early days of the game, it would be pretty unrecognizable in content compared to today's version. Rugby did not start like basketball did, with a complete set of laws handed down from on high. What happened was that the early attempts at codification reflected what was already occurring on the pitch. As the game spread throughout the world, modifications were instituted to ensure continuity.

Over the years, many laws have been changed to promote specific strategic objectives, to rein in wayward practitioners of dubious techniques, and to correct imbalances in the way offense and defense interact. The best way to understand this process is to take a close look at a specific law relating to one part of the lineout that has undergone radical changes in the last few years.

The lineout is a means of restarting play after the ball has gone into touch, or out of bounds. One team throws the ball in as both teams' jumpers are lifted to precarious heights in an attempt to gain possession and produce a quick ball for the back line to use. Lineouts have become an intricately choreographed phase that requires coordinated timing from everyone involved. But it wasn't always so.

Until 1999, lifting in the lineout was done surreptitiously under the guise of supporting the jumper, who had to rely on good old-fashioned vertical leaping ability and natural height to secure the throw-in. There was also a lot more contact between the two teams and fewer clean takes that allowed the ball to be spun out wide in a hurry. When the law changed and lifting was brought into the open, a whole new set of skills had to be learned and the sport of rugby gained by highlighting its enormous collective capacity for ingenuity and the athleticism of its players. As of this writing, no serious advocates are calling for a return to the older, slower, less exciting incarnation of the lineout law.

Of course, unintended consequences always accompany any change, and lifting was no exception. If lifting was legal in lineouts, then why not on restart kicks? Seeing jumpers positioned at various points on the pitch with individual lifters ready to propel them skyward in hopes of cleanly fielding the kick is now common. This law change has also made the game more interesting and put more strategic emphasis on what was a neglected area of play.

Then, some coach or player somewhere had the bright idea of lifting jumpers to snatch penalty and conversion kicks out of the air before they could clear the crossbar. This strategy actually worked a few times over a couple of seasons, but it proved too much for the traditionalists at the IRB. The Laws Committee deemed that it contravened the spirit of the law governing penalties (a viewpoint we agree with) and added an amendment that made the practice illegal. This example demonstrates how the laws are evolving with the game — but never at the expense of the all-important ethos of the sport.

Reading the law book

We played rugby for many years before ever actually holding a copy of the laws in our hands and daring to look inside. Because we didn't know any better, we spent years believing incorrect interpretations and committing penalties for unknown reasons, which generally limited our effectiveness for our teams. Knowledge of the laws came from older, more experienced players who spouted knowingly about "hands in the ruck," "offside at the tackle," and other vague terms. In retrospect, what we heard varied from almost right to completely wrong.

Delving into the law book opened up a whole new world. Referees' calls that previously seemed unfathomable were suddenly made clear. Confidence soared at the breakdown, where strength and technique were supplemented with an almost magical sense of knowledge. Our enjoyment of the game expanded exponentially as the mysterious shield of ignorance surrounding referees' decisions melted away.

Our advice for any aspiring rugby player, coach, referee, or fan is to get a copy of the laws and dig in. Versions can be downloaded from the Internet, but going to the IRB's official Web site (www.irb.com) is best, so that you know the version is up-to-date. Getting your hands on a hard copy is a little more difficult but not impossible.

Building up your knowledge

You don't have to spend long days and nights poring over the laws — far from it. However, an hour or two going through the main points of the law is time well spent. You'll begin to have a better understanding of what the referee is doing on the pitch if you've done your homework. In fact, you're more likely to know what's going on than some of the players, many of whom, sad to say, don't have a clue what the referee is going on about.

A good way to familiarize yourself with the laws in action is to focus on the referee during a game. Watch his every move, and try to figure out why he makes the decisions he does. Through close observation, you'll get to know the various signals and recognize the types of play that lead to important decisions (all 45 of the referee signals are found later in this chapter).

You can quickly enhance your knowledge of the game by approaching the referee at the reception following a local match — most of them love the game every bit as much as the players do and enjoy talking about it. Also, referees are probably the most cooperative and friendly group to deal with in the rugby world, and are always eager to help people improve their knowledge of the laws of the game.

Approach referees in a friendly manner that reassures them you aren't going to start arguing the merits of a decision they just made. You'll soon find yourself immersed in the intrigue of what actually happened at the bottom of a ruck, or why a certain transgressor was judged to be offside. You'll begin to understand the finer points of some laws that were once absolutely bewildering.

Another way to increase your level of understanding is to ask questions of your coach, who is often a good source of information about the laws. You may find that coaches are instant experts on referees, even though their views may be more derogatory than flattering. For all this, however, most coaches have a good basic knowledge of the law book — it's an essential requirement if they want their team to succeed. (See Chapter 18 for more information on coaches.)

Your coach should tell you during training sessions if you're doing something that would cause a referee to come down on you like a ton of bricks. If you repeat the offense in a match, your coach's behavior toward you is going to be less congenial, to say the least. Finding yourself banished to the reserve bench is a good indication that your knowledge of the laws is flimsy and you need to spend some quiet time with the law book. Just as a lack of knowledge of the laws can hurt your team immensely, an understanding of them will reap enormous benefits.

Introducing the Match Officials

Running the game is a tough job that often attracts more criticism than praise. The referee is the main player in this drama, but she has help from other members of the refereeing fraternity who are there to make her job easier. Collectively, the referee, the touch judges or assistant referees, the substitution official, and the television match official (TMO) are known as the *match officials.* (If you aspire to become a referee or a touch judge, check out Chapter 20 for all the details.)

The referee: The one with the whistle

Whether you're a player or a spectator, the referee is the person to watch. The referee is the single most important person on the field during a game. The primary function of the referee is to manage the match and help create a spectacle for the fans to enjoy.

The referee is the official who has the ultimate power over what occurs in a rugby match. What he says, goes. He is the sole judge of fact and law during the match. The referee's position is probably the most demanding of all, requiring a broad depth of knowledge, a high level of fitness, and a very thick skin.

Players prefer referees who don't talk down to them. No one likes a dictator. The best referees understand what the players are doing and, whenever possible, try to let the game flow. Referees should be firmly in control without feeling the need to constantly assert their authority. This is a tough balance to strike for any referee. The ultimate accomplishment for a referee is when, at the end of the match, no one remembers who held the whistle.

Referees are passionate about the game and fervently believe they have the best job in the world. The top-level referee's job has been transformed by the advent of professionalism. Full-time referees are now needed to work the various competitions around the globe. In the past, police officers, school teachers, and business people volunteered their time as referees. Now a small but expanding group of professional referees who work matches all over the world exists, covering competitions from the Six Nations to the Tri Nations to Super Rugby. (For a description of these tournaments, see Chapter 14.) Travel is often long-distance — Southern Hemisphere referees sometimes officiate at Northern Hemisphere matches, and vice versa. The reward is that they get to spend time in some of the most entertaining cities in the world — while getting paid well for doing something that they thoroughly enjoy.

The vast majority of referees are, and will always be, amateurs. Regardless of their status, however, the same duties and responsibilities are entrusted to them. Before the match, they conduct a coin toss to determine which team will kick off and which end the other side will defend. They also do a pre-match inspection to ensure players are in compliance with the relevant laws on equipment and clothing.

During the match, the referee is the sole judge of fact and law. Referees' decisions are final, with no appeal to a higher authority available. Referees are additionally charged with keeping the official time and score, sending players off for serious offenses, and regulating the comings and goings of substitutes and replacements. In all these duties, they're assisted by fellow refs in subordinate roles, depending upon the level of match being played. (The further one travels down from the highest echelons, the less likely it is that a referee will have two other referees as touch judges.) A referee is allowed to consult with the other match officials, but the final decision in all matters is the whistle-blower's alone.

Your rugby-playing experience will be far better if you try to keep the referee happy — antagonizing the person with the whistle is not a good idea. Rugby players should always treat referees with respect and address them as "Sir" or "Madam." One of the ways that rugby maintains its reputation for sportsman-like conduct is a zero-tolerance policy toward players and coaches at any level who are not civil in dealing with the referee. The badgering and brow-beating of officials that occurs in other professional sports is totally unacceptable in rugby and is contrary to the spirit of the game.

To prevent being targeted by the referee, act as if you never intended to break the law, never question a ruling unless you're the team captain, and be courteous at all times.

Touch judges and assistant referees: The ones with the flags

The term *assistant referee* is a new one used by the IRB and refers to touch judges who are also trained referees. They have all the same duties as touch judges, plus they're entrusted to provide referees with any assistance needed to fulfill their responsibilities. In practical terms, professional or high-level domestic matches may feature assistant referees appointed by the organizing union, whereas lower-level contests are likely to have touch judges provided by the competing teams.

The two touch judges, one on each side of the field, play a very important role in a rugby match. As the name indicates, their primary responsibility is determining where a lineout has to be formed and which team throws the ball in to the lineout after it has gone into touch (we cover lineouts in Chapter 9).

The touch judges have to determine exactly where the ball crossed the touchline, which team was the last to touch it, and which team will throw the ball back in. They signal this by standing at the spot where the lineout is to be taken, raising a flag overhead, and pointing in the direction of the team that will throw it in.

A further duty is judging whether or not penalty and conversion kicks have been successful. To do this, the touch judges move to a spot behind each upright that gives them the best view of the kick. If the kick goes over the crossbar and between the posts, they raise their flags to indicate that fact.

Assistant referees also act as the referee's second and third pair of eyes. They advise the referee whenever they witness incidents of foul play that the referee didn't see. At the provincial and international levels, an assistant referee is in radio contact with the referee and can alert her via a microphone built into the touch flag. In matches at the lower levels, an assistant referee alerts the referee by holding the flag horizontally and pointing infield at a right angle to the touchline.

After you've watched a few games, you begin to realize that the touch judges and assistant referees are almost as important as the referee, and have to be as fit and alert as the one with the whistle.

The substitution official: The one with the numbers

In the not-so-distant old days of rugby, the 15 starting players of a match were usually the same players who finished it. In international matches, a doctor used to have to certify that an injured player was no longer able to continue before he could be replaced. With the liberalization of the substitution law, which encourages coaches to make numerous changes as a strategic matter of course, the need arose for an extra official to supervise this activity.

The *substitution official,* sometimes called a *reserve touch judge* or assistant referee, handles the parade of players entering and exiting the pitch for trips to the blood bin or the sin bin, and the subbing and replacing of individuals from the reserve bench. For changes made by the coaching staff, this official holds up two numbers, one for the player leaving the game and the other for the one joining it, letting spectators and the referee know exactly who is contesting the match at all times.

The duties don't stop there, though, because the substitution official has to be wary of teams trying to get around the various substitution laws through nefarious means. And the reason why this person has to be a qualified referee is that on rare occasions the match referee will suffer an injury and have to be replaced by one of the touch judges, necessitating the substitution official's move up the ladder to touch judge.

The TMO: The one with the video screen

At most major rugby matches involving professionals, a referee is also required for a fourth important job, the *television match official (TMO),* or *video referee*. The TMO spends the game in a quiet room somewhere in the stadium perched in front of a television set. You may be thinking this sounds like quite a cozy little job, but keep in mind that the video referee has to be an actual referee because the job requires someone with an intimate knowledge of the laws.

The video referee's role has expanded from when it was first introduced. Initially, only in-goal decisions could be considered and the referee had to ask specific questions of exactly what she wanted to be reviewed. The original purpose was basically to determine whether or not a try had been scored, as well as other in-goal issues, but that responsibility has evolved into helping the referee to identify players who have been involved in committing foul play.

Scoring a try

When referees are uncertain whether a player has properly grounded the ball on or over the tryline, they make a hand signal that resembles a mime outlining a large imaginary box, to indicate a television screen. This means they've asked for the video referee to watch a replay of the incident and determine whether someone actually scored a try. At the same time, the referee contacts the video referee via a radio microphone hookup and explains what he wants the video referee to look for. Usually the video referee watches the play several times before informing the referee whether a try was scored. Occasionally, the replay won't definitively show the incident in question; in this case, the TMO will send it back to the referee without a recommendation. Either way, the final decision rests with the referee on the field.

Identifying foul play

The TMO has the added burden of figuring out who was involved in an incident of foul play if the offender couldn't be singled out by the referee or the touch judges. The referee contacts the TMO and asks for help in unmasking the offender. In this case, the video referee can look only at the incident specified by the referee.

Recognizing the Referee's Signals

If you're watching the match on television, you have the advantage of being able to listen to the referee's calls, because they now wear microphones. Having the referees miked allows you to hear what they say to the players in the heat of battle; it also lets you eavesdrop on their conversations with touch judges and the TMO.

Many signals a referee makes are somewhat understandable because they mimic the infraction being called. Referees give signals to indicate what penalties have been given, all scoring plays, and whether a team has been awarded a free kick or advantage in play. The referee also signals when the clock is stopped. While the time left in the game is often shown on the scoreboard, remember that the referee is the final arbiter of time — what the referee says, goes.

Some signals are not so easily understood, though, and may take a little time to identify. But don't worry; the signaling system becomes very clear when you can identify each specific signal. The signals you'll see the referee make during a rugby match are shown in Figure 5-1.

Figure 5-1: The referee's signaling system.

Intentionally bringing down a ruck or maul

Entering a ruck or a maul in front of the back foot and from the side

Unplayable ball in maul

Prop drawing down opponent

Prop pulling opponent

Wheeling scrum more than 90 degrees

Foot-up by front row player

Throw-in at scrum not straight

Failure to bind fully

Handling ball in ruck or scrum

Throw-in at lineout not straight

Closing gaps in lineout

Barging in lineout

Leaning on player in lineout

Pushing opponent in lineout

Offside at scrum, ruck, or maul

Offside at lineout

Obstruction in general play

High tackle (foul play)

Offside option: penalty kick or scrum

Offside under 10-meter law or not 10 meters at penalty and free kicks

Dissent (contesting referee's call)

Award of drop-out at the 22-meter line

Punching (foul play)

Physiotherapist needed

Stamping (foul play: inappropriate use of boot)

Ball held up in-goal

Timekeeper to stop and start watch

Doctor needed

Bleeding wound

Chapter 6

Understanding the Fundamentals

*U*nderstanding the fundamentals of the game is the first step to becoming a full-fledged rugby enthusiast. Whether you're a player, spectator, parent, or coach, being familiar with the basic principles makes every rugby experience better and more fulfilling.

When you first watch rugby on TV or in person, it can appear confusing as 30 players run around the pitch in what appears to be semi-organized chaos. Their collective actions are mysteriously orchestrated by the whistle-blowing referee, who shouts indecipherable commands and periodically stops and starts play at seemingly random spots on the pitch. That's how we first saw rugby as well, attracted to the overall physicality of the sport but lacking even the most basic grasp of what was happening.

Our knowledge of the game developed from asking questions of more erudite fans along the sidelines and using the trial-and-error method on the playing field. Many lightbulbs of awareness have gone off in our heads over the years as murky concepts suddenly became clear while watching and playing in countless matches. In this chapter, we discuss the object of the game, detail the skills that every rugby player needs, and clarify some of the most confusing rugby regulations, so you'll be able to bypass the initial confusion stage and move right into understanding the action.

The Object of the Game

The game of rugby has one simple objective — to score more points than the opposition. This is an aim common to most ball sports, but where rugby differs is that the laws of the game prescribe that it be done by carrying, passing, kicking, and grounding the ball, and, most important, by observing fair play and doing it all with a sporting spirit.

Although individual positions have specific duties, all players are allowed to participate in offensive and defensive aspects of the game and thus must have a universal set of skills enabling them to do so.

Accumulating points in rugby can be done only by possessing the ball, either in scoring tries or kicking goals. This has led coaches and strategists down divergent paths with the same endpoint. Some focus on building excellent defensive teams that can withstand pressure and ultimately create enough turnovers and mistakes to produce opportunities to score points. Another school of thought stresses attacking prowess, placing a premium on creativity and speed.

Both approaches attempt to build squads that can capitalize on the concepts of interaction between offense and defense inherent in the laws of the game. The best teams are ones that master both disciplines and easily transition from one mode to the other. Too much emphasis on either discipline leads to a concentration of players without sufficient overall skills, exposing exploitable weaknesses.

Running with the ball

Western Montana has become a hotbed of high school rugby, with new teams springing up every year all across the region. Through my membership in the Missoula All-Maggots club, I've had the opportunity to work with many of these teams as a visiting coach. Most of the youngsters taking up the game in Montana are also football players, so they're no strangers to rough contact and tackling, but what I've been most struck by is how much they all enjoy catching and running with the ball. A lot of the newcomers are used to playing both offense and defense, but very few of them have ever tucked the ball away and run at or over a defender. After they experience this thoroughly exciting aspect of rugby, they're hooked on the sport. The additional skills and fitness that football players gain from exposure to rugby definitely helps them on the gridiron, but more important, it gives them a chance to play a game that they'll be able to participate in throughout their adult lives, regardless of their size or athletic ability.

Running, Passing, and Kicking

Because the key to rugby is scoring points, the obvious requirement is to move the ball toward the opposition's half of the field either to ground the ball in their in-goal for a try or to get into range to successfully make a kick at goal. All the while, the defense attempts to stop this progress downfield. The three ways that teams change their position on the field are by running, passing, and kicking the ball.

Running

Any of the 30 players on the pitch can run with the ball to their heart's content, provided they can maintain possession. Being a valued ball-runner entails never losing possession of the ball, either when tackled or by throwing errant passes. Unless you're superhuman, odds are pretty good that you're going to be tackled before you reach the tryline. To avoid being brought down, you can pass the ball backward to a teammate who is behind you.

Passing

Requirement number one in passing the rugby ball is that all passes must go either backward or exactly horizontal, often called a *flat pass*. This standard is in relation to a team's own tryline, not the position of the player. If a player throws the ball and it travels parallel to the tryline, then it's a legal pass. If the ball's arc takes it anywhere behind that parallel line, then this pass is perfectly acceptable also. (Illegal forward passes are discussed a little later in this section. A variety of passing styles are explained in Chapter 10.)

Kicking

The third method of advancing the ball downfield is by kicking it. Every player is allowed to kick the ball, but most coaches want this chore to be handled by backs unless circumstances dictate otherwise. A number of different types of kicks exist, but they fall into three general categories: short, medium, and long. (We go over these kicks in greater detail and give them specific names in Chapter 10.)

Short kicks, whether along the ground or in the air, are usually designed to be regathered by the kicker and then carried farther. These kicks make sense when the defensive line has come up fast and flat, cutting down the space and time available to run or pass the ball through them.

PLAYER TIP

Creating space

By first running and then passing the ball at just the right time and place, you can draw the defenders to you, thereby *creating space* for your teammate to carry on with the charge. The ability to create space, or to entice the defenders in your immediate area to focus on you and therefore forget about your supporting teammates, is a critical skill that can make a good player into a great one. If you can draw the defenders slightly away from where the attack will come next and then time your pass perfectly, you'll have created space and unlocked the secret to winning rugby. The key

here is that you never want the player receiving the pass to be in a worse attacking position than you were. Passing the ball should be done to accomplish something. Simply passing because you're about to be tackled, without considering whether the receiver is in a position to advance the attack, won't help your team and may get your best buddy injured.

In rugby parlance, throwing a ball that forces your teammate into a defenseless position as he attempts to catch it, setting him up for a monstrous hit by the tackler, is called a *hospital pass*.

Medium kicks are mostly booted high in the air to test the catching abilities of the opposition under pressure as members of the kicker's team converge on them. If the chasers, or the fastest of the kicker's teammates, get there in time, they can contest the ball in the air.

COACH TIP

Kicking also plays a crucial role in field position. Because scoring points from your half of the field is harder, you need a reliable kicker who can punt it long with good accuracy to move play into your opponent's half of the pitch.

Long kicks are meant to gobble up large chunks of territory in one fell swoop. When a team is backed up behind its own 22-meter line, these kicks are generally intended to go over the touchline so that play can be restarted with a lineout. At other times, long kicks are supposed to stay in the field of play and are followed up by marauding defenders to attack the ball-carrier before her teammates can retreat in time to help out.

What Can Go Wrong?

If rugby just involved players running, passing, and kicking the ball up and down the pitch unopposed, it would be about as exciting as lawn bowling. What makes the sport a thrilling spectacle is that for every player attempting to run, pass, or kick, a corresponding player is doing his darndest to prevent that from happening. When athletes collide in any competitive endeavor, errors are bound to occur, especially if the goal of one team is to force the other into making mistakes. In rugby, these mistakes have specific names — and the two most common involve ball-handling.

Knock-on

The most recognizable form of a knock-on looks very much like a fumble in football. A *knock-on* happens when a ball-carrier loses control of the ball for whatever reason and it goes forward (meaning toward the opponent's dead-ball line) and touches any other player or the ground before the player can regather the ball. If the ball goes flat or backward, that's not an infraction. The same is true if a player bobbles the ball in the air but is able to haul it back in before it touches the ground or any another player.

A knock-on is also called when the ball hits a player's arm or hand — whether they're trying to catch it or not — and bounces forward. The distance the ball travels forward is irrelevant; it can be a couple of centimeters or 9 meters, and it's still a knock-on. Barely nudging the ball ahead with your hand while trying to pick it up is the same as having it ripped from your grasp in a tackle.

A ball that bounces off a player's head, chest, or shoulder is not a knock-on, provided that no hands or arms are involved. Getting hit in the face with the ball when it's passed to you is embarrassing — but it's a relief when the referee shouts, "Off the head, play on!"

The one exception to the knock-on law is when a player is trying to block, or charge down a kick. The law is written to reward aggressive play, so if the ball hits the outstretched hand or arm of a player who's attempting to block a kick, it's not an infringement as long as the player doesn't try to catch it.

If play stops after a knock-on (see the advantage law section for when play stops and when it doesn't), the non-offending team gets to put the ball in at a scrum on the spot where the knock-on occurred. A knock-on then, in effect, is usually a turnover by the team that had the ball.

Wise coaches always place an emphasis in training on practicing the basic handling skills. The better your team handles the ball, the less likely they are to knock it on during a game.

Forward pass

Throwing the ball forward — meaning toward the opponent's dead-ball line — is strictly prohibited. If you pass the ball and it travels forward as it leaves your hands, you've made a *forward pass*. From the safety of the sidelines, a forward pass seems eminently preventable. But in the heat of battle, passing the ball forward is easily done. Location on the pitch becomes jumbled, and pressure from tacklers can be intense, causing wayward passes that are intended to follow the tenets of the law but somehow run afoul of it.

Mistakes — intentional and otherwise

Rugby referees have to be some of the most perceptive beings on the planet, because they're called upon to determine intent as well as assign blame for mistakes on the field. A number of errors, when they occur in general play and there is no hint of purpose behind them, result in a scrum to the non-offending team. A knock-on is one such case. If, however, the referee thinks a player intentionally knocked a ball on in an attempt to spoil the offensive move to keep it from going quickly out wide, that is dealt with by awarding a penalty to the other side — giving them possession and a better tactical position than a scrum.

Once again, an exception exists. If the ball is thrown backward and hits the ground and then bounces forward, it's not an infraction. The same exception applies if a pass is released backward and the wind catches it and takes it forward. You are responsible for only what you do with the ball, not what the ground or the elements cause it to do.

A good way to judge whether a pass is forward or not is to imagine a line running through the ball that is parallel to the goal lines at either end of the field. A pass that goes along that line or behind it is legal; a pass in front of it is illegal. (The same standard helps determine whether a ball has been knocked on.)

The Tackle Law — Where Football Ends, Rugby Begins

When football emerged from the sport of rugby early in the 20th century, the biggest initial change was the concept of ending each play when the ball-carrier was tackled. In football, that's the signal for everyone to stop playing and head back to their respective huddles and spend the better part of the following minute getting ready for the next five seconds of action. In rugby, after the ball-carrier is tackled the game continues and gets even more interesting. What happens next may seem muddled and disorganized, but if you know what to look for it's actually well orchestrated and usually follows several different laws that govern the tackle situation, or what is known as the *breakdown*.

The tackle situation and continuity

For years, rugby administrators at the International Rugby Board (IRB) have been fiddling around with the tackle laws in a bid to quicken the game. The admirable intention has been to speed up the process of making the ball available for further play. Concerned that matches were being slowed down by unsightly pileups of bodies fighting for the ball, the lawmakers have tried to simplify things. The result has been the assigning of responsibilities to both the tackler and the tackled player which, if unfulfilled, draw the referee's whistle and the awarding of a penalty. Even though the changes have been somewhat effective, this is still the most contentious area of the game.

The tackle law is written like this: "A tackle occurs when the ball carrier is held by one or more opponents and is brought to ground. A ball-carrier who is not held is not a tackled player and a tackle has not taken place. Opposition players who hold the ball-carrier and bring that player to ground, and who also go to ground, are known as tacklers. Opposition players who hold the ball-carrier and do not go to ground are not tacklers." The definition of "brought to ground" includes a player who is on one knee, sitting on the ground, or on top of another player.

The tackled player

When players are tackled, they must immediately let go of the ball when their bodies hit the ground and their momentum stops so that play can continue. Lying on the ground and keeping a tight hold of the ball is illegal. Tackled players must either pass the ball immediately or release it at once by placing it on the ground in any direction (ideally, the ball should be placed backward, but that isn't always possible).

When the tackled player has released the ball, she must attempt to roll away from the area — which in practice means that she can't lie on top of the ball, and can have no further involvement in play until she regains her feet. If the tackled player tries to play the ball in any way, or prevent others on their feet from playing it, while still on the ground, she is liable to be penalized.

As a ball-carrier, your primary goal is to not lose possession of the ball for your team, whether you're on your feet or on the ground. Therefore, the best thing to do when being tackled is to manipulate your body position so that you fall with the tackler on the opposite side from where your teammates are. That way, when you release the ball back, your team will have first crack at securing possession and the opponents will have to step over both the tackler and you to grab the ball. (We offer more tips for the tackled player in Chapter 7.)

The tackler

When a player tackles an opponent and they both go to ground, the tackler must immediately release the tackled player. Then he must immediately get to his feet or move away from the tackled player and roll away from the ball. After the tackler gets back on his feet, he can play the ball on the ground from any direction. Exactly how far away the tackler must roll isn't defined, but the law is clear that he must not interfere with play until he's back on his feet. If he makes the mistake of grabbing the ball while he's still on the ground, he attracts the whistle and the opposition is awarded a penalty.

If by the time he gets to his feet a ruck is already formed, he can't then play the ball because he is now subject to the ruck law, which we discuss fully in Chapter 7. After a tackle, all other players must be on their feet when they play the ball. Players are on their feet if no other parts of their body are supported by the ground or by players on the ground.

Tackling no-no's

In addition to the restrictions we describe in the previous section, the following rules also apply:

- A player can't stop a tackled player from passing the ball.
- A player can't stop a tackled player from releasing the ball, or from getting up and moving away from it.
- A player isn't allowed to pull the ball from a tackled player before the tackled player has released it.
- A player may not fall on or over the tackled player.
- A tackle can't be made when the ball-carrier is held by one opponent and a teammate of the ball-carrier binds onto that ball-carrier, because a maul has been formed (see Chapter 7 for more on the maul).

What happens if the ball doesn't come out? Sometimes so many bodies are heaped together on the ground that neither the tackler nor tackled player can move away no matter how hard the players try. If the ball becomes unplayable at a tackle, the referee orders a scrum, with the put-in given to the team that was moving forward before the stoppage. If no team was moving forward, the scrum put-in goes to the attacking team. Most tackles turn into rucks soon afterward — we cover how and why that occurs in Chapter 7.

The Advantage Law — When Play Stops and When It Continues

When you watch a rugby match, you'll notice that some of the things we describe in this chapter happen, yet play doesn't stop. Even those who are more familiar with the game may ask, "Why not?" The answer is because of the *advantage law*, which allows play to continue even after an infraction has been committed. The goal of the law is to keep play flowing by minimizing stoppages. The referees who tend to earn the highest accolades in the public's eyes — meaning they're the least complained about — are the ones who properly use this critical piece of judicial wisdom.

The advantage law is easy to understand if thought about in the right way. Simply put, when one team commits an infraction, the other team is afforded the opportunity to gain an advantage from the mistake. Instead of immediately blowing the whistle for every little blunder, the referee lets play continue, waiting to see if the non-offending team can profit from the miscue.

Imagine, for example, that a player from the United States is running with the ball and is tackled hard by a player from Canada. When she hits the ground, the ball spills forward from her hands. That's a classic knock-on. But instead of stopping play with a whistle blast, the referee calls out "Advantage Canada" (or more likely identifies the team by the color of jersey the players are wearing) and points an arm in their direction. Now the Canadian team knows they can try to make the best of the situation on attack. If they're successful and can capitalize on the error, the referee will call out "Advantage over," and the contest progresses without play being interrupted. If they're stopped or otherwise stymied in taking their opportunity, the referee will blow the whistle and bring the teams back to the spot of the infringement for a scrum, where the ball will be put in by the Canadian scrumhalf.

So what exactly does a team have to do to gain an advantage? Referees consider two criteria: territorial and tactical. To illustrate, we go back to our North American example.

To gain a territorial advantage, the Canadian team would have to advance the ball beyond where it was originally knocked on by the American player and end up gaining more territory than if the referee had ordered a scrum. They could accomplish this by running it downfield or kicking it and having it go out farther down the touchline. Territorial advantage gained must be clear and real — the possibility of gaining it is not enough to forestall a stoppage in play.

A tactical advantage can be gained by a team having the freedom to use the ball as they wish. In the same example, if the Canadian team decided to pass the ball out wide along the back line to give their winger some space to run, they may have gained a tactical advantage even if they didn't get past the point of the original infringement. Referees have to ask themselves, "Was the team able to make a conscious choice to employ a tactic that would have gained them an advantage?" Whether or not the option was successful is irrelevant.

Tactical advantage is harder for referees to judge than territorial advantage because it involves more interpretation, whereas a territorial gain is easy to discern with the naked eye.

One of the oldest coaching sayings is directly related to advantage. Savvy coaches from the international level down to the beginners always encourage their charges to "play to the whistle." Newcomers to the game often see an opponent make a mistake and immediately let up, assuming that the referee is going to blow the whistle. If you train your team members to continue playing at full speed, they'll have more chances to cash in on the opposition's errors. Besides, you never know if the referee will see every infraction.

The advantage law takes precedence over the rest of the laws because it's responsible for cutting down on the number of times the action is halted for inevitable infringements. Advantage can be played for all but five situations in a game of rugby; these instances are safety-oriented, and four of them deal with scrums.

A whistle must be blown at once with no consideration for advantage when

- ✔ A player is lifted in the air in a scrum.

- ✔ The scrum collapses.

- ✔ The scrum is wheeled around more than 90 degrees.

- ✔ The ball comes straight out the other side of the tunnel from where the ball was put into the scrum by the scrumhalf.

- ✔ The ball, or a player carrying it, touches the referee.

- ✔ The ball has gone into touch or over the dead-ball line.

Players with a good tactical head on their shoulders have figured out an interesting use of the advantage law that may help you score some extra points for your team. If you're within range of the goalposts and you hear the advantage call, try to make a drop goal. If it goes over the post, great, you've added three points to your team's score. If you miss, it's no big deal, because the referee will bring it back to the original spot of the infraction. When you're trying this, be sure you take the drop right away while the advantage is still on, otherwise you may waste a shot at goal that you could have gotten from the penalty kick.

Observing the Offside Law

Without doubt, the most important rugby law involves what is offside and what is onside in general play. Like soccer, rugby is a sport that revolves around the offside law. The main difference is that in soccer, offside is only really a concern near the goals, whereas in rugby, offside is in operation from end to end and sideline to sideline.

Spectators and players alike are often totally bewildered by the offside law, but it really is quite simple, as we explain.

In general play

A player is *offside* in general play if he is in front of a teammate who is carrying the ball, or in front of a teammate who last played the ball. If you are behind a ball-carrying teammate, you are *onside*.

Players who are offside are temporarily out of the game and should either stay where they are or get back onside. Figure 6-1 shows a team moving toward the opposition's tryline, with two players in the offside position.

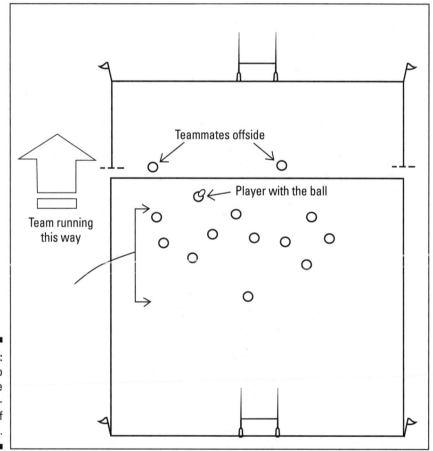

Figure 6-1:
Players who are offside are temporarily out of the game.

To get back onside (and thus be able to take part in the game again), a player must retreat behind the ball. A player can return to being onside in one of four ways:

- ✔ The offside player runs behind the teammate who last kicked, touched, or carried the ball.
- ✔ A teammate carrying the ball runs in front of the offside player.
- ✔ A teammate who has kicked the ball forward runs in front of the offside player.
- ✔ A teammate runs past the offside player toward the opponent's tryline.

A player can also be put onside by a member of the opposition in three ways:

- ✔ An opponent carrying the ball runs 5 meters.
- ✔ An opponent kicks or passes the ball.
- ✔ An opponent intentionally touches the ball but doesn't catch it.

When an offside player can't avoid being touched by the ball or by a team-mate carrying it, the player is *accidentally offside*. If the player's team gets no benefit from this (meaning that no potential tacklers were blocked by the action), play continues. If the player's team does benefit because the offending player shielded the ball-carrier from a defender, a scrum is formed with the opposing team putting in the ball. The same applies when a ball-carrier passes the ball to a teammate who is in front of her. If it's accidental, it's remedied with a scrum to the opposition.

A good way to remember this law is to imagine you're the player with the ball. Everyone who is on your team and who is behind you is onside, and any teammate who is in front of you is offside. That should give you a better understanding of the most mysterious law of rugby.

Being penalized for going offside

At some stage of the game, all players find themselves offside. However, remember that players aren't penalized for being in an offside position unless they

- ✔ Interfere with play.
- ✔ Move forward toward the ball.
- ✔ Fail to comply with the 10-meter law (we talk about this little beauty in the next section).

If the referee catches you offside — and you're offending — he awards the opposition a penalty (we discuss all the options after a penalty has been awarded at the end of this chapter). When a player knocks the ball on, a teammate who happens to be in front of him can be penalized for playing the ball if he prevents an opponent from trying to play on.

Offside players must be careful that they're not caught *loitering*. This quaint rugby term refers to someone who is standing or retreating in an offside position and preventing the opposing team from playing the ball as they wish. Former South African whistle-blower Andre Watson — now the director of referees in his home country — popularized the term *lazy runner* to denote this individual. If you find yourself in this situation, either fall back or get out of the way completely, or you'll attract the ire of the referee!

The offside law may sound rather tricky, but one simple solution applies if you're concerned about getting a penalty for being offside — get back behind your teammates before rejoining the fray.

Crossing the 10-meter line

Players are penalized if they fail to comply with the 10-meter law. This law applies when a player kicks the ball ahead and a teammate is standing in an offside position in front of the kicker. The offside player is prohibited from moving toward the opposition or going within 10 meters (11 yards) of where the opponent is waiting to play the ball.

The offside player is considered to be illegally taking part in the game if she is in front of an imaginary line that runs the width of the field, which is 10 meters in front of the opponent waiting to play the ball, or from where the ball lands. The offside player must immediately retire behind the imaginary 10-meter line. If she doesn't, the referee penalizes her for being offside and intentionally obstructing an opponent by awarding the opposition a penalty.

Figure 6-2 shows a player who is inside the 10-meter line and who must move back behind it or be penalized.

While retiring, the offside player cannot be put onside by the opposing team. However, before the player has moved the full 10 meters, the player can be made legal by any onside teammate who runs in front of her. The key here is that she must be retreating when passed. If she is standing there waiting, she can't be put onside.

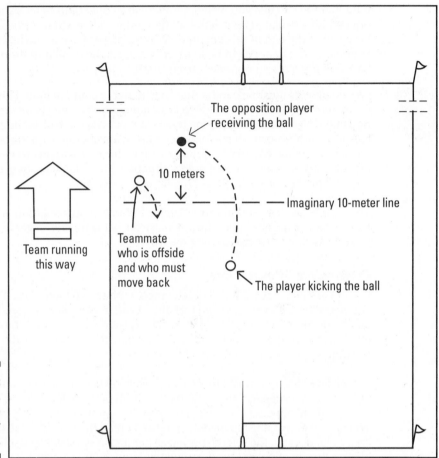

The opposition player receiving the ball

10 meters

Imaginary 10-meter line

Team running this way

Teammate who is offside and who must move back

The player kicking the ball

Figure 6-2:
Move back, or break the 10-meter law.

From set pieces

The offside laws are slightly different for the *set pieces* — which are scrums and lineouts. At a scrum, the offside line for the defending team is a line parallel to the dead-ball line that is 5 meters (5.5 yards) behind the team's hindmost foot in the scrum. This foot usually belongs to the number 8, so all of the back-line players have to stay 5 meters behind this player's back foot. This law is in place to ensure the team that wins the ball has clear space to use it (we give more comprehensive details about the scrum in Chapter 8).

At a lineout, two separate offside lines parallel to the goal lines for each team exist. One offside line is for the players taking part in the lineout (the ones standing there waiting for the ball to be thrown in). Until the ball has been thrown in and has touched a player or the ground, this offside line runs down the middle of the two sets of forwards on a line from where the ball was thrown. After that, the offside line is wherever the ball is. Basically, this is to keep players from crossing over the initial line until the ball can be played. Players in the lineout are also prohibited from crossing the 15-meter mark infield before the ball is thrown in. If they do so, they're considered to have left the lineout and are thus offside and subject to penalty.

The other offside line applies to the players not taking part in the lineout, usually the backs waiting for the ball to be passed out to them. For the backs, the offside line is 10 meters (11 yards) behind where the ball is being thrown in from, or their goal line if that is nearer. Until the lineout is over, the back-line players can't advance beyond that line. If not closely watched by the referee, backs are naturally inclined to edge forward in anticipation of getting their hands on the ball or putting themselves in a better defensive position to stop the expected attack.

At tackles, rucks, and mauls

The offside laws for tackles, rucks, and mauls are similar to those highlighted in the preceding section, with minor differences specific to the nature of each situation. After a tackle is made, if a tackler gets to his feet and plays the ball before a ruck has formed no offside line exists and the tackler can play the ball from any direction. Any other player attempting to pick up the ball must enter the area from a position on his side of the tackled player, no matter when he gets there. This forces other players to get back behind the tackle before playing the ball.

The sight of the ball on the ground must hit a certain circuit in some players' brains that turns them from thinking individuals to starving hyenas after a piece of meat, willing to risk anything to possess it. Not getting back behind the offside line before entering the tackle area will more often result in a negative outcome than in a successful stealing of the ball. The best thieves at the tackle situation are the ones who use their wits first and their quickness second.

A *ruck* is the term used when the ball is on the ground and at least two players from each team are in contact over it. After a ruck has been formed, two offside lines exist. Each offside line runs through the rear foot of the player farthest back in the ruck, parallel with the goal line. A player may join the ruck alongside the last player — but not from the side, or she is liable to be penalized. If you aren't part of the ruck, you can't be in front of this line. (We provide more information about rucks in Chapter 7.)

Rucks aren't neat, tidy things, so sometimes the temptation to help out in a hurry is greater than the discipline needed to join in at the proper place. Keep in mind that winning the ball only to have it given back to your opponents by an offside called against you doesn't help your team.

In a *maul,* which happens when a player carrying the ball is held by one or more opponents, virtually the same story is played out: One or more of the ball-carrier's teammates bind on the ball-carrier, and everyone involved is on their feet. Once again, two offside lines parallel to the goal lines exist, one for each team. Players joining the maul have to do so from behind or alongside the hindmost foot of the player bringing up the rear of the maul. If you aren't joining the maul, you have to stay behind this last player's foot. (Mauls are discussed in more detail in Chapter 7.) In most mauls, you can usually find an inviting place to slot in on the side, but you must resist the urge to do so.

Being offside at any of these phases of play is punishable by a penalty awarded to the non-offending team at the spot where the player was judged to be offside.

Playing Foul

The laws are written with an eye toward proportional punishment, reflecting a widely held belief that the penalty should fit the crime. The foul play law has four parts — obstruction, unfair play, repeated infringements, and misconduct — with progressively stiffer sanctions meted out to wrongdoers.

Obstruction

The first level of foul play is *obstruction*. When a player and an opponent are running for the ball, the players can't charge or push each other, except when they're shoulder to shoulder. Other players can't run in front of the player carrying the ball or block the tackler. This transgression is dealt with by calling a simple penalty. Obstruction is generally considered to be a heat-of-the-moment type of offense.

Unfair play

The second level of foul play is *unfair play.* These are intentional actions in direct opposition to the laws and result in a penalty and sometimes a warning that a player who continues said behavior will be severely dealt with. A player can't waste time by making the ball unavailable to an opposition player, throw the ball into touch or over the dead-ball line to slow the game down or prevent an attacking movement, or repeatedly commit the same penalty. If done subtly, the best players can get away with these callous infractions by hiding their intentions from the referee, but normally that works only once.

Repeated infringements

The third level of foul play is *repeated infringements,* which are judged to be even more cynical and disruptive than unfair play. Rucks and the tackle area seem to breed this type of behavior. After a player or a team has committed several of the same infringements, drawing a penalty each time, they are cautioned. If the behavior persists, the player must be shown a yellow card.

A yellow card forces the player into the sin bin (like the penalty box in hockey) for ten minutes to think about his evil ways, forcing his teammates to soldier on with 14 men on the field. If he doesn't demonstrate he's learned his lesson upon returning to action, the next step is a red card, signifying total banishment for the remainder of the match.

Misconduct

The fourth level of foul play is reserved for the most serious type of misconduct. A player cannot punch, strike, stamp, trample, kick, or trip an opponent. A player must not tackle an opponent above the shoulders, pick up and then dump the ball-carrier on her head or shoulders, tackle an opponent who has jumped into the air to catch a high ball, or late charge someone who has kicked the ball. A *late charge* means to tackle or hit someone late, or well after the ball has left the area. Depending upon the severity of the misconduct, most often reflective of the referee's perception of malicious intent on the part of the offender, either a yellow or red card is issued.

With the advent of television coverage at almost every major match, players guilty of misconduct are also subject to citing commissions that can issue suspensions and fines for an offense that the referee or the touch judges didn't see. Citing commissions usually consist of three officials who conduct a hearing with the offending player present to determine whether the player should be suspended for the offense. If the commission rules against a player, he or she may be suspended for further matches, depending upon the severity of the misconduct and the player's previous disciplinary record.

Taking Penalties

A multitude of actions on the rugby pitch can cause the referee to award a penalty. The primary result of being awarded a penalty is that your team gets possession of the ball and a choice of options on how to use it. The decision on what to do on the field rests with your captain, and the choice is governed by field position, how the match is progressing, time left, and the score.

The captain on a rugby team is responsible for making all the on-field decisions during the match, and must be a rugby-savvy individual with a command of the strategic nuances of the game.

Kicking at goal

When your team is awarded a penalty kick, one of the options is to take a shot at scoring three points by attempting a penalty goal. To do this, the captain or kicker informs the referee that the team wants to kick for goal. After this option is chosen, no other options are allowed. Unless a law states otherwise, the mark for a penalty is at the place of infringement. On a penalty-kick attempt, the opposing team must stand still with their hands by their sides from the time the kicker starts his approach until the ball is kicked. After receiving the tee from the sidelines, he has a one-minute time limit on taking the kick. When the ball is kicked, it's live again and in play.

The decision to take a shot at goal is determined by a number of situational factors. The game score, time remaining, kicker's range, and relative difficulty of scoring tries all figure large when considering whether to kick for goal.

Kicking for touch

Another option is to gain territory by kicking the ball downfield into touch. Normally a ball kicked into touch results in a lineout with the other team throwing the ball in, but on a penalty kick possession is retained by the kicking team. The key is to make sure the kick actually goes out of bounds. Most teams decide to do this if they're out of the range of their goal kicker or if they need to score more than three points.

Choosing a scrum

A third choice for the non-offending team is to have a scrum formed at the place of the infringement with their put-in. This is a strategic decision that is usually made when there isn't enough time left to choose a lineout or when a team doubts their ability to get the ball to their jumpers. Also, an attacking scrum is a very difficult situation to defend against — even more so when the spot of the penalty is close to the defending side's goal line.

Taking it quick

A *quick tap* occurs when the non-offending team immediately kicks the ball through the mark and continues play as soon as a penalty has been given by the referee. *Through the mark* means that the kicker must kick the ball a visible distance at or directly behind the spot where the penalty has been awarded. If the kicker is holding the ball, it must clearly leave her hands. If the ball is on the ground, it must clearly leave the mark.

Taking a quick tap can be an extremely effective weapon because the opposition's defense has little time to react and realign. However, this choice should be used judiciously, because when you take it quick, you're giving up a shot at three points, or a chance to gain territory.

A team also has the option of kicking through the mark and attempting to run the ball straight at the opponents or to use a designed play, particularly when they're close to the tryzone. This type of quick tap is referred to as a *tap and go*.

Free kicks

An award for a lesser degree of infraction, usually for technical violations rather than conduct, is called a *free kick*. The signal for a free kick also differs from a penalty, signified by a bent arm raised in the direction of the team that will get the ball (refer to Chapter 5 to see what this looks like). A free kick gives the non-offending team possession but with far fewer benefits than a "straight-arm" penalty. A scrum is one choice available on a free kick, but kicking for goal isn't. When kicking for touch from a free kick, possession isn't retained at the ensuing lineout and ground is gained only if the kicker is behind his team's 22-meter line, making this an unattractive choice (the hows and whys of lineouts are covered in Chapter 9).

Chapter 7

Playing the Game

• •

• •

At the heart of rugby is the notion that in every situation there must be a fair contest for the ball. The laws of the game have changed over the years to promote this goal, and as a result the game has become faster and more technically demanding of all the players on the pitch.

The modern game is meant to be continuous and fast-moving with as few stoppages as possible — which would be easily accomplished if players just ran around from end to end, but the confrontational nature of the sport demands that one team try to stop the other from advancing whenever possible. This inevitably leads to contests for the ball that develop spontaneously after each tackle. Understanding what happens after a player has been tackled is at the core of developing a thorough knowledge for both fans and players.

The key to being a good rugby player is to understand the strictures governing each particular part of the game, and then have the skills to excel in those areas. The key to understanding the game as a fan, then, is to be able to recognize what is happening as a match progresses, and to understand why the referees make the decisions they do.

In this chapter, we start where the game begins, with kickoffs and restarts, then give further details on the seemingly complicated activity that accompanies a ball-carrier being brought to ground. That leads us to a comprehensive examination of the breakdown, followed by a closer look at the laws governing rucks and mauls. (These parts of the game may seem chaotic at first glance, but when we explain them you'll see how organized they really are.)

Getting Started

Starting a match is a facet of the game that has undergone a significant change in the last few years. At one time, a place kick was used to start each half. At some point, somebody clever read the law and saw that it allowed for a tee (approved by the union sanctioning the match) to be used for this purpose. This led to a frenzy of plastic tee designs that ended up looking like traffic cones. The goal of using a tee was to help get the ball as high in the air as possible to make securing it much easier for the kicking team. Sensibly, the International Rugby Board (IRB) stepped in and mandated that all kicking restarts would from then on be *drop kicks*, which are kicks where the ball is dropped from the hand and hits the ground before the kicker's foot comes into contact with it. (Refer to Chapter 2 for an example of this type of kick.)

Kickoffs to begin each half

A kickoff is the first opportunity for both teams to contest possession of the ball. Before the game, both captains and the referee meet and toss a coin. The winning skipper chooses either to kick off or defend an end. (If the captain decides to kick off at the start of the first half, the other team will do so at the start of the second half.) The choice of ends is especially important when the wind is a factor.

Kickoffs are taken from the center of the halfway line (refer to Chapter 2 for details about the lines on a rugby pitch). Most pitches have a half-meter dash line to mark this spot, and referees will often direct wayward kickers back to this spot if they attempt to go astray. If the ball is kicked from in front of the halfway line, or too far from the center, the referee can order that the kick be taken again.

Every player on the kicker's team must be behind the ball until it's struck (Figure 7-1 shows the formation of the players in a kickoff). Players are allowed to get a running start, but their timing has to be right so that they don't inadvertently pass the ball before it's airborne. If they're judged to be in front of the kicker, a scrum is formed in the center of the field with the opposition getting the put-in. This inexcusable mistake drives coaches nuts because it gives a great attacking opportunity to the other team.

The players on the receiving squad (the team that isn't kicking) must line up behind their own 10-meter line. The receiving team has a distinct advantage over the team kicking because the players are able to lift the locks (refer to Chapter 4 for more details about this playing position) up in the air to take the ball, while the kicking team has to rely on regular jumping. (Remember, the kicker's teammates have to charge down the field after the ball; the opposition has the ball coming to them.)

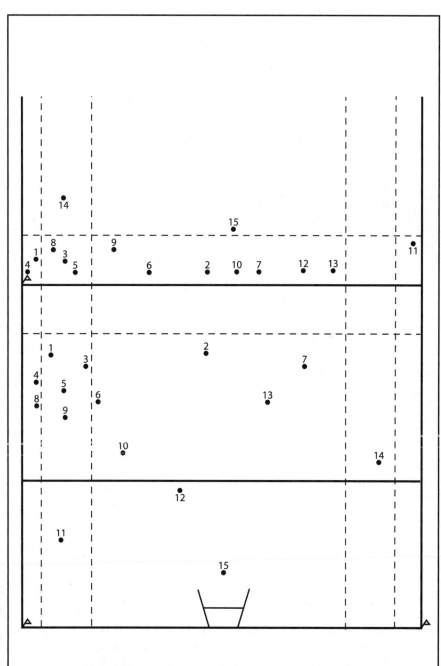

Figure 7-1:
Kickoff
formation.

The ball must reach the opponent's 10-meter line for the kick to be legal. Remember, the place where the ball hits the ground doesn't factor in to determining whether it has traveled the required 10 meters. (See Figure 7-1 for the alignment of the kicking and receiving teams.)

If the kick crosses the 10-meter line in the air and is then blown back across the line by a stiff breeze, it's play on! Even if the kick doesn't reach the 10-meter line, you keep playing, because the receiving team can choose to play the ball and you need to be ready to tackle them. If the ball fails to reach the 10-meter line and isn't played by the receiving team, the referee will give them the option of having another kickoff or a scrum at midfield.

Your goal as the kicker is to put enough air under the ball to let your team-mates charge downfield and secure it before the other team can do so. The temptation is to try to kick the ball exactly 10 meters, but this is unwise because if the ball doesn't go at least that far the receiving team can choose to have a scrum.

A ball that is kicked off directly into touch, or out of bounds on the fly, gives the non-kicking team three options. They can have the ball kicked off again, take a lineout on the halfway line, or have a scrum at midfield (with their put-in). A kickoff that goes into the in-goal area and is immediately grounded also produces a choice of a re-kick or a scrum at center.

Unless your team is getting pummeled in the scrums, instruct the captain to always take the midfield scrum over another kickoff. The scrum is a vastly superior attacking opportunity for your side because the key back-row defenders are required to stay bound-in while scrummaging, which provides more space for your backs to operate in the midfield. (For all the details about scrums, see Chapter 8.)

Restarts after scores and 22s

In addition to beginning each half, kickoffs are used to restart the game after either team has scored a try, penalty try, penalty goal, or dropped goal. A great feature of rugby is that when you score, you automatically get another chance to regain the ball because the non-scoring team kicks off to the one that added to their scoreboard total. The same regulations that control kickoffs also apply to restart kicks.

A 22-meter drop-out (a drop kick) is used to restart play after the ball is grounded in the in-goal area by the defending team if the attacking team caused it to go in there. This usually happens if a missed penalty kick is caught and grounded by the opposing team, or if the ball goes over the dead-ball line. Another way the ball can end up in the defending team's in-goal area is when an offensive player kicks ahead in general play and loses the race to touch it down.

A 22-meter drop-out can be taken anywhere behind the 22-meter line — and, as with a kickoff, everyone on the kicker's team has to be behind the ball. The defense has a little more leeway here and can attempt to block the kick as long as they don't actually cross the 22-meter line in doing so.

If you're the player taking the drop-out, you can prevent your teammates from being offside (in front of the ball) by doing two things before you kick it. First, look both ways to see if any of your teammates are in front of you. If they are, wave them back. When they're all behind the ball, signal that you're about to take the restart before you kick it.

Just like kickoffs, if the ball crosses the 22-meter line in the air and is then blown back, play continues. Similarly, if the ball doesn't reach the 22-meter line you still need to remain vigilant, because the receiving team can choose to play the ball even if it doesn't cross the line.

If the kicker gives the drop kick a bit too much juice and it goes directly into touch on the fly, the receiving team can either take another drop-out or opt for a scrum midfield on the 22 or a lineout at the 22-meter line.

Nothing gets under the skin of your forward pack like overcooked restart kicks that go directly into touch, forcing them to defend a scrum from a disadvantageous position. So, if you've been entrusted with the kicking duties and want to keep on good terms with the big folks up front, be sure to keep your drop-outs within the field of play.

Another recent strategic development involves players drop kicking the ball a foot or so over the 22-meter line and regathering it immediately. This is perfectly legal because the law requires only that the ball cross the line — 1 inch or 50 yards are both acceptable.

The Tackle Situation

Unlike football, where the contest comes to a screeching halt after every tackle, in rugby tackles are part of a continuing sequence of play. Without proper regulation what happens at the tackle situation can degenerate into constant stoppages and continual blowing of the referee's whistle. The laws have evolved to prevent this from taking place, and to turn the tackle situation into a transitional phase for the next positive use of the ball.

In rugby, a tackle is made when a ball-carrier is brought to ground and held there. (A tackle also occurs when the ball touches the ground while the ball-carrier is being held, or when the player is being held and is lying on another player.) *Brought to ground* means no longer on your feet, which includes having one knee down. Simply put, if you're held and don't have both feet on the ground, you're tackled. Being knocked to the ground without a tackler holding on isn't a tackle, and you're free to get up and run some more. But if you're held, a different set of laws takes over and you've got some serious responsibilities to take care of.

The tackled player

The ball-carrier who is brought to ground is known as the tackled player. The first requirement of the tackled player is to immediately make the ball available. The tackled player can place the ball in any direction, but the best choice is to direct it toward supporting teammates and away from opponents. The key is to release the ball under control, so that your side has the best chance to recycle possession. If able to do so, a tackled player can also pass the ball at once. In practice, this means that as soon as the ball-carrier comes to a stop on the ground it's time to release the ball.

The most important thing to remember is that when you've been tackled you can't hold on to the ball, especially if a player on his feet is trying to take it from you. The continuity theory in effect here is that if a player isn't on his feet, he can't play the ball anymore, so he has to make it available for other players to use.

The error that most new players make in running with the ball is that they don't plan for being tackled. A good player avoids tackles whenever possible but prepares for their eventuality by positioning her body so that when she is brought down she has control over the outcome. This means securing the ball on the way down to stop it from being ripped away, using strength to go to ground with her body between the tackler and the ball, and placing the ball so her cohorts can maintain possession for the next phase of attack.

The tackler

The tackler is also charged with making sure the ball is immediately available for other players. The tackler's first act after going to ground must be to let the tackled player go so that the ball can be freed. A player can't wrestle the ball-carrier for possession while they're both on the ground. Holding the ball-carrier tight on the ground will draw the referee's whistle just as quickly as not releasing the ball.

The second duty is to get away from the ball. Letting go and then using the body to cover the ball up or slow it down is both illegal and dangerous because it will draw unfriendly boots to the tackler's prone figure.

The tackler is also restricted from any contact with the ball until he is back on his feet. Getting back up is the best course of action, because it allows the tackler the chance to pick up the ball. Unlike subsequent players who enter the area, the tackler is free to play the ball from any position as long as he has regained his feet. This advantage usually lasts only for a short time, until players from both sides arrive and change the nature of what's happening.

Just because your feet are on the ground doesn't necessarily mean you're "on your feet" for the purpose of playing the ball after the tackle. If any part of your body is supported by someone on the ground, the law is the same as if you were flat on your back — you're not allowed to play the ball.

Stealing the ball after the tackle is one of the most effective ways to create turnovers in general play. Coaches should teach all of their players, from fullback to the front row, how to quickly get back on their feet after making a tackle so they can legally contest for possession of the ball. Then they should demonstrate the low-body position they'll need to reach in with both hands and steal the ball off the ground. Make sure players understand that as others arrive and the ruck forms, they need to obey if the referee yells, "Ruck formed, no hands" (we cover the rucking rules later in this chapter).

What happens next?

In a perfect world, no need to stop play at a tackle situation would exist, because tacklers would release tackled players immediately, the ball would come free, and play would continue. It isn't always that cut-and-dried on the pitch, however, and the laws outlining what happens next reflect that reality. The term *breakdown* is a catchall for the multitude of things that can happen from when the ball-carrier is brought down to when the ball is next played.

Breaking Down the Breakdown

Whenever the ball is on the ground after a tackle it's a free ball and both teams have full rights to it. The events at the breakdown are the hardest to adjudicate because everything happens so fast and the referee's vision is routinely obscured by players flying in and bodies piling up on the turf. More penalties are called at the breakdown than in any other part of the game. The key to successful work at the breakdown is for players to be well coached, self-disciplined, and fully cognizant of the applicable laws.

When we first started playing rugby, the breakdown was a complete mystery. Not knowing the law made distinguishing between times when behavior was legal and when it was seriously wrong impossible. The easiest way to improve your overall game is to know the tackle, ruck, and maul laws. Knowledge is power. More energy is wasted at breakdowns by players who don't know what they're doing than in any other area of the game.

Tackle, Ruck, or Maul?

Every rugby spectator, and we mean *every* rugby spectator, has at some stage become befuddled and bemused figuring out the differences among a tackle, ruck, or maul. Don't worry — you're not alone. We didn't pick this one up for at least five years!

A tackle is something that starts with two or more players on their feet, one of them carrying the ball, and ends up with them on the ground. As soon as a tackle happens, however, a new phase usually takes its place. This depends on what happens to the ball when it's released or passed. Tackles more often than not end up morphing into rucks as more players arrive at the breakdown.

The difference between a ruck and a maul is that in a ruck the ball is on the ground, and in a maul the ball is off the ground in the hands of a player. To put it simply: off the ground — maul; on the ground — ruck.

Roughing It in the Rucks

A *ruck* is formed when two or more players, at least one from each side, are on their feet over the ball in physical contact with each other after a tackle has been made or when the ball is on the ground.

The player who has been tackled with the ball is allowed to place it on the ground, or push it toward her teammates. She must do this immediately after going to ground. The referee allows her momentum to come to a halt, then the ball must be released. The tackled player can usually get away with one good rollover, but a second one is likely to be penalized. If the player hangs on to the ball too long, perhaps to allow her teammates time to catch up or to prevent a defender from poaching the ball, the referee blows the whistle and awards a penalty to the defending side.

The first players to arrive at a ruck have to bind to each other or the opposition, as shown in Figure 7-2. The players grab each other around the shoulders or waist, or whatever body part is handy, and then try to step over the ball. The players on both sides of the ruck can attempt to drive the opposition back and away from the loose ball, but under no circumstances can they play the ball with their hands.

Launching your body into a ruck like a Scud missile is illegal and dangerous. Good form and body position are more important than brute strength at rucktime. You need to stay low and balanced, keeping your shoulders above your hips and your head up as you go over the ball to secure possession. A well-placed, concentrated shove is vastly superior to the head-down charging rhino technique.

When the ruck is formed, the prime aim is to remove the ball. Players use only their feet to rake the ball back to a waiting teammate, and aren't allowed to touch the ball with their hands. Alternatively, the attacking group of players can drive forward, stepping over the ball and clearing defenders away from it, making the ball available for the waiting scrumhalf, who decides how the team attacks next.

Players must not make deliberate contact with an opponent who is on the ground. Kicking or raking an opponent who may have fallen isn't tolerated, and can result in the referee sending the offender off the pitch. This is called *stamping* and is dealt with harshly.

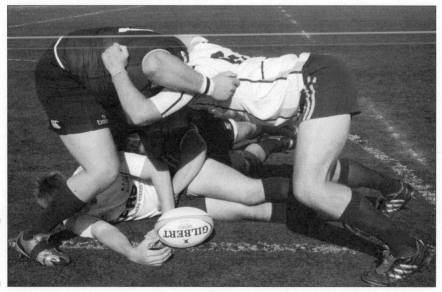

Figure 7-2:
Forming
a ruck.

The ball is won from the ruck when the attacking players successfully bind together, drive forward over the ball, and make it available for the halfback at the back of the ruck, who then distributes it. Good rucking means quickly providing the ball to the scrumhalf, which in turn allows the backs to attack before the defense can realign. If the opposition is denied time to realign before the next attacking wave, their defense is likely to have holes for your backs to exploit.

Rucking rules

Attacking from the ruck can be highly effective and sometimes devastating, but it's also an area where countless infringements occur. The scope for foul play in a ruck is enormous, and referees strictly enforce the rules. The whistle is blown if players who join a ruck

- ✔ Come from an offside position. The offside line at a ruck is the hindmost foot of the last player in the ruck.
- ✔ Come into the ruck from the side. Even if you're onside, you still must enter the ruck from behind the last player's foot.
- ✔ Loiter at the ruck. If you're not part of the ruck, you must retire behind the offside line.
- ✔ Use their hands to mischievously get the ball back to their side.
- ✔ Use their legs to prevent the ball from being played.

Players aren't allowed to kick the ball back into a ruck, because after the ball comes out the back of a ruck it must leave that area. As the ball is coming out of a ruck, no player is allowed to fall on or over it.

One of the most common ruck infractions is when a defensive player gets his hands on the ball before the ruck is formed but can't quite rip it away. After the ruck is formed, the referee will usually shout out, "It's a ruck, no hands" or something to that effect. Then the defensive player must be disciplined enough to let the ball go to prevent the whistle.

Kick the ball, not the player

In rugby, the term *mountaineering* is used to describe the act of players unnecessarily attacking an opponent with their feet. Mountaineering usually involves a situation where players stomp all over an opponent who has fallen and is lying near the ball.

A player must strictly ruck for the ball and not ruck other players. If you're attempting to free the ball using a raking motion where your boot is moving primarily backward as opposed to straight down, you may not get into trouble with the referee but you're still opening yourself to a possible penalty. If your boot is aimed at the ball and it unintentionally collides with a body lying near the ball, nowadays chances are you'll draw a whistle. If you strike an opponent with your boot and she's a long way from the ball, you'll find yourself in a lot of trouble and possibly be sent to the sin bin for ten minutes. Stamping directly down onto the legs, the body, or, worse, the head of an opponent who's lying helpless on the turf is unsportsmanlike.

Remember, malicious acts have no place in rugby, so keep your rucking technique within the spirit of the game. The ruck law generally has been interpreted differently by referees throughout the world, but recently the IRB has made efforts to bring all countries into line and stamp out the practice of over-vigorous rucking.

Stay on your feet

Perhaps the most important law is that players joining or forming a ruck must have their heads and shoulders no lower than their hips — otherwise, you could be putting yourself in danger. At rucktime, the goal is to stay on your feet, and entering with your head down decreases your strength and may lead to serious injury.

Players in a ruck must be on their feet, and they must endeavor to stay on their feet. A player can't deliberately

- Fall or kneel in a ruck.
- Collapse a ruck.
- Jump on top of a ruck.

Rucks can be unsteady and sometimes collapse, especially when players use the wrong technique, causing them to lose their feet. For a ruck to be successful, players have to be well drilled, well coordinated, and disciplined — and know the laws.

Directing the ruck

The most important player at the ruck is the scrumhalf, who directs proceedings by telling her forwards exactly where to go. The scrumhalf is usually the only person who can actually see where the ball is, how many opposing players are committed to the ruck, and where the defense is positioned. She can then decide if more of her forwards are required at the ruck, whether the ball should be released or retained, and exactly where her teammates need to concentrate their efforts to ensure they get the ball back.

"Ruck formed, no hands" — listening to the ref

There is an old saying in sports that you have to play to the officials. For example, umpires in baseball sometimes have their own strike zones, and the key is to understand those peculiarities and make the needed adjustments. In rugby, no situation is more difficult to adjudicate consistently than the precise moment when a tackle transforms into a ruck, especially when bodies are flying everywhere. When defending players get their hands on the ball after the tackle but can't clear it, and then the ball-carrier's supporters make contact with them, a ruck is formed. At this moment, referees are taught to loudly declare, "Ruck formed, no hands!" This command specifically warns the player who has his hands on the ball that if he doesn't immediately let go, he will be penalized.

Suddenly letting go of the ball after you've done all of the hard work to steal it is incredibly difficult, but release it you must, as soon as you hear those four words: "Ruck formed, no hands." The thing to remember is that you need to listen to the referee and adjust your play to comply with his commands and overall management of the game.

After the ruck has been formed, the scrumhalf is basically the foreperson, telling the forwards where to go, what to do, and whether they're being successful in getting the ball back to her. An experienced scrumhalf focuses the forwards' energy and attention on the area where it's needed most.

Working the pick-and-go

A successful attacking strategy from a ruck is the called the *pick-and-go*. In a pick-and-go move, the ball-carrier strategically places the ball some distance back from his prostrate body. Hot on his heels are several teammates, who step over the ball and quickly drive their opponents off it.

Another attacker, who now has a clear run to the ball, bends down, picks it up, and charges ahead until being tackled, setting up yet another ruck or another pick-and-go. This tactic, if done properly, can be carried out over and over, allowing a team to gain ground and keep the defense off balance.

Mastering the Maul

A *maul* is formed when a player who is carrying the ball and is on his or her feet is held by one or more opponents. In addition, at least one teammate must be attached to the player holding the ball. This phase of play is illustrated in Figure 7-3.

Figure 7-3:
Forming a
maul.

Mauls are mostly used as an attacking ploy from lineouts (see Chapter 9 for more details about lineouts). The coordination and cohesion at the lineout is perfect for forming a maul because the forwards involved are all right in the area and ready to bind and drive ahead.

The speed of a maul isn't the most significant element. Slow, steady progress where everyone is in sync tends to produce better results than a bunch of forwards with their heads down going at full gallop. Mauls are occasionally created when a player carries the ball into a would-be tackler and then turns to face her supporting teammates in an effort to protect the ball and stop it being wrestled away by an opponent. Teammates can grab the ball-carrier between the waist and shoulders to protect her from the opposition and retain possession of the ball. The goal is to keep driving forward while moving the ball to the back of the maul for immediate use when the scrum-half deems it's time to do so. This is the one time in rugby when it's legal to be playing while in front of the ball.

A central feature of any good maul is proper binding by all participants. The tighter you are with your teammates, the more force you can exert and the harder it is for the opposition to stop or split you apart. The other indispensable element is communication. Everyone should know where the ball is and where it's going to maximize its protection and sharpen the focus of the attacking platform.

Mauling laws

To the spectator, mauls can look totally confusing, like an out-of-control amusement ride. On the pitch, though, a well-executed maul can ensure that one team totally controls the game. It requires an enormous amount of dedication and discipline, and a proper understanding of the laws.

An important part of the maul law is that players can join a maul only from an onside position. The mauling manual includes other basics such as the following:

- ✔ Players who are in a maul must endeavor to stay on their feet. Referees regard collapsing a maul or jumping on top of it to be dangerous play. This is an obvious penalty.

- ✔ Players aren't allowed to remove an opponent from a maul. Dragging an offside player out of the maul is prohibited; remember, enforcing the law is the referee's job.

- ✔ While in a maul, the ball-carrier can go to ground but must make the ball available immediately upon doing so. Players must respond accordingly when a maul goes to ground and it becomes a ruck.

The two main types of mauls are driving mauls and rolling mauls, which evolve after the maul has been formed.

Attacking from a driving maul

When the attacking team tries to drive through the opposition, the tactic is called a *driving maul.* The ball is usually carried by a player in the second line of the maul to protect it from the opposition. The players in the front line of the maul stay relatively upright, with their teammates behind them, adopting a lower body position so they can get better leg drive and better leverage to push the maul forward. In effect, the maul becomes a driving wedge charging straight ahead, but the big difference is that the ball is being held by one of the players and isn't on the ground.

What makes the driving maul so effective is that the defenders not involved in opposing the maul are required to constantly move backward to stay onside. Backpedaling defenders are much easier for your back line to beat. The key to taking full advantage of maul possession is to have your scrumhalf use the ball before the maul stops moving forward.

In the old days, mauls were allowed to stop and start repeatedly and seemed to go on forever. Then the IRB changed the law, mandating that when a maul stopped, the ball had to be used immediately or it was a turnover. This de-emphasized the use of the maul as an attacking strategy, much to the detriment of the game. Recognizing and remedying the unintended result, the IRB compromised and now allows a maul to stop once. The team in possession then has five seconds to start moving again or produce the ball.

This is a good law change because mauling is an important component of a team's physical presence on the field. If your side can regularly drive forward using a controlled maul, your opponent will be physically taxed and mentally demoralized because it takes much more energy to stop a maul than it does to attack from one.

Using a rolling maul

A *rolling maul* occurs when the attacking team transfers the ball into the hands of a player on one side of the maul where the opposition appears weakest or has the least number of players. His teammates roll around to that side, pushing the player with the ball forward in a fairly good imitation of a cyclone. This type of maul resembles a slowly spinning top, with one player rolling onto another, enabling the maul to move forward as the ball is transferred from one player to the next.

When executed properly, a rolling maul is a powerful attacking weapon because it's so difficult to defend against (especially when the team in possession changes its direction, going from one side of the field to the other). Most of the time the opposition has its work cut out just trying to stop the rolling maul from advancing, and has no real chance of getting the ball back. Whoever is currently holding the ball watches for the moment when the opposition defense in front of him is in disarray. He then peels off and takes the ball into the open field once again.

Directing the maul

As with rucks, the scrumhalf acts as the coordinator at mauls. She doesn't get directly involved in the maul but stands behind, right next to the action. The halfback looks for opportunities, decides where the opposition defense is weakest, urges her forwards on, and tells them where to go. She advises her teammates where they should join the maul, and indicates who needs support to ensure that the maul keeps moving in the desired direction.

Stopping the maul

A good maul is difficult but not impossible to stop. When trying to stop a maul, the first thing to do is try to turn the ball-carrier or tear the ball away and gain possession for your team. (This is easier to do in mauls that occur spontaneously than in planned ones from lineouts.)

When the maul is near the sideline, the best option is to try to concentrate your opposing shove at an angle to force the attacking side out of bounds. Burrowing your way into the opposition's maul through the front is also legal, as long as you remain on your feet and don't come from an offside position. This maneuver has to be attempted right away, though, because when the ball starts being funneled to the back it's impossible to get to.

If you can't get the ball or drive the maul over the sideline, then you have to stop its forward progress. You can do this by hitting the leading edge of the maul with full force, at an angle lower than the opposition players who are driving at you. Be careful not to lose your feet and drag others down with you — that can cause the maul to collapse, which will result in a penalty and possibly a trip to the sin bin. A strong back and superb body position are required to stop a maul that already has momentum.

Chapter 8

The Art of Scrummaging

The scrum is rugby's signature element because it is unique in the world of sport. It's an easily identifiable part of the game, involving more than half the players on the field — two packs of eight battling for possession of the ball. Nothing comes close to the sheer power generated by eight players bound together as one with a singular purpose. Maximizing the combined force of all the forwards is the most technically challenging part of the game. It's also the most physically demanding, as the exertion required to compete in repeated scrums drains the life out of your body faster than any other aspect of play.

Because every game has numerous scrums to restart play after minor infringements, consistently winning its own scrums is absolutely vital for a team. Scrums are often described as the engine room of rugby, delivering a team's prime power source. A team that's dominant in the scrum is usually well on its way to a win, because what happens in this area of the game affects so many other aspects of the match.

In this chapter, we demystify the scrum by providing an inside look at the heart of rugby's least understood phase, so you can compete safely and win the battle up front.

Scrum Isn't Synonymous with Mayhem

If you watch other sports on television, you may hear the occasional commentator refer to a spontaneous pile of disorganized bodies on the ground as a scrum. Nothing could be further from the truth. The reality is that a scrum is a very well organized and synchronized activity where every player involved has a specific set of skills, roles, and responsibilities. For a scrum to be successful in restarting play, all players must remain on their feet. Scrummaging takes strength, technique, aggression, and courage — it certainly isn't a haphazard melee.

We cringe every time we hear or see uninformed announcers and sportswriters use this term inaccurately, because it reinforces negative stereotypes about the game and belittles one of rugby's most intriguing features. Scrummaging is an esoteric art form, practiced out of the limelight but thoroughly appreciated and respected by knowledgeable coaches, fans, and the other participants on the field.

Scrummaging is an intense, precise endeavor, where technique reigns supreme over brute strength. Your pack can boast eight incredible hulks, but if they can't work together in a coordinated fashion they'll be well and truly beaten by a side of average-sized players who have their act together.

A scrum formation is like a battering ram: The front row (made up of three players) is reinforced with five more players strategically placed behind them in positions that best stabilize the formation and push the opposition backward. To make this configuration work, every player has to have proper alignment and balance, sufficient expertise to adapt to pressure and movement, and enough strength to withstand the force generated by eight individuals working as a unit to mercilessly smash them.

Becoming a good scrummaging team takes countless hours of repetitive drilling together as a unit. This practicing can be done against either a scrum machine or an opposition pack. Training should be broken up into two types, each with different goals. The first is concentrated on correct binding, foot positioning, leg angles, balance, and spine alignment. All players are unique in the power they can generate from their body shape, so figuring out how to feel comfortable in the scrum while maintaining maximum effectiveness is the priority in these sessions. The second type of workout involves repetition in engaging hard, pushing as a pack, breaking up and running to a spot, and then reforming as quickly as possible to simulate the activity in a match. Undertaking this kind of physical conditioning is useless, though, if the proper techniques and muscle memory haven't been sufficiently developed.

My first time packing down

I first played rugby at Occidental College in 1987 under the guidance of Coach Michael Godfree. Like many coaches who were backs in their playing days, the scrum was somewhat of a mystery to Michael. He knew immediately that I was a prop, of course, but was somewhat vague on what I was supposed to do when it came time to scrum down. My total instruction in propping consisted of another player directing me to "get in there and push."

With one week of training under our belts (where we were mostly introduced to basic skills like passing and tackling), the many rookies on that year's Oxy squad faced off on a Saturday against Long Beach State, then a Southern California powerhouse. I played tighthead prop and came up against an Australian guy with a full beard who must have been about 30 years old. Every scrum was an adventure in survival. He lifted me in the air, bent me in half so that I was kissing my knees, twisted me like a wet towel, and hit me so hard on every engagement that I'm sure I ended up several inches shorter. None of this would be legal now, but at the time it was considered the price to pay for being a rookie front-rower.

My day ended with a split cheek that required eight stitches — suffered in a tackle, not a scrum — and the next day I was sore in more places than I had ever been in my entire life, but I was also hooked on propping and still am to this day. It's the most directly confrontational position on the team and requires heart, strength, stamina, and a desire to not get individually beaten. Mastering how to do it right is a long journey of experimentation and setbacks, but in the end the ability to confidently prop up a scrum is the most satisfying of rugby pleasures.

Sections of the Scrum

The basics of scrummaging include knowing how to correctly bind together as the scrum is formed, using good body positioning prior to and after the engagement, winning the ball, and providing a solid platform for launching the attack (Figure 8-1 shows the formation of a scrum). The best way to explain the scrum is to go through the individual positions, describing how the players are arranged and what their responsibilities are.

The front row

The formation of a scrum starts with the hooker (number 2), who is the central figure of the whole affair. After the referee marks the spot where the scrum will take place, the hooker moves there and raises his arms, enabling the two props (numbers 1 and 3) to bind onto the hooker. The props then slide their inside shoulders under, up, and through, so that they end up in front of the hooker's shoulders. The hooker then binds onto the props by gripping each of them by their rugby jersey, with his arms across their backs so that the three are closely bound together (see Figure 8-1 for how the front row binds).

Figure 8-1:
Binding
together:
The front
row gets
ready for a
scrum.

The front row is where the scrum is usually won and lost. A bad front row can't be saved by a good second row. A good second row, however, can make a good front row into world-beaters.

The members of the front row must be solidly bound together at the shoulders and hips in a scrum because the opposition's goal is to split them apart. The force exerted on the front row from the players behind them and the opposing scrum is enormous, and any weakness in binding will be ruthlessly exposed and exploited. Practicing correct scrum formations should be part of your team's training routine. Strong scrums mean fewer injuries and more chances to beat the opposition.

When they're all linked up, the three front-row players bend their knees, sink their hips, and prepare to withstand the pressure when the second row and back row bind-in behind them. They also look directly into the eyes of the opposition's front-rowers in readiness for the battle ahead.

Playing in the front row requires specialized skills, so each player must be suitably trained for the position. For safety reasons, not just any reserve can come off the bench and slot in up front. Without proper instruction and experience, the front row can be a dangerous place. If you're training to play prop, being able to play on both the tight- and loose-head sides is best — because you never know when you may be called upon to do double-duty in a match.

The term *hooker* isn't a pejorative one but instead refers to the action undertaken by this player when the ball is put into the scrum. He hooks it with his foot to be channeled to the back of the scrum for use by the scrumhalf or the number 8.

The props derive their names in the same fashion, because they "prop up" the hooker. The terms "loose-head" and "tight-head" refer to the placement of their heads when the scrum comes together. The loose-head is just that: loose on the outside. The tight-head has her noggin sandwiched in tight between the opposition loose-head and hooker.

The second row

While the front row is getting ready, the two locks in the second row (numbers 4 and 5) place their inside arms around each other, gripping onto their jerseys at waist level. They bend forward and place one shoulder against the back of the hooker's upper leg just below the buttock and the other in the same spot on either the tight-head or loose-head prop, depending on which side of the scrum they're on. When the locks' shoulders are properly positioned, their heads should poke out between the props' and hooker's hips. Their heads should be slightly raised so they have full vision of the ball as it travels through the scrum.

The lock then thrusts his spare arm (the one that isn't holding on to his second-row colleague) between the prop's legs and grabs onto his waistband. This bind has changed over the years — the locks used to put their arms around the prop's hips. Both locks going down on one knee before engaging was also common, but this too is becoming a rarity at the highest levels.

Most international locks now get into position behind the front row without going down on one knee. As a lock, you can try this style by keeping both feet on the ground and bending deeply at the knees and the waist before you bind to the front row. The advantage of this technique is that as the scrum engages, your feet are already planted and ready to lock out, and you don't have to reposition them after the engagement.

The back row

After the second row is bound in, the two flankers (numbers 6 and 7) bind onto the second row. They reach across the backs of the locks with their inside arms and grab a handful of the locks' jerseys while using their inside shoulders to apply pressure to where the props' buttocks meet their hamstrings.

On an offensive scrum (where their team has the put-in), the two flankers are responsible for keeping the ball from escaping out the sides as it's being channeled back and for keeping the props in tight to the hooker. On a defensive scrum, they're more involved in pushing forward and their angles at engagement change to reflect this.

In attack, the flankers need to always keep their eyes on the ball until the scrum is over so they can support the number 8 if she picks up the ball, the scrumhalf if she darts around the fringe, and the backs if they crash back toward the forwards. On defense, the breaks need to focus on where and when the ball is coming out of the scrum, so they're ready to immediately disengage from the scrum and be there to stop the ball-carrier if necessary.

The last piece of the back-row puzzle is the number 8. This player slots in at the back of the scrum, driving forward with both shoulders against the backsides of the two second-rowers. To help stabilize and hold the locks together, she binds her arms around the outside of their hips and puts her head between their bodies.

The number 8 has more to do at the end of the scrum than at the beginning. She must coordinate with her scrumhalf as to what their plan is for each ball she receives. If the scrum is moving forward, the task is much easier, but if it's static or moving backward, the difficulty level rises. Whether she is picking the ball up from the back and taking it on herself, passing to her scrumhalf, or giving her scrumhalf protection, she must be sure-handed and a quick decision maker. She is also charged with controlling the ball with her feet at the back to keep it from emerging too early or in an untidy fashion. This ability to manage the ball at the base of the scrum with her feet is a skill unique to the number 8 position.

The ninth forward — the scrumhalf

Because the scrumhalf is responsible for much more than just putting in and removing the ball from scrums, and despite the fact that he's technically a back, forwards will sometimes pay the little guy a huge compliment by referring to him as the ninth forward.

The scrumhalf is crucial for effective attack and defense from scrums. This player is the direct link between what happens at the scrum and how the ball is delivered to the back line. If a scrum is barely holding off the opposition's push, the scrumhalf must adapt and be faster in distributing the ball. If the scrumhalf's team has the upper hand, the player can vary the attack and take advantage of opportunities off the edges of the scrum.

On defense, the scrumhalf first puts pressure on his opposite and the other number 8 to prevent them from easily clearing the ball. He's also called upon to make tackles when the offense targets his side of the scrum for attack.

Communication with the number 8 is vital to successfully transfer the ball from the back of the scrum to the back line. This transition from set play (scrums or lineouts) to general play depends upon how well in sync numbers 8 and 9 are in all situations.

Engagement

By this stage, the eight forwards should be bound together into one powerful unit. Before a scrum can begin, the referee makes sure the scrumhalf has the ball and then begins a series of four calls:

1. **Crouch:** Commands the players in the front row to dip down so that their shoulders are slightly above hip level.

2. **Touch:** Makes the props reach out and touch their opposite on the shoulder to ensure the front rows are no more than an arm's length apart.

3. **Pause:** Lets the front-rowers get set and ready to come together (see Figure 8-2 for an example of this).

4. **Engage:** The two teams charge into each other so that the heads of the front-rowers interlock with those of their opposite numbers.

Next time you watch a match, listen carefully when the scrum engages and you'll hear bodies colliding and players grunting as they exert themselves to the limit. Sometimes, you'll also hear the pack calling out a cadence in unison to coordinate their shove.

Figure 8-2: The two packs are ready to engage.

Following the engagement, all 16 players in the scrum flex their legs forward and keep their backs straight.

The area on the ground that is formed between the two packs is called the *tunnel,* and is where the ball will be put in by the scrumhalf. If the scrum rotates, or moves off the mark too far and doesn't immediately stabilize, the referee will usually reset the scrum. Until the ball leaves the halfback's hands the scrum must be stationary, and neither team can push until the ball is inside the scrum.

The put-in

Holding the ball in both hands, the scrumhalf prepares to throw it into the tunnel. When she is ready to begin, the hooker signals for the number 9 to deliver the put-in. When the scrumhalf gets the signal, she puts the ball in play. The throw-in must be done right away, and if the scrumhalf delays putting in the ball, the defending side is awarded a free kick. The ball must be thrown in with a single forward movement, without any spin on it. Trying to trick the opposition with a fake put-in is strictly prohibited.

This is a case where what's written in the law book and what happens on the pitch is very different. The law says that the ball has to be put straight down the middle of the tunnel, but in practice this almost never happens. As long as the put-in is not too far on the side of the offensive team the referee will usually let play continue. This makes it very difficult for the defensive team to steal possession at scrumtime.

The contest for possession

The scrum begins when the ball leaves the scrumhalf's hands. After the ball touches the ground in the tunnel, any front-rower may use either foot to win possession of the ball. What isn't allowed is for any front-rower to have a foot in the tunnel before the ball is put in by the scrumhalf.

Hookers develop individualized styles of winning the ball, but the key is having a quick strike and soft touch on the ball so that you maintain good control of where it goes. Play around with different styles to see what feels the most comfortable. When you find a technique that works for you, practice to perfect it — you will find it easier to win the ball when your movements are deliberate, not spontaneous.

After the ball has been hooked, the ball is then channeled backward between the two second-rowers toward the number 8, who then holds it in the scrum with his feet until he or the scrumhalf decides to play it.

Whatever happens in the scrum, no one is allowed to touch the ball with their hands until the ball has been cleared. A scrum is over when the ball comes out in any direction (except out the tunnel), or when the number 8 unbinds from the scrum and picks up the ball.

Laws at Scrumtime

The laws governing scrums are constantly being tinkered with in the interests of producing a fair contest for the ball and ensuring safety. First we give you some of the general restrictions, and then we move on to more specific rules.

When a scrum is called after an infringement, it's set wherever the infraction occurred (unless the infraction happened within 5 meters (5.5 yards) of the touchline or the tryline. In such cases, the scrum begins 5 meters in from those lines).

A full scrum has eight players from each side, but is legal with as few as five participants. The opposition isn't required to reduce its numbers to match the other team when players have been sent off or because of injuries.

In cases where front-rowers are injured and no more suitable replacements are available, the referee will call for *uncontested scrums* (for safety reasons), which means that the scrums come together gently and the team putting it in always wins the ball.

Binding and releasing

Every player in the scrum is required to bind onto a teammate with at least one arm until it ends. When any player binds onto a teammate in a scrum, that player must use the whole arm from hand to shoulder to grasp the teammate's body. Placing only a hand on another player isn't satisfactory binding. Proper binding prevents flankers from disengaging early from a scrum and gaining a defensive advantage.

Props are the only players who are permitted to grab an opponent. Loose-head props bind onto the opposing tight-head props by placing their left arms inside the right arms of the tight-heads and gripping the back or side of the tight-heads' jerseys. The loose-head must not grip the chest, arm, sleeve, or collar of the opposition tight-head. Loose-heads must not exert any downward pressure in order to keep the scrum from collapsing. (See the next section for more details about collapsing.)

Tight-head props bind onto the opposing loose-head props by placing their right arms outside the left upper arms of the opposing loose-heads. Using their right hands, tight-heads must grip the loose-heads' jerseys. They're also not allowed to grab anywhere else or force the scrum down. All other players in a scrum have to bind onto a lock's body with at least one arm. Everyone has to stay bound until the scrum is over.

Collapsing

If a scrum collapses and goes to ground, the referee must blow the whistle immediately to ensure that players stop pushing. This is a safety precaution and is one of the few situations where advantage can't be played. (Chapter 6 explains when advantage *can* be played.)

A few rules focus on preventing scrums from collapsing. Front-row players must not

- Twist or lower their bodies.
- Pull opponents, or do anything that is likely to collapse the scrum, either when the ball is being thrown in or afterward.
- Fall or kneel in a scrum.

A lot of leeway exists between what is actually written in the law and what happens in most scrums. As long as the scrum doesn't collapse and the ball comes out, most referees won't spend too much time scrutinizing everything that goes on in the front row. They will, however, strictly penalize any voluntary collapsing of the scrum because of the dangerous nature of this act.

You can't spend too much time working on your front-rowers' scrummaging technique. Regardless of the laws, opposing players will employ a variety of tactics that can result in a collapsed scrum. Your players need to know how to counter these moves and remain on their feet.

Driving in and up

Front-row players are prohibited from lifting an opponent and can be penalized for doing so deliberately. Regardless of who's responsible, if a player in a scrum is lifted in the air or is forced upward out of the scrum, the referee must blow the whistle immediately to stop players from pushing. Lifting was banned by the International Rugby Board (IRB) because it can cause serious injury. Sometimes, though, players pop out of their own accord because they're under too much pressure. This move can also be penalized.

Feeding

The scrumhalf is supposed to throw the ball straight down the middle of the tunnel between the two front rows, but this almost never happens. On the infrequent occasion when a scrumhalf is penalized for this infraction, it's called *feeding* and results in a free kick to the opposition.

Lax enforcement of the law against feeding has made stealing a put-in at the scrum a rarity. When you successfully hook the opposing team's throw-in, that's called a *tight-head,* or *taking one against the head.*

The scrumhalf is also prohibited from *dummying,* or faking a pass, when the ball is ready to be removed from the scrum. If the scrumhalf reaches in and puts her hands on the ball to take it out, then emerges without it and fakes a pass, she can be both tackled and penalized.

Strategic Scrummaging

In addition to securing possession, the scrum can be an outstanding attacking weapon. The primary goal of any pack is to at least be able to win your own scrum put-ins and provide a good platform for your backs to use the resulting possession. This is why most coaches will tolerate a prop that isn't the most effective player around the park if he is a good scrummager. Losing your own ball on scrums is a recipe for disaster on any team, and is certain to be ruthlessly exploited by the opposition.

The scrum has become a multi-faceted attacking platform in different positions and situations, especially now that the offside line for players not involved in the scrum is 5 meters (5.5 yards) behind it. The key to using the scrum effectively is having your pack players be well versed in a number of different techniques and options depending upon what you're trying to accomplish.

Attacking from the scrum

What makes a scrum the ideal set piece to launch an attack from? First, the opposition's best defenders, their back-rowers, must remain bound to the scrum until it's over. This limits their range because getting into the open field takes them longer. It also gives the offense the element of surprise because they can probe with either backs or forwards. Second, because the offensive back line of the team with the put-in is much closer to the point of attack on a scrum, the defense has less time to react to planned moves.

The best attacking position is a scrum in the middle of the field. This position forces the opposition to split their backs because they don't know which side the thrust will come from. Ideally, your scrummagers will push the opposition backward during the scrum, which puts them into reverse and makes defending even more difficult. Any team worth its salt should be able to win almost every one of its own scrums throughout a match, which gives players an air of confidence about starting the offense at scrumtime.

A scrum set near the sideline creates a natural attacking avenue down the *blindside,* or the short side, of the field. The reason why teams target the blindside is that it's less congested with defenders than the wide side of the field. Typically, the blindside is guarded by the weak-side wing, who's left all alone to stop the advance. Teams look to create a mismatch down the blindside, with a back-row forward charging at a wing. Nothing is more tantalizingly tasty to a back-rower than a lone wing isolated one-on-one between him or her and the promised land.

Wheeling the scrum

Purposefully turning a scrum by a concerted effort of your pack is called *wheeling.* When the other team has the put-in, wheeling is a way of creating a turnover. If you can wheel the scrum past 90 degrees (so that the tunnel has passed beyond a position parallel to the touchline), it has to be reset and this time your team gets the put-in. (See Figure 8-3 for an example of wheeling the scrum.)

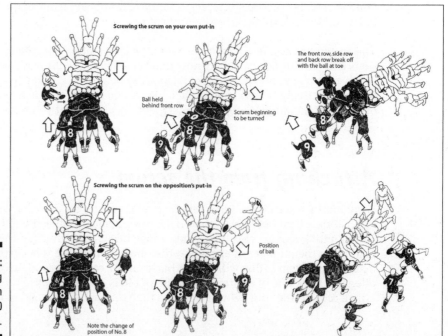

Figure 8-3:
Wheeling
the scrum
past 90
degrees.

Situations also arise where a team will want to wheel its own scrum. When close to the goal line, wheeling causes one of the flankers to be rotated farther away from the point of attack. Remember, they have to stay bound until the scrum is over, and are thus at the mercy of the wheel.

Another time to use the wheeling technique is when you attack down the blindside. The main pack defender in this circumstance is normally the blindside flanker (who is closest to the short side of the field). If the flanker's shoulders are allowed to remain parallel to the tunnel of the scrum, she is in perfect position to stop a scrumhalf or the number 8 who charges down the short side. As the scrum wheels around, the blindside flanker is forced to go with it, making the tackling angle more difficult.

Wheeling can be used to create turnovers at key times during a match. For example, if your opponent has the put-in on their 5-meter line (that is, near your tryline), turning the scrum past 90 degrees gets you the ball in an excellent attacking position with little risk involved. Late in the match when defending under your posts, attempting to wheel their scrum is a risky choice, but if you have confidence your pack can work the wheel, you may get the ball and prevent the opposition from getting a try.

If your scrum is getting repeatedly wheeled, you can counter by having your front row step sideways in unison against the direction of the wheel. The motion looks like a crab walking sideways, which is why it's called *crabbing*. Instead of the scrum continuing to rotate on its axis, crabbing causes the scrum to move sideways, stopping the wheel.

Getting a shove on

If your team possesses the power and skill to win every one of your put-ins, the next step is to strive for physical domination of the opposing pack. This helps immeasurably in the execution of your goals in all other phases of play.

Initially your team should attempt to push the opposition off its ball at every opportunity in the scrum. Even if your players are unsuccessful at winning the opposition's ball, driving the other team backward is an important defensive tactic. Doing so forces the opposing scrumhalf and the number 8 to play the ball more quickly and under more pressure, often leading to rushed passes and mistakes in getting the ball to the flyhalf. It also causes their entire back line to edge backward while yours can be moving forward, thereby stifling the opponents' attack.

The same idea can be used as an offensive tactic. If your team can consistently shove the other team's scrum back, it puts the opposition's defenders on the *back foot,* meaning they have to retreat to stay onside. This opens up more attacking options and demoralizes the opposition.

Pushing it over the edge

If you have a scrum near your opponent's goal line, you can attempt to score a *pushover try*. After the ball is hooked and channeled back under the number 8's feet, the scrum slowly advances toward the tryzone while the number 8 keeps the ball in, controlling it with his feet. When he thinks he can score, the number 8 picks it up and crashes over the line to ground the ball.

Scoring a pushover try is rare at the international level but much more common in club matches, where the scrums are more likely to be one-sided. There's nothing more uplifting than completing a pushover try — and nothing more demoralizing than being driven back into your own in-goal area.

In a physical sense, domination at scrumtime boosts your forwards and drains the other team's. This means less energy for them during rucks and mauls, further enhancing your conquering capabilities.

Chapter 9

Lineouts: Restarting from Touch

*1*f you appreciate the aerial artistry of basketball, you'll love the lineout. It features the timing and technique of a jump ball with a twist unique to rugby — the jumpers are allowed to be lifted to even greater heights by their teammates. This results in a visual treat where players are hoisted high into the air and a competition for possession takes place a dozen feet off the ground.

Lineouts are the primary method of restarting play after the ball has gone over one of the touchlines (and therefore out of bounds). Lineouts always take place on a touchline and are instantly recognizable by the two parallel lines of players who face the sidelines waiting for the ball to be thrown in. (Refer to Chapter 2 for full details about the touchlines.)

For most of rugby's history, lineouts were a confused jumble of bodies that usually ended up producing more stoppages than quickly usable balls. The introduction of legal lifting has made the lineout one of the more entertaining parts of the game, where true competition for possession flourishes. In little more than a decade, the lineout has been transformed from an unsightly phase that favored one-dimensional players to a dynamic display of athleticism, strategy, and teamwork.

This chapter unlocks the secrets of this highly competitive part of the game. We give you a full description of the lineout, detail the variety of roles played by those involved, and explain the rules the players must follow. Plus, we provide insight into the tactics that make the lineout a thing of beauty, and finish up with an examination of prohibited behaviors.

Determining When a Lineout Occurs

The lineout is used to get play going again after the ball has gone over a sideline and into touch (out of bounds). How or why the ball went over one of the sidelines doesn't matter; if it goes out of bounds, play is restarted with a lineout (we explain the one exception at the end of the chapter). Whether the ball is kicked out, carried out, or driven out, or simply rolls unattended over either of the touchlines, a lineout is the prescribed way to reignite the action. That part is easy — where it gets more difficult is in determining when a ball actually has gone into touch, thus necessitating a stoppage in play.

So how can you tell if the ball is out of bounds? The touch judges are the arbiters of this question. If they deem the ball has gone into touch, they raise their flags to indicate this fact to the referee, who then blows the whistle.

Basically, the touch law states that any time the ball, or a player carrying it, comes into contact with the touchline or the ground beyond it, it's in touch. If the ball crosses the touchline in the air and is then blown back or caught by a player in the field of play, it's not in touch.

Understanding Where a Lineout Takes Place

Lineouts always take place on a touchline. The exact location varies depending on factors such as where the ball went out of touch and how it got there.

In cases where a player is bundled into touch with the ball or an errant pass trickles over the line, figuring out where the resulting lineout will ensue is easy — it happens at the place where the ball crossed or came into contact with the line. The touch judge will then stand at that exact spot with a raised flag and not move to either side until the lineout is over.

The law gets more complicated when the ball is kicked into touch by a player on either team. When the ball is kicked out, the spot for the lineout is determined by where the ball was kicked from and how it went out of play. (See Figure 9-1 for a diagram explaining touch and throw-in locations.)

Directly into touch

When the ball is kicked out of bounds and it doesn't touch the ground or another player on its way out, it has been kicked straight out or *directly into touch*. The location of the kicker determines where on the sideline the lineout will be held.

✔ If the player who kicked the ball out of bounds is on or behind his own 22-meter line, the lineout is formed where the ball went over the line (refer to Chapter 2 for an explanation of the 22-meter line). This is a strategically profitable kick because it gains territory. However, if the ball is passed from a point in front of the 22-meter line to a kicker standing behind the 22-meter line, the place for the lineout restart is the spot from where the ball was kicked.

✔ If the kicker is in front of her own 22-meter line when the ball goes directly into touch (kicked out *on the full*), the lineout is taken from where the player made the kick. This means the team doesn't gain any territory — and the kicker loses friends. (Tired and emotional forwards hate having to run back to where a player has kicked the ball out on the full.)

✔ If the player kicks the ball out of bounds on a penalty kick (to gain territory and set up an attacking lineout), it doesn't matter where the ball is kicked. The lineout takes place where the ball goes over the touchline.

✔ If the player kicks the ball directly into touch from a free kick but is in front of his 22-meter line, the team does not gain any territory. The lineout is taken from where the player kicked the ball — so make sure you know the different signals for a penalty kick versus a free kick (refer to Chapter 5 for all the referee signals).

Indirectly into touch

When the ball bounces infield or hits any part of a player before going out, it has been kicked *indirectly into touch*. When this happens, the place where the ball was kicked from doesn't matter; the lineout is taken at the point where the ball crossed the line.

If you have at least one foot either on or inside the 22-meter line, you're considered to be behind the 22-meter line. If you catch the ball outside your 22-meter line and then take it back behind the line before you kick it, you won't gain the territory. Also, if you're outside the 22-meter line and pass the ball to a teammate who *is* behind the line and she kicks it into touch, you gain no ground and the lineout is taken from where the ball was kicked.

On a penalty kick where a player opts against kicking for goal and instead kicks for touch to gain yardage and set up an attacking lineout, the location where the kicker is standing on the field doesn't matter. The lineout takes place where the ball went over the sideline. (See Figure 9-1 for examples of touch and the place for the throw-in.)

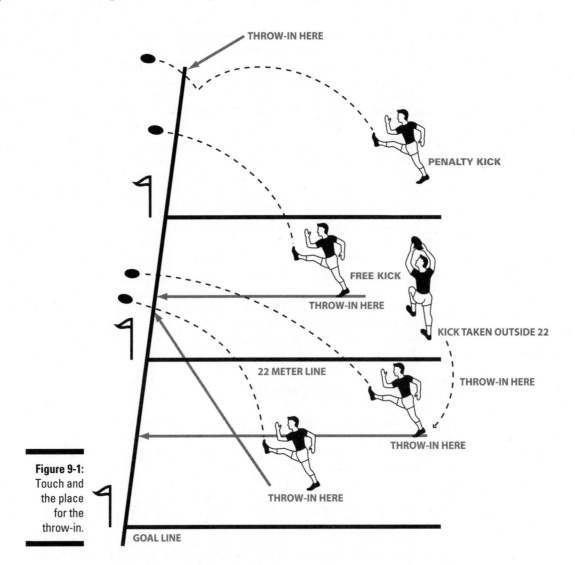

THROW-IN HERE

PENALTY KICK

FREE KICK

THROW-IN HERE

KICK TAKEN OUTSIDE 22

THROW-IN HERE

22 METER LINE

THROW-IN HERE

THROW-IN HERE

GOAL LINE

Figure 9-1:
Touch and
the place
for the
throw-in.

Figuring Out Who Gets the Throw-in

The law determining which team gets to throw the ball in at the lineout is
straightforward. Whichever team last kicked, touched, or was in possession
of the ball before it crossed the touchline loses possession. A member of the
other team will get the honor of throwing the ball to the players in the lineout. (The team awarded the throw-in at a lineout has the advantage, because
they know where the ball is going.)

Telling which player was the last to have contact with the ball isn't always easy, so the touch judges are required to keep up with play and follow the progress of the ball as it makes its way up and down the pitch. When the ball goes into touch, one of the touch judges signals by raising the flag and pointing with his free arm in the direction of the team that will throw the ball in at the resultant lineout.

The exception to this law is when a penalty has been awarded. In this case, the non-offending teams know that they will get the throw-in. (Remember, players can kick the ball directly into touch during a penalty kick and take the lineout where the ball leaves the playing area, gaining territory for their team.) This is especially common when a team is backed up in its own end and wants to advance the ball, or when it's near the opposition's tryline and needs to score more than three points. (Refer to Chapter 2 to find out about the point system.)

When you carry or kick the ball into touch it amounts to a *turnover,* because the other team gets the throw-in. This enables tacklers to use the sideline as a 16th defender, by driving the ball-carrier into touch whenever the runner is near the sideline.

One of the most common errors for inexperienced ball-carriers is not being conscious of where they are in relation to the touchline. When coming into contact with a defender within 5 meters (5.5 yards) of touch, players should lower their body position and lean infield to prevent the defender from driving them out. This is easily practiced with a ball-carrier, a defender or two, and a sideline.

Lining Up for a Lineout

In its simplified form, a lineout consists of two straight rows of designated players from each team who line up facing the sideline. The ball is thrown in between the two lines, and the players attempt to secure it for their side to use. When the two groups get into position for a lineout it looks haphazard and casual, but the exact opposite is true. Every move and placement, from the initial location of each individual to the spacing between them and where they end up, is choreographed with attention to detail.

A lineout doesn't officially begin until the ball is thrown in, but the process starts as soon as the ball goes into touch. First, the lineout has to be correctly formed, then a decision on each team's strategic intent is internally taken. This is followed by the actual execution of the play and the distribution of the ball, all without running afoul of the law. A lineout isn't over until the ball is passed or run out of the area between the 5- and 15-meter lines (except when a ruck or maul forms after the ball is thrown in; then the lineout isn't over until that phase has cleared the initial line of touch).

Forming a lineout

A lineout is considered formed when at least two players from each team are lined up at the spot where the ball went into touch. The players from the competing teams face the touchline in two straight rows, with a space of 1 meter (1.1 yards) between them. Like in a scrum, this area is called the *tunnel* or *gap*. The middle of the tunnel should be at the spot where the ball went out, called the *line of touch*.

The lineout exists in a contained area. The front boundary is 5 meters (5.5 yards) from the touchline and is marked by the 5-meter line. The rear limit is designated by the 15-meter dash lines, giving each team a total of 10 meters (11 yards) to work with. Every player who is part of the lineout must stand between these two points. Two players who are exempt are the player throwing the ball in and the receiver, who stands at least 2 meters (2.2 yards) behind her line of players. The defense is also allowed a receiver, plus a person to mark the thrower, usually the opposing hooker. This player must stand 2 meters from the line of touch and 2 meters from the 5-meter line. (Figure 9-2 illustrates a typical lineout formation.)

The number of players taking part in the lineout is determined by the team that has the throw-in. The number varies depending on personnel and strategy. (In the 1999 World Cup, Ireland used a 14-man lineout against Argentina!) A standard lineout has seven players in the line and one player throwing the ball. A lineout formation with fewer than the standard eight forwards is referred to as a *short lineout*.

On offense, each team decides the best tactical way to win its lineout and can vary its numbers throughout the match. The opposing team can choose to have fewer players in the lineout, but it can't have more. On the offensive team, after a player becomes part of the formed lineout she can't leave it. The defense has a little bit of leeway here. If it sends seven players to the lineout and the offense puts fewer in the line, a corresponding number of defenders can leave without being penalized, provided they do so in a reasonable amount of time.

Calling the play

Just like a quarterback in football calling an audible at the line of scrimmage, a certain player (it varies from team to team and can be the hooker, the receiver, the captain, or anyone else in the lineout) is given the important task of making the calls. Timing and coordination are key aspects of successful lineout play, so making sure that everyone involved knows exactly what the plan is on each throw-in is absolutely vital.

Figure 9-2:
Contesting
possession
in the
lineout.

Before every lineout, the attacking team decides who the ball will be thrown to and what he'll do after winning it. For example, a particular call may mean that the second jumper will receive the ball and then everyone is supposed to form a maul and drive forward. The lineout caller uses a code system to let everyone on his team know what is about to happen while preventing the opposition from knowing what they're up to.

At training under the coach's direction, the lineout players work on a system of codes for various plays. The system may involve numbers or code names, but it has to be understood by everyone to prevent confusion. A throw can be short, long, looping, or bullet-like, depending on the signal or code words used. Some teams are even more sophisticated and have more than one player calling signals to confuse the opposition. Only they know which calls are real and which are decoys. Your code should be simple but flexible enough to accommodate all of your lineout schemes, without requiring that your team be loaded with secret code breakers — you want to confuse the opposition, not your own players!

Breaking the code

For the first several years of my rugby career, I played for Occidental College and the Oxy Olde Boys. Because the two teams had significant interchange between them, we used the same lineout calls. A series of words and numbers would be shouted out by the hooker, but only the second digit of the second number determined where the ball was going. The code was

(continued)

(continued)

very simple, and not too tough to grasp. Later, when I played for other clubs, I was exposed to more complex coding systems that I adapted to without too much trouble.

I first ran into problems during my years playing in Latvia, especially in training with the national team. Their calls were a mix of Latvian and Russian numbers interspersed with slang. I never could keep them all straight, so ultimately the lock I was lifting, Wilmars Sokolovs, would wait until the calls were done and then he'd tell me in English where the ball was going! Problem solved, because he and I were usually the only English speakers on the pitch.

A few years later in Northern Ireland, I ran into other issues while training with Ulster and playing for Portadown. Ulster's system involved various code words that I had real difficulty understanding because of the thick accent of their hooker. Most of the time I'd figure it out, but occasionally I'd find myself lifting the wrong man or being in the incorrect spot, which greatly displeased the coach.

The Portadown club used countries, beers, and banks to signal where the ball was going, and after numerous training sessions I'd thought I had everything memorized. During the first match, though, I ran into trouble with a call I'd never heard before, and I guessed it had to be a country. Scotia, however, turned out to be a bank.

When I first started coaching the Oxy women's team, I took the easy way out and had my players make dummy calls with the hooker indicating where the throw was actually going by holding the ball in her left or right hand, or both.

Ultimately, the call is unimportant. What really matters is that the lifters and jumpers are in unison and that the hooker can hit the target. Adding in a sufficient variety of lineout looks will also keep the opposition guessing just enough to prevent them from consistently stealing your throw-ins. Getting the fundamentals right will enable a team to win their lineout ball on a regular basis, regardless of whether the other team knows where it's going.

Throwing in the ball

The throw is usually made by the team's hooker, but anyone on the side can restart play if necessary. To be effective, the hooker has to have the ability to vary her throws from quick hard ones at the front, to higher ones in the middle, to more lobbed ones to the back of the line. For a throw to be legal, it has to travel at least 5 meters (5.5 yards), straight down the middle of the tunnel. The thrower can't step onto the field of play before releasing the ball. The referee normally allows a throw that is slightly off center, but not a throw that blatantly favors the receiving team's side. The ball leaving the hooker's hands signals the official beginning of the lineout.

The player who throws the ball in must be consistent and precise in her delivery so she can hit her jumpers with regularity. Timing is of the essence to prevent the opposition from getting their hands on the ball. Mastering the technique of throwing in can be very difficult. The skill requires excellent hand-eye coordination and a good sense of spatial anticipation. The thrower needs to visualize the apex of the lifted player's hands as the target and throw to that spot before the jumper actually gets there. The beginner will miss the mark most of the time and provide the opposition with a chance to steal it. Throwing in can be extremely frustrating even for professional players, who go from hero to zero from one week to the next on the strength of their throwing accuracy.

Hookers need to practice throwing at every training session. They should start with both feet about half a meter behind the touchline, so they can step forward on their follow-through without stepping onto the field. Work on hitting all the spots where your jumpers will be using varying amounts of loft and zip to avoid defenders. The thrower needs to be in tune with each jumper's technique and preferences. If the wind is up at training, rejoice and take advantage of the inclement weather to have your hooker work on adjusting her throws to account for the force of the breeze.

Aspiring hookers can never get enough throws at training. Because recruiting a pack of forwards to come over for a few hours while you play a one-sided game of catch with them is unrealistic (at least without a well-stocked cooler), the best thing to do is find a wall or set of goalposts to throw at. Make marks at different points on the target that approximate the varying maximum heights attainable by your jumpers, and then alter your distance from them to simulate their different positions in the line. Then, throw until hitting them all becomes routine.

Taking the throw

To help a jumper get as high as possible in the lineout, his teammates can lift him heavenward. The catch is that they're also responsible for bringing him safely back to earth.

The best result in a lineout is for the jumper to cleanly catch the ball. This isn't always possible, so the next best thing is to tap the ball back to your side in hopes that the receiver or another lineout player will be able to secure it. When they're up in the air, lineout jumpers can use either their inside arm or both arms, provided they're over the head, to grab or redirect the ball. When the ball is taken, the jumper should turn his body on the way down, so that he's facing his teammates when his feet touch the ground. This allows the other forwards to bind-in around the jumper to protect the ball from the opposing pack and also provides a good mauling platform.

The opposition's jumpers try to figure out where the ball is likely to go and then try to launch themselves to the right place to win the ball. Defensive lifting is even more challenging, because the lifters never know where their jumpers will take off from. Contesting the lineout works best when you have instinctive leapers with excellent timing — plus a scouting report on the opposition's lineout tendencies!

Starring Roles in a Lineout

The lineout requires an array of unique skills that must be performed with precision to successfully compete. Just like casting for a theater company, the lineout performers must be able to play various parts and be versatile enough to switch roles when the situation demands. The players involved in lineouts are almost always forwards, and they're usually required to fulfill multiple duties at various times during the match. (Refer to Chapter 4 for details about the positions of the players discussed in the following sections.)

Jumpers and lifters

Before players were allowed to lift one another in the lineout, each player had a designated position that rarely varied. The advent of lifting led to more strategic lineouts, and now most teams will lift at least three different jumpers in various places up and down the line. To confuse the opposition, they may also switch around the roles of players and use jumpers as lifters.

Winning squads used to be the ones with the tallest players who had the longest arms. Now the dominant teams are the ones with the most accurate throwers and best coordination between jumpers and lifters.

Jumpers

Lineout jumpers are still usually the two locks and the tallest of the backrowers. Whoever they are, they have to possess balance in the air, excellent core strength, and good hands. Jumpers should have good footwork so they can quickly move into several different positions in the line. Part of their craft includes faking jumps to draw their opposite off the ground, and also not giving away their true intentions when they're going to get the ball.

The responsibilities of the lifters are as important as those of the lineout jumpers. One lifter is positioned in front of the jumper and one behind her. They must work in tandem and be perfectly coordinated to ensure that the jumper reaches the top of her leap a split second before the ball gets there. (Figure 9-3 shows a jumper being lifted.)

Lifters

Lifters need to be strong and able to confidently lift some of the biggest players on the field. Hoisting a 240-pound man more than 6 feet in the air and then holding him there until he catches the ball isn't easy!

PLAYER TIP

Two similar techniques are used to lift a jumper, depending on whether you're in front of him or behind. When you're the front lifter, the key is to stay low and close to your jumper with your knees bent and your butt lowered. Support the jumper by gripping the thighs just above the knees so you can attain the maximum lift possible. The lifting power needs to come from your legs and not your arms or back. After the player jumps, extend your arms straight over your head and use your legs to push the jumper up even higher. When he reaches the zenith of his jump, your arms are locked out straight over your head. Although the basic technique of lifting with your legs and extending your arms is the same for the back lifter, your contact point with the jumper is different. The back supporter grasps the jumper's legs, just beneath the buttocks. The back lifter has the primary responsibility of providing the initial thrust to help get the jumper airborne.

Figure 9-3:
A tight view of the lifters' binds.

The receiver

The receiver position has traditionally been filled by the scrumhalf. This makes sense because after the ball is won, she's the best person to distribute the ball to the waiting back line. Recently, though, teams have successfully expanded the role of the receiver by making her into another lineout jumper. From her position 2 meters (2.2 yards) behind the players in the lineout, the receiver is allowed to enter the line before the throw-in.

Even if the receiver isn't going to enter the line, she still has to be a player with great hands because she is invariably called upon to consolidate loose possession. When the receiver is a forward, teams will also use her to attack right away after a lineout or provide a critical shove to get the maul moving forward when the jumper comes down.

Movement in the lineout

The concept of movement in the lineout is also a relatively new one that has flourished since the introduction of lifting. Movement of jumpers and lifters up and down the line is used to prevent the opposing jumpers from settling in one particular place to contest the throw-in. When a team's jumpers are on the move, stealing the throw is harder for the opposition because they don't know when the movement will end or where the ball is going.

A moving jumper can reach greater heights than a stationary one. Coordinating a moving jumper, two lifters, and the throw-in to all converge on one spot at the same time takes a lot of practice, but when it's done right it looks effortless and is an incredibly graceful display of power and athleticism.

Keystone Kops in the lineout

Not all modern lineout developments have been good. Some coaches and players have become too fond of trying to outsmart each other by devising complex and elaborate lineout tactics — and sometimes they outsmart themselves. Wacky lineout maneuvers that have players running this way and that (some making dummy runs, and others being used as decoys) can appear comical. In the end, the lineout looks like a totally out-of-control Keystone Kops routine where everything goes wrong and the opposition wins the ball. Nothing is worse than running through a series of moves and then having the referee blow the whistle to penalize your side for delaying the throw. The best strategy is to keep unnecessary movement to a minimum, making it sharp and accurate with a definite purpose.

Talking Tactics Down the Line

The lineout has become an elaborate action-adventure, with designated jumpers, special jumps, decoy moves, and more subterfuge than a James Bond movie. The basic aim, though, remains unchanged. Every team wants to set up a good platform to launch their attack. The key is to be able to execute different forms of incursions equally well, so as to keep the opposition off balance. When the jumper has his mitts on the ball, the options are limitless.

The element of surprise is one of the best weapons available to a team at a lineout. If the defenders are unclear about what form the assault will take, positioning themselves appropriately is tougher. Just when they get ready to counter one tactic, you throw another one at them, thus increasing the overall effectiveness of both moves.

Peeling off

One effective lineout play involves the jumper tapping the ball down to a moving (or *peeling*) forward. The peeling player has to stay within a meter of the lineout until receiving the ball, but can then cut upfield around the front or rear edge of the formation. The key here is to get past the lineout defenders quickly and thrust immediately into the back line. Timing is essential to pulling this move off, but because the peeling player is already moving and the defenders are static it can lead to clean breaks.

Throwing to the front

Hitting a non-jumper at the front of the line is an option when your traditional jumpers are having trouble securing the ball. For this to work, the defenders must be concentrating on the jumpers, leaving the player at the front unguarded. The opposing hooker will generally be able to tackle this player as she goes down the blindside, so the real benefit comes from the player who receives the ball being able to pass it back to her hooker, who is all alone with room to run.

One cheeky variation for throwing to the front of the lineout involves the front lifter getting in position to support the front jumper, but then just as the ball is thrown, she turns around to face the hooker and receives the ball via a quick low throw. The key to pulling this off is having the player taking the ball position herself slightly infield, to make sure the ball travels at least 5 meters (5.5 yards) before she moves forward to take it.

Setting up the maul

Lineouts are a particularly good time to initiate a driving maul (refer to Chapter 7 for details of the maul) because all the required players are in close proximity and the defense is preoccupied with stealing the throw-in. As soon as the ball is taken and the jumper is returned to earth, the other forwards bind in to form the maul and start pounding ahead with concerted effort. Getting the ball out of the jumper's hands and moved quickly back is important, so that the opposition has no chance to take it away.

An effective lineout tactic is to get a maul going (which sucks in defenders) and then immediately spin the ball wide. This gets the defense moving in the wrong direction and creates chances for your backs to break through. An extra benefit of successful mauling from the lineout is that teams will sometimes stop contesting the throw-in and concentrate exclusively on stopping the maul.

Quick off the top

The standard method of distributing the ball from the lineout is to bring it down, consolidate it, and then have it ripped off the jumper and transferred to the scrumhalf. For a speedier way of getting the ball to the back line, the jumper can toss the ball directly to the scrumhalf as soon as the catch is made, saving valuable seconds. This requires a jumper with excellent balance in the air and a deft passing touch. If the jumper can't cleanly take the ball with two hands, the ball can also be redirected using one hand (either way, this move is called a *tap down*).

Every tactical lineout move has a multitude of variations that can be adapted to your team's strengths. Don't try to pull off stunts that your players can't effectively perform. Get the basics right first, and then experiment with adding more options.

Things You Can't Do

More than any other area of the game, the lineout is all about being controlled in your behavior. The lineout law is the longest one in the book, detailing a laundry list of prohibited actions.

The primary focus is on the thrower's responsibilities. For a lineout to be legal, the ball must be thrown straight down the tunnel and travel at least 5 meters (5.5 yards), and the thrower can't step into the field before he releases the ball. The opposition can't prevent the ball from going at least 5 meters.

Attention then shifts to the other players in the lineout and what they can't do. As a general rule, they aren't allowed to hold, push, grab, or in any way make contact with the opposition across the line of touch. Contesting the ball is okay, but you can't do so by taking out the other player in the air. When the jumper is in the air, leave him alone! The same goes for the lifters; they have to be left alone until they bring their jumper down. Using an opponent to gain leverage for a leap is also on the banned list of techniques.

Other violations involve the offside lines at the lineout. Before the ball is thrown, the offside line is the middle of the tunnel; afterward, it's the ball itself. A lineout isn't over until the ball is passed or run out of the area between the 5- and 15-meter lines. When a ruck or maul forms after the ball is thrown in, the lineout isn't over until that phase has cleared the initial line of touch. For players not in the lineout, their offside line is 10 meters (11 yards) back from the line of touch, and they can't advance until the lineout is over.

Taking It Quick

At the beginning of this chapter, we say that one exception to using the lineout to get play going again after the ball goes out of bounds exists; it's called *taking it quick* (when a player opts to quickly throw the ball back into play instead of waiting for a lineout to form).

A quick throw can be used to restart play when the ball has gone into touch, but several restrictions govern this practice. A player on the team who will get to throw the ball in at the lineout can instead opt to throw it in quickly from anywhere behind the line of touch as long as the lineout hasn't already been formed. The thrower has to use the exact same ball that was previously in play, and it can't have touched anyone on the sideline, including touch judges, ball boys, photographers, spectators, and so on.

The beauty of a quick throw is that it allows you to reignite the attack right away without letting everyone get realigned. Defenders often use the time after the ball has been kicked out to rest and regroup, making it a perfect time to launch an unexpected foray. (So, after a long clearing kick, the first concern of the chasers should be preventing a quick throw-in. This is easily accomplished by following the ball downfield and marking the player who picks it up.) The only danger of a quick throw-in is that you can't count on support from your teammates unless you advance the ball to where they are.

Quick tosses can be straight, or be thrown back toward the attacking team's goal line, but they can't be thrown in forward toward the opposition's goal line and they must travel at least 5 meters (5.5 yards). Taking it quick also has a unique aspect in that players can throw the ball in to themselves so long as it travels the required 5 meters.

Taking it quick can be a good decision when the kicking team has outkicked their coverage. This occurs either when the kicker really nails the ball and it carries beyond where the player's teammates can cover or when the chasers fail to get downfield to play defense. Take it quick only if you have ample time and the right opportunity presents itself. Otherwise, because the majority of lineout balls are retained by the team with the throw-in, you're better off letting the forwards do their thing and taking the moment to catch your breath.

Chapter 10

Individual Skills

*I*n established rugby countries, playing the game starts at a very young age. The skills necessary to become a complete player are introduced and developed over time, building a solid foundation onto which tactical acumen can later be added. Coaches with a lifetime of experience guide youngsters through the essential steps to rugby proficiency as they grow and mature.

In North America, players tend to pick up the game later in life, and coaches lack the deep reservoir of knowledge relied upon so heavily by nations where rugby is an imbedded part of the sporting culture.

Instruction in our part of the rugby universe runs the gamut from extraordinary to almost nonexistent, and when it's offered ends up necessarily being more concentrated into a shorter time span and more reliant upon trial and error while playing. As a result, sometimes even the best players who excel on superior athleticism tend to lack complete skill sets.

Rugby is a game where everyone must possess basic skills, regardless of position. Players are expected to instantly switch from offense to defense and vice versa throughout a match. One-dimensional players deficient in fundamental running, passing, kicking, or tackling skills have no place on a rugby team.

In this chapter, we explain the basics of how to run, pass, kick, and tackle so you can understand the different techniques players use. We also provide plenty of tips so you can fill in any gaps in your game and perfect your rugby craft.

Running Rampant

Running is an integral part of the sport, essential to playing both offense and defense. Though there's certainly nothing wrong with speed, if you can't adapt your running style to handle and pass the ball properly you'll actually hurt your team more than help. Some of the best rugby players aren't the fleetest of foot, but they fulfill their positional responsibilities by practicing good form.

When carrying the ball, you need to be constantly thinking of where the defenders are and what your supporting players are doing in relation to your movements. On top of all this, you need to always be mindful of your primary goal — not to lose possession of the ball.

Running in an upright position may work on the track, but try it in a rugby game and you'll get seriously thumped. The best running position for rugby is to lean forward for balance and effective weight distribution. The rugby running style enables you to adapt to whatever is going on around you. You need to be able to quickly react to the situation at hand, changing directions, accelerating, slowing down, and moving in all sorts of ways a lower body position facilitates. Lowering your center of gravity allows you to react more quickly on the fly.

Running at full pace with the ball takes a little practice before you feel entirely comfortable. When running in the open field, hold the ball in both hands in front of your body. This position allows you to pass to either side of your body and keep the defense guessing. If you have to get ready to pass the ball, it's usually too late to do so.

When you can't avoid being tackled and no one is there to pass to, shift the ball into your outside arm and hold it tight against the side of your body. Tacklers often target the ball in contact with the goal of dislodging it from your grasp, so you need to hang on to the ball to keep the bad guys from stealing it.

To preserve possession throughout the tackle situation, practice running into contact while carrying the ball under one arm, tucked or cradled between your arm and rib cage or armpit where it's protected from the opposition's defending players. Carry the ball in the arm farthest away from the defender, and you can use the other arm to either fend off your opponent or push away from him when he attempts to tackle you. As you make contact, keep your body between the ball and the tackler. When you're brought to ground, you have to release, but remember that you're entitled to place or immediately pass the ball, so don't relinquish it too early.

Receiving a pass on the run

Receiving a pass is difficult at first because so many things are happening at the same time. When the elements are broken down and methodically practiced with precision, your ball-handling errors will be dramatically reduced. The receiver should catch the ball while maintaining an awareness of the defenders in order to choose the best option.

Whenever you're running in support of a ball-carrier, think about where space may be created and how you can exploit it if you get the pass. This is a very subtle and elusive skill that comes from game experience and watching world-class players. Because humans can look in only one direction at a time, your sense of the defensive team's presence and where the gaps are likely to be is primarily gathered through your peripheral vision.

Prior to receiving a pass, look at the passer and verbally communicate that you're ready for the ball to be delivered. Before the ball is passed, reach out with both hands with your palms facing the passer and your thumbs together to provide a target and get ready for the ball's impending arrival. As the ball nears, extend your arms to meet the ball and catch it with your fingers while watching the ball into your hands. When a teammate passes to you, don't take your eyes off the ball until after you catch it. One of the most common mistakes is momentarily losing sight of the ball at the last second to sneak a peek at the defense. Changing your focus too soon may cause you to knock-on — and then get knocked silly — as you attempt to regather your fumble. (Refer to Chapter 6 for full details about the knock-on.)

Side-stepping the tackler

A *side-step* occurs when a ball-carrier heading in one direction suddenly changes course and heads off on a different path. This move is one of the easiest and most effective ways of getting past an opponent. A good time to use a side-step is when you're running with the ball and a defender lines you up for a one-on-one, open-field tackle.

To set up the side-step, run directly at a would-be tackler, which will cause the player to slow down while preparing to make the tackle. Just before the collision, slow down a bit and tuck the ball under one arm for safety (see Figure 10-1a). If you want to side-step to your right, drop your body weight onto your bent left leg, planting the foot firmly on the ground. Drop your shoulder to your left, and then drive hard off your left leg and push away in a sideways direction to your right (see Figure 10-1b). (To add to the deception, before you push off toward the right, feint with your upper body to make your opponent think you're about to go left.) When you've side-stepped around your opponent, accelerate to full speed and continue your run. The key is to slightly reduce your pace before you make your move and to explode off the driving leg to create as much distance as possible between you and the defender.

Figure 10-1:
Stepping
out with the
side-step.

Although the side-step may sound a bit like a fancy move from a '70s disco movie, it's a great skill in rugby because if it's done well the defender in front of you looks pretty foolish grabbing thin air as you cruise by.

Curving into the swerve

If you have the pace and space to run around your marker, the swerve is the move for you. The *swerve* is similar to the side-step, involving the ball-carrier initially running directly at the defender and then curving away just before contact. The ball-carrier usually makes only a slight swerve of the body, and if done at high speed it can be very effective in getting past a defender.

To swerve to your right, first bob to the left with a slight turn of the shoulders as your right leg moves forward. Then take a long stride across the running line with your left leg and move your body away to the right as your right leg comes through. The key is to swerve as close as possible to the tackler to force her to commit, reducing the player's reaction time to adjust and make the play.

Fending off forcibly

Occasionally, despite our svelte physiques and blistering pace, even your esteemed authors sometimes fail to completely evade all 15 defenders. When contact becomes inevitable, you can use the tackler's momentum to your advantage by using your arm to push the tackler away, which is called *fending off*. This is a move common to both the rugby pitch and the football field.

To fend off a tackle, carry the ball in one arm, then just before the collision, turn your body so that your free arm is facing the direction where the contact is coming from. As the defender attempts to make the tackle, thrust your free arm directly at the closest part of the defender's body, usually his head or shoulders (see Figure 10-2b). Push the tackler away and down to stop his momentum (see Figure 10-2c). This action gives you leverage to push yourself off the defender, so you can pick up speed and accelerate away before the would-be tackler has time to recover. (See Figure 10-2 for more detail about the tactics described here.)

Figure 10-2: Fending off a would-be tackler.

Going into a hit and spin

In the *hit-and-spin* move, the ball-carrier commits to contact and then bounces off and spins out of harm's way. Run at the tackler, get lower than your soon-to-be victim, and drive your shoulder hard into the player's upper body while keeping your feet under you. As you bump off the tackler, spin or roll away. The spin is made by quickly twisting, swiveling your hips, and turning your back on the tackler.

When attempting a hit-and-spin move, the more space you create with the initial bump-off, the easier it will be to spin away from your opponent. The key here is to keep your arms free so that the ball can be distributed if the tackler is able to hang on and stop your progress.

Throwing the dummy

A *dummy* is simply a fake pass. By throwing a dummy, you lead your opponent to believe you're going to pass the ball to a teammate, but at the last minute (just as your opponent changes direction to follow the ball) you pull it back and continue running.

This move involves faking the pass with your eyes, arms, and body, while maintaining awareness to see if the defender bites on the misdirection. When the tackler takes the bait and commits toward the receiver, pull back the ball and cut upfield. If you don't do a good enough job of selling the dummy, get ready to be hit hard by the tackler.

Notable running styles

The greatest single example of running rampant in recent memory was New Zealand's rugby colossus Jonah Lomu, knocking over everyone in sight to score repeatedly in the 1995 World Cup. Lomu simply ran through, straight over, or around everyone and everything.

Players both past and present use guile and brilliant changes of pace and direction to make them extremely dangerous when they have the ball in hand. Because very few are blessed with Lomu's size, strength, and agility, the key to successfully running the ball is to use your head to beat the tackler. Smashing the tackler but losing control of the ball is a victory for the defense. You can't expect to make every defender miss, but if you're mindful of your body position in the tackle, are able to maintain possession, and provide a recyclable ball for the next phase of attack, you've done your job as a ball-carrier.

Passing with Panache

Passing the ball is one of the most elementary of rugby skills and should be the first one taught to all newcomers. The goal of passing is to provide a ball that is easily caught by a teammate who is in a better position to continue the attack.

When preparing to make a pass, hold the ball upright in both hands with a hand on either side of the ball, fingers spread wide with the thumbs up to ensure control and balance. When you're ready to pass, swing the ball across your body in the opposite direction of the target (so, if the pass is going to the right, first swing the ball to the left side of your body). Then swing your arms and shoulders back toward the teammate you're passing to, and release the ball. The ball should leave your hands quickly and with a snap (see Figure 10-3).

Making a good pass means you involve your whole body and are well coordinated. Other factors that are critical to a good pass are the following:

Figure 10-3:
Passing the oval ball.

✔ **Accuracy:** Accuracy is vital. When you throw the ball to your teammate, don't throw it directly to him, throw it just slightly in front of him so that he can run on to it and collect the ball at pace. Having to speed up to catch the ball is much better than having to slow down. A good pass travels on an upward arc that your teammate can catch somewhere between his waist and his chest. If he has to bend over or leap to get the ball, his stride will be broken and the defenders can more easily close on him.

For better accuracy and distance, increase the rotation on the ball by bending your arms and turning your wrists slightly as you release it. Your two pinky fingers should be the last digits in contact with the ball.

✔ **Velocity:** Speed is important. Throw the ball with some velocity to ensure it maintains its height and doesn't drop before reaching the player who is going to receive it. A pass that is headed downward is twice as hard to catch as one that is going up. When passing in tight spaces, don't put too much mustard on that hot dog, or the receiver will struggle to control the ball.

✔ **Tactical awareness:** Pass only when your teammate is in a better position to continue the attack. Passing the ball to someone who is surrounded by defenders is not only pointless but also dangerous. A good rule to think of is that you're responsible for your pass and for the next one as well; don't pass the ball if the player you're passing to won't have the opportunity to pass it on — unless, of course, she's streaking down the sideline for a try.

Bringing tactics into play

After you've figured out how to pass, the next step is understanding when to do so. One of the most basic tactical skills is drawing the defender and then passing before you get tackled. *Drawing the defender* means getting the tackler to commit to you, which prevents him from covering other attackers.

If the player with the ball passes it too early, the defender may have enough time to change direction and chase down the receiver. To prevent this, lure the defender to commit by running at him. Then before you reach the defender, who is preparing for the tackle, pass the ball to a teammate who is in a better position to continue the assault.

The ball can be passed much faster than players can run across the field. To demonstrate this principle, challenge your fastest player to run the width of the pitch in pursuit of the ball while it's being passed along the back line. If your team's passing skills are adequate, the ball will always beat the player. This is also known as *letting the ball do the work.*

Spiral pass

A *spiral pass* is made when you put some spin on the ball, causing it to rotate as it moves through the air. The hand farthest away from the direction in which the ball is about to be thrown moves up over the ball as it's thrown, which makes the ball spin. (If the ball is being passed to the left, the right hand comes up over the ball, giving it a counter-clockwise top spin, as shown in Figure 10-4.) The advantage of a spiral pass is that it flies straighter and flatter because it's aerodynamically superior to a ball that doesn't have any spin.

Figure 10-4: Spinning out with a spiral pass.

Cut-out pass

When you pass the ball out along the line and deliberately skip the receiver next to you, it's called a *cut-out pass*. The pass travels right in front of the adjacent player, but instead of reaching out and taking the ball, she fakes grabbing it and lets it fly by to the next player in the line. The phrase *two-man cut-out* means that the ball-carrier has thrown the ball past the first two players next to her in the attacking line, sending it instead to the third player in the line.

For example, the flyhalf may pass the ball beyond the inside center and outside center, and straight to the wing (refer to Chapter 4 for an explanation of where each player lines up on the field). This is usually a predetermined move, but can be executed spontaneously if the passer sees the space outside.

If you're the player being cut out, do your best imitation of someone expecting to get the ball in order to deceive the opposition. The pantomime includes having your hands ready for a pass, running in your usual position in the back line, and sometimes includes breaking the silence with a loud "Now!" just as the passer releases it. The pass needs to be a fast spiral one because speed ensures that the cut-out is effective. The ball has to be thrown quickly and accurately so that the outer backs have the maximum amount of time to do something with it before the defense can react.

Lob pass

A *lob pass* is a high, looping pass that goes just over the outstretched arms of the opposition. This type of pass is used when you're on attack and find yourself crowded by defenders who are running in the passing lanes between you and your support. The only way to pass in this situation is to lob the ball over the defender's heads to one of your teammates.

Pop pass

A short floating pass in close quarters is called a *pop pass*. It's a versatile transfer where the pass is carefully weighted to allow the receiver to easily take the ball without breaking stride. The ball is passed using one or both hands. Start low and lift your arms and wrists to pop the ball up to the receiver. This should not be a bullet or flat pass, and should have a little loft under the ball so the receiver can catch it between his waist and shoulders.

If you find yourself caught in the tackle but your hands are still free, you can use a pop pass to deliver it to a teammate who's running close by in support. The goal is to make the pass as easy as possible to catch, because your receiver is likely to be charging through a tight gap and needs to focus on where the defenders are coming from, not on reaching for a wild pass. Scrumhalves often use the pop pass off the fringes of rucks and on tap penalty plays to transfer the ball.

Dive pass

When you dive forward and pass the ball from underneath your body with a scooping motion, it's called a *dive pass*. This pass is mainly used by scrumhalves, usually at the back of the scrum, when they find themselves under pressure from the defense and need to get the ball away very quickly. Because you're diving away from pressure when it's made, the dive pass also creates a little distance between you and the nearest defender.

Scrumhalf pass

The *scrumhalf pass* is the standard type used by the number 9 to distribute the ball. The essential elements for this pass are that the scrumhalf has her feet behind the ball and her weight initially over it. By staying on her feet and taking a step toward her target, the scrumhalf builds momentum without a time-consuming backswing. When executed properly, the ball goes straight to the target, quickly and with a nice trajectory, making it easy to catch.

The scrumhalf should be your team's best passer. She's responsible for passing the ball from set pieces and distributing it out of rucks and mauls.

Through practice, scrumhalves figure out exactly how to get the ball to their closest teammates. The skill is acquired through hours of training, where the scrumhalf throws the ball to the flyhalf, centers, and wings without looking to see where they're positioned (rugby telepathy, if you like). Scrumhalves have to be the master of every type of pass because they're often forced to improvise when getting the ball out of tricky situations.

Kicking Cleverly

Despite the fact that rugby emerged as a handling game from soccer, kicking still plays a central strategic and tactical role. Kicking in the oval game takes a variety of forms and is used primarily to gain territory, restart play, or score points. Although all kicks are similar in that you launch the ball with your boot, they diverge greatly in technique depending on what you're trying to accomplish.

If you're just starting to coach youngsters or beginners, you can do your team no greater service than making sure every player has fairly good kicking skills. You can guarantee that sometime, somewhere, in a game, every player is going to be called upon to kick the ball. Nothing is more pleasing than seeing a tight forward forced into a situation where his skillful footwork is suddenly called upon in a desperate circumstance and he delivers flawlessly. It may be the only time he ever puts boot to ball, but when it comes off it's a thing of beauty.

An adept kicker is an asset to any rugby team, and like every other basic skill, becoming an effective kicker requires heaps of practice.

Spiral punt kick

The *spiral punt* is an all-purpose kick that is usually the first one you practice. The basic skill looks just like an NFL punter kicking it away on fourth down. The best method for punting the ball is to make it spin off your boot (shown in Figure 10-5). This corkscrewing action is extremely effective, because as the ball leaves your boot it goes the longest distance and is very accurate.

When you want to kick the ball deep into opposition territory with a *clearing kick* (a kick that clears the ball out of your end), the spiral punt is the best kick to use. It's also easy to master. Here's a step-by-step approach to doing it right (see Figure 10-5 for more details):

1. **Hold the ball in both hands well out in front of your body, at an angle so it can spiral off your foot when kicked.**

2. **Drop the ball at an angle of about 30 degrees toward the center of your body (see Figure 10-5a).**

3. **Shift your weight onto your non-kicking foot, which is aimed at the target, while drawing the kicking foot back (see Figure 10-5b).**

4. **Swing your kicking foot straight through so that it strikes the ball along its long axis, and point the toe of your boot out as you make the kick.** You can adjust the flight of the ball by changing the angle of your foot and the point at which the ball is struck in its fall. After the ball is dropped onto your foot, your boot should move slightly across the ball, somewhat like a corner kick in soccer. Watch the ball move all the way onto your boot, and then follow through.

5. **Extend the arm on the opposite side of your body for balance.**

If the kick is done properly, the ball will spiral off your boot. The spiraling effect makes the ball go farther and straighter than the usual punt kick (which usually floats in the air with less distance gained). A right-footed kick will cause the ball to spin clockwise from left to right, and vice versa for a left-footed kick.

Just like a good golf swing, you don't want to kick the ball too hard. Through trial and error, you'll quickly discover just how much force you need to accurately propel the ball the full distance. When you have the right technique and can regularly hit the ball's sweet spot, you'll be amazed at how far a rugby ball can fly.

Figure 10-5:
Kicking
a spiral
punt for
distance
and
accuracy.

Up and under

An *up and under,* or a *Garryowen,* is similar to the spiral punt but is modified for a different purpose. The kicking technique is the same except that the ball is held in the hands so the point and not the side of the ball is facing down. On impact, your boot makes contact with the pointed end of the ball (see Figure 10-6). The goal is to keep the ball in play and put it high enough to provide hang time for your chasers to contest the ball as it returns to earth. The strategy behind an up and under is that it tests the nerve and concentration of the recipient's fullback and forces the opposition's forwards to retreat.

When making an up and under, you have to weight the kick so that the ball comes down just outside your opponent's 22-meter line. That way, the player trying to catch the ball has to deal with tacklers and pray for support from forward teammates. If the ball goes inside the 22-meter line, the receiver can call for a *mark,* like a fair catch in football, which stops play and gives the opponent a chance to kick the ball away.

Figure 10-6:
Testing the
opposition
with an up
and under.

Chip kick

A short punt kick that's calculated to go just over the head of an advancing defender is called a *chip kick*. The goal of a chip kick is to regather the ball in the open space immediately behind the opponent.

Taking a chip kick on the run is particularly difficult and requires a deft boot, but that's when the option usually presents itself and is hardest to defend against. Chip kicks work because the laws prohibit a defender from impeding any player who has just kicked the ball in his or her efforts to regain possession.

When chipped with just the right touch, the ball will often be caught by or bounce up for an attacking player to regather and continue the attack. Chip kicks are used when the defense is up flat with superior numbers, because after you kick the ball they've got to leave you alone.

Grubber kick

A short punt kick that travels low across the ground is known as a *grubber kick*. The goal is to create top spin on the ball, causing it to quickly roll forward on the pitch, end over end (as shown in Figure 10-7). This is a good tactical kick when done properly, because the ball scoots along the ground and can bounce in any direction at any moment. Chasers have the advantage in gathering the ball because they're reading the bounce as they follow it and are less likely to be thrown off by an unpredictable hop.

To make a grubber kick, drop the ball and strike its back half just before it hits the turf so it skips low along the ground (see Figure 10-7). This kick is an effective tactic when the opposing defensive players are coming up fast and you want to put the ball in behind them.

Drop kick

Attempting a field goal during general play is called taking a *drop kick.* Slotting a drop goal is rare, but it gives your side another scoring option when you're near your opponent's goal line and can't break through to score a try.

To take a drop kick, move forward with the ball in both hands, plant your non-kicking foot, and draw back your striking leg as you drop the ball onto the ground. It should land on the pointed end and bounce straight back up a couple of inches. The place to drop the ball for a right-footer is about the width of your hips to the right of your planting left foot.

Figure 10-7:
Rolling out a grubber kick.

The object is to contact the ball with your boot a split second after it rebounds off the ground. Timing the kick and being able to control the dropping of the ball takes a very long time to perfect.

Over the past couple of seasons, before training started and while everyone else was getting their kit on, we developed a little fantasy game where we simulate the final drop goal from the Rugby World Cup 2011 . . . the Eagles are down by two, it's the last movement of the match, and the 40-something ageless wonder — out of nowhere! — gets the ball and squares up for the match-winner. He strikes the drop, the jam-packed Eden Park crowd holds its collective breath — and it's good! The Eagles win the Webb Ellis Cup! (We can dream, can't we?)

Goal kick

Goal kicking involves placing the ball on a kicking tee, making your approach to the ball, striking it, and then following through. Contests between evenly matched teams are usually won by the side with the more accurate goal kicker. Having a reliable goal kicker in your team is a necessity, not a luxury. Goal kicking is a specialist skill, so usually only a few players can handle the responsibility. Having more than one kicker is important; if the main kicker is injured, a suitable replacement is already on the field.

Virtually all kickers in the modern game use the round-the-corner style for kicking goals. The main elements are a measured approach (or *run-up*), planting the non-kicking foot, striking the ball, and following through. As shown in Figure 10-8, goal kicking requires the following step-by-step approach:

1. **Position the ball on the kicking tee.** The usual way to place the ball for a kick is to stand it on end, angled forward toward the goalposts you're aiming for.

2. **Walk back from the ball.** Take about four paces backward, and then right-footed kickers take two paces to the left. If you kick with your left foot, take two paces to the right.

3. **Approach the ball in a slight arc, in a slow relaxed manner, with your eyes focused on the part of the ball you intend to contact.** Coming at the ball in a slight arc gives the required curl to the run as you approach the ball from the left (if you kick with your right foot). The curl to your run-up creates a slight right-to-left action on the ball when it's in the air, helping its trajectory and keeping it in line. The curl also improves the distance of the kick.

4. **Push your hips forward with the final stride, plant your non-kicking foot, and extend your arms for balance.** The last stride with your non-kicking foot must be the longest, with your planted foot ending up slightly behind and the width of your hips away from the ball. The planted foot should be aligned with the toes pointed at the goalposts.

5. **Swing through, and kick the ball.** Strike the ball on its end where the four seams come together with your kicking foot. The top of your foot (near the big toe and instep) contacts the bottom of the ball, driving it forward and up. Extend your foot as you swing your leg through, pointing in the direction of the target. Your chest should be facing the target at impact.

Goal kickers can come from any position, so if you think you've got the knack for it, practice your goal kicking — you never know when you may be drafted into the role.

Figure 10-8:
Goal-kicking
technique.

PLAYER TIP

Goal kicking requires hours and hours of practice to get right. So get a ball, go down to the local park, and experiment until you're comfortable with a goal kick that suits you. Concentrate on the ball until after the moment of impact by keeping your head down and your eyes on the ball. Always remember to follow through when kicking for goal. The follow-through ensures that the balance and coordination needed to put the ball through the goalposts is maintained.

If you carefully watch the world's leading goal kickers, you'll notice they each have their own particular style. From teeing-up the ball to approaching it, from striking the ball to following through, a myriad of techniques will work. The one thing leading goal scorers have in common is that each time they kick for goal they display the exact same routine and a relaxed kicking motion. So encourage your players to experiment and develop their own style to make kicking for goal routine.

Tackling Tough

In football, the object of tackling is simply to bring the runner to the turf by whatever means necessary, because that immediately stops play. In rugby, taking down the ball-carrier is only the first part of a sequential contest for possession that begins with the tackle itself.

Because the rugby tackler's job only starts with bringing the runner down, players must always be mindful of body position throughout contact to increase their team's chances of creating a turnover (stealing possession of the ball). This difference is particularly significant when trying to coach former football players, who tend to opt for the big hit instead of being focused on winning the ball.

For a beginner, the prospect of having to tackle someone is often daunting. Great emphasis should be placed on teaching newcomers how to tackle properly. *Tackle bags* (large, vinyl-covered bags filled with foam) are used to help players perfect their techniques without getting hurt and to ensure they get it right before they actually have to tackle in a match.

The key to teaching how to tackle or developing the ability is to break down the activity into its basic elements and then work slowly to build a progression of drills that simulate the skill. Even though you'll start out on your knees, you need to walk before you can run when it comes to tackling training. When you have a solid understanding of the basics and confidence in yourself, tackling can become one of the more enjoyable parts of the game. Bear the following in mind:

> ✔ **The fear factor:** You can overcome the fear of injury. Naturally you may think that trying to stop a rampaging forward who is charging straight at you is going to inflict damage on your person, but the reality is that you won't get hurt if you tackle correctly.
>
> ✔ **The focus factor:** To be a good tackler, you must possess the ability to block everything else out of your mind as you prepare to make the tackle. Tackling is a precise battle of mind over matter.

The real secret of tackling tough is to convince yourself that you can do it. When you overcome that hurdle, you'll discover your size or shape really doesn't matter — you can effectively tackle any opponent and not get hurt.

When tackling, don't be cautious or half-hearted about it. Those who don't tackle with 100 percent commitment are the first to get hurt; those who trust their instincts become great tacklers and a vital asset to the team.

Developing a good tackling technique takes time, but it's not difficult. When you've acquired the skill, you can improve it at training sessions — even the best players regularly return to the tackle bags to keep their tackling techniques up to scratch. As with running, passing, and kicking, different types of tackles require different techniques.

Front-on driving tackle

A *front-on driving tackle* is used when a ball-carrier is running directly at you. To make a front-on driving tackle correctly, follow these steps (see Figure 10-9):

1. **Assess the situation as your opponent approaches.** Figure out the best type of tackle for the situation and which shoulder you're going to use to hit the opponent, then convince yourself that you're going to be successful.

2. **Lean forward and use one of your shoulders to aim at the spot where you want to hit your opponent.** As you prepare to tackle, push forward with your shoulder, targeting the spot where you want to hit, as shown in Figure 10-9a. You're not allowed to tackle above the line of the shoulders, so aim between the hips and the knees.

3. **Use your legs to drive into your opponent.** Launching your tackle from a balanced, low position with both feet on the ground helps you to generate as much power as possible when you drive your shoulder into your opponent. Good tackling begins with the lower body and is finished with the upper body.

4. **Keep your head aimed to the side of your opponent's body.** Your head position is very important. Your head should be up and your back should be straight. By choosing a shoulder to tackle with early on, and by placing your head to the side, you'll avoid flying knees and elbows that you would have taken if your head was in front. Never use your head as a weapon like in football.

5. **Drive into your opponent, grabbing him or her tightly around the waist.** Drive hard into the ball-carrier to push him or her backward and upward. Wrap your arms tightly around the ball-carrier and hold on (see Figure 10-9b). Smashing the opponent isn't crucial in rugby; making sure you bring the ball-carrier down, even if you get dragged a few meters, is more important.

6. **Try to get the ball from your opponent.** Keeping a strong hold on your opponent so he or she can't get out of the tackle, try to get some part of your hand, arm, or body on the ball. Doing this can help dislodge the ball from the ball-carrier's grasp.

7. **Try to regain your feet and win the ball.** When you're both on the ground, you must release the ball-carrier and immediately attempt to regain your feet and try to steal the ball before anyone on the other team arrives at the breakdown.

Start beginners off slowly by kneeling, standing, stepping, walking, jogging, and then finally running into tackle drills (see Chapter 18). This allows them to grasp the elements of the tackle slowly and builds their confidence.

Figure 10-9: Making a front-on driving tackle.

Side-on tackle

When the ball-carrier is trying to run around you and turns slightly sideways, you'll want to use a *side-on* tackle. A *side-on tackle* is made when you aim your shoulder at the ball-carrier's hip, just below the waist, and place your head behind or alongside the player's inside buttock (in other words, cheek-to-cheek). After hitting the ball-carrier with your shoulder, put your arms around the player's thighs and squeeze tight. Keeping a strong grip on the thighs has the effect of dragging your opponent down.

When making a side-on tackle, never put your head across the body of the runner, as you're likely to catch a driving knee or thigh on your noggin. If you've played football, you've been coached to put your head in front of the player, so you'll need to adapt your tackling technique for safety. Keep your head behind the ball-carrier and away from danger.

Tackle from behind

Another variation of the driving tackle is the tackle from behind. When chasing the ball-carrier from behind, the tackler targets the area just above the knees, as shown in Figure 10-10. The tackler's arms encircle her opponent's thighs with a firm grip, which effectively traps her legs and drags her down.

Figure 10-10: Diving in to tackle from behind.

Ball-and-all tackle

When the you tie up the ball and prevent the runner from passing in contact, it's called a *ball-and-all tackle*, or *smother tackle*. The advantage of this technique is that you slow down the runner's progress while hindering his ability to recycle the ball. The objective is to at least prevent the ball-carrier from quickly passing the ball to anyone else.

The technique can be made from the front, chest to chest, from behind by wrapping your arms around the runner, or any other way you can pin the ball in the tackle. A successful ball-and-all tackle will prevent the ball from being passed by your opponent, so it can be transferred to another player only after you both go to ground and he releases it.

Stationary tackle

The *stationary tackle* is similar to the ball-and-all tackle, but here the ball-carrier is running right at you while you're stationary. By preparing yourself for the front-on impact — and, when it comes, holding on tightly — you can topple your opponent forward and over your body using the ball-carrier's momentum.

Use the stationary tackle if you're a smaller player confronted by a large forward. If you hold on doggedly and vigorously, you can upset your opponent's balance.

Ankle tap

Even if a ball-carrier has blown by you, you're still allowed to hit her feet with your hand in an attempt to trip her from behind in a last-ditch effort to bring her down.

An ankle tap takes perfect timing and an effective tap, but it does work. Usually the defender makes a diving attempt at the ball-carrier and tries to disrupt her stride by smacking one of her ankles inward, so that it collides with the other leg and trips the runner. When you ankle tap a player, getting right back to your feet and pursuing her is essential, because as soon as she regains her feet she can take off running again.

Chapter 11

Tactics and Teamwork

*N*orth America is home to plenty of athletes, but developing instinctual rugby players is a challenge. Even when the basic skills are mastered, North America lacks the key decision makers in critical positions that other countries produce in abundance. For example, the tactical awareness of a 15-year-old New Zealander is typically miles ahead of a 25-year-old North American, because North Americans start playing the game so much later in life. This places an extraordinary burden on North American coaches to open their players' eyes to the tactical possibilities available to them.

As a coach, you need to fully appreciate what your players can and can't do and then develop a style of play that best suits your strengths. Conducting a brutally honest appraisal of your side and a balanced evaluation of the opposition before each game will assist you in developing the most appropriate game plan for every match.

We're not going to promote a particular type of playing style in this chapter because we'd rather give you the information to make an informed decision based on what kind of talent you have at your disposal. In this chapter, we provide you with a framework for establishing a game plan, talk about adapting to the elements, detail how to put points on the board, and give you a structural way to defend against all comers.

Creating a Game Plan

The most important element in any rugby team is that all of your players have a solid grounding in basic skills. Planning complicated moves and intricate defensive systems is useless if your charges can't pass, catch, and tackle. After the essentials are taken care of, it's time to move on to strategic concerns. (Refer to Chapter 10 for full details about running, passing, kicking, and tackling.)

The burden of choosing a particular strategy rests with the coach. Implementing a sophisticated game plan will work only if the time is taken to explain all aspects of it to the players so that they understand the concepts they'll be asked to carry out on the pitch.

The most important first step in attack and defense alike is to devise a good plan. Everyone in your team must understand the plan and know what is expected of them. Winning teams concentrate initially on working out the best method for overcoming the opposition, no matter what style they play. Whether they are simple or complex, plans have to involve the whole team because any weak link will be ruthlessly exploited by the opposition.

You also need to know which of your players are capable of adapting their game on the fly in case you need to alter the plan during a match. Your number 8, scrumhalf, and flyhalf should all be able to make in-game adjustments, so keep that in mind when selecting players for those key positions. A game plan doesn't have to be complex to work, so don't feel the need to script every play like a football coach does. Keep it simple, and stick to what the team does well.

Understanding your team's strengths and weaknesses

The first step in assessing your team's strengths and weaknesses is to look at the size, speed, and fitness of the players. This can be done by testing on the pitch and in the weight room. Simple physical evaluations will give you a good idea of which players are your fastest, strongest, and most fit.

Your players' level of experience also helps in the decision-making process. Maturity and knowledge of the game are vital parts of a successful squad. When you've got a good handle on your players' physical abilities and match experience, you're ready to select a team and start building a strategic foundation.

Just as every player possesses unique talents, each rugby team has a distinctive character that defines how it will play. To fully evaluate your side's strengths and weaknesses, break your players' performance down into its various elements. Assess the set pieces, rucking and mauling, how effectively they contest possession, and their overall competence in general play.

When you examine your side's character, look at both the positive and negative components of their play:

- ✔ Do you have a strong forward pack that usually wins their own scrums and provides good, clean ball at the back, or are they being pushed around and barely getting the ball out?

- ✔ Are your forwards adept at rucking and mauling, or is the breakdown a source of frustration, turnovers, and penalties?

- ✔ Do you have reliable jumpers in your lineout who consistently win possession and occasionally steal the ball from the other team, or do your jumpers struggle to win their own throw-ins and concede the opposition's?

- ✔ Are your back-rowers getting to the tackle situation and making an impact there, or are they late, indecisive, and ineffective?

- ✔ Can your flyhalf and fullback read the game and make good tactical decisions, or do they lack the vision to make the correct choices under pressure?

- ✔ Do you have backs with the skills to move the ball quickly who use their pace to cross the gain line, or is every trip down the line a retreating exercise waiting for the next knock-on?

- ✔ Do your backs tackle well in the open field, or are they a line of matadors?

Your appraisal needs to be totally impartial. This is a time for clinical observation focused on what your players can and can't do. Put aside your preconceived notions to institute a style of play that takes advantage of your team's talents and minimizes their deficiencies.

Winning the set pieces

The best way to guarantee that a team has every chance to beat an opponent is to have a solid forward pack, which means that the forwards must attempt to dominate in all areas of play. At the very least, these players must hold their own in scrums and lineouts, win the ball in tackle situations, and get the ball out to the back line.

If your team can't get or keep the ball in rugby, winning is impossible. Forwards are responsible for winning possession of the ball a majority of the time, so building the strongest pack from the best athletes available is logical. A solid but unspectacular back line will perform exponentially better when they are working behind a dominant set of forwards. If the forwards are poor, however, a great back line will be wasted.

The primary focus of any pack is to be able to win their own scrums. This takes hard work, dedication to the task, and countless hours of training time. Shortchanging scrum practice is a recipe for disaster. Putting out a team of fantastic backs who never get the ball because their forwards are getting steamrolled is one of the most frustrating experiences in the game. To keep this from happening, scrummagers must feel confident they can win their own ball before moving on to other tasks. (Refer to Chapter 8 for a rundown of requirements for a strong scrum.)

If you have a dominant tight five (two props, the hooker, and the two locks) that consistently drives the opposition off the ball, scrums will be attacking platforms for your side no matter which team has the put-in. On the other hand, if you're being beaten and pushed around up front, you need to adjust your game plan to minimize the damage.

After scrums, the lineout is the next most important set piece confrontation. Timing, teamwork, and accuracy of movement and throws are the key factors to winning the ball at the lineout. Even teams that lack height and gifted jumpers can be productive at the lineout as long as they work together as a unit. (Refer to Chapter 9 for full details about lineouts.)

If you're winning your lineouts with regularity, a whole host of attacking options will be opened up. Start with the driving maul, transition to a rolling maul, and, when they make adjustments to stop it, try the peel into midfield or down the blindside. (Refer to Chapter 7 for details of driving mauls and rolling mauls, and refer to Chapter 9 for info on peeling.)

If you're consistently losing the lineouts on your team's throw-in, you've got a serious problem and need to change your approach. Try throwing deep beyond the 15-meter line or to the front lifter to mix things up. Even if you lose these throws, the opposition isn't likely to make a clean steal. If you're not having any success contesting the opposition's throws, concede the throw-in and concentrate on stopping their mauls instead.

The most overlooked set pieces are kickoffs and restarts. A normal match usually has at least four or five opportunities for each team to secure possession in this way. Unfortunately, these set pieces are often worked on infrequently, if at all, by many lower-level teams. Being ready to contest kickoffs and restarts and having a definite plan for getting the ball and distributing it to the right players during these set pieces will markedly improve your team.

Well before each game, take your captain aside and discuss what options should be chosen in every situation. Do you prefer a scrum, a lineout, or a re-kick if the restart doesn't go 10 meters? When you have the choice, do you want to kick for touch to gain territory and restart play with a lineout, or elect to set a scrum to get things moving again? These decisions require a sense of how you expect to match up against the other team and will invariably need to be refined on the fly as the match unfolds. If your captain has the game plan down, making the right choices becomes much easier.

Playing the ten-man game

The *ten-man game* refers to a strategy in which a team focuses play around the eight forwards, the scrumhalf, and the flyhalf. (The backs are usually neglected and hardly see the ball.) The object of the ten-man game is to keep the ball in tight among the pack and drive directly through the heart of the opponent's forwards.

Playing the ten-man game is a tactical decision to consider when the players on your team have a clear advantage over the competition up front but are comparatively weaker in the back line and out wide, or when the conditions are wet or windy. This type of game requires a totally dominant pack, a scrumhalf who provides good service, and a flyhalf who kicks the ball accurately, efficiently, and deep. As for the rest of the backs, they are primarily selected for their defensive prowess and ability to prevent turnovers.

In the ten-man game, the forwards usually keep the ball in hand, especially if they can gain territory by using driving mauls and quick rucking. If that doesn't work, the scrumhalf passes the ball to the flyhalf, who will then kick the ball either toward the sideline to get a lineout or in front of the forwards for them to chase and contest for possession.

The flyhalf kicks for the sideline, knowing that his team has enough good lineout jumpers to win the ball even if the opposition has the throw-in at the lineout. Inevitably, through turnovers and good defense, the team can get close to the opposition's tryline and score the points required for victory.

These tactics aren't pretty — the ball is hardly sighted in open play, and watching a big bullocking forward bustle his way over the line from a few meters out isn't exactly a moment of aesthetic beauty. Nevertheless, playing the ten-man game often ensures victory under the right circumstances.

The ten-man game isn't commonly used anymore at the international level, although South Africa still practices a version of it. The speed of the modern game and the importance of teams having fast, expressive backs make the ten-man game an anomaly at the highest level. The ten-man game, even though grounded in solid principles, isn't the most entertaining spectacle for the masses — but to those who fully appreciate the subtlety of the battle up front, it's awe-inspiring stuff that can be every bit as riveting as a 100-point tryfest.

The teams that still play the ten-man game do so for important reasons. Teams with powerful packs and reliable lineouts and scrums find it a comfortable way to dominate possession and territory while wearing down the opposition.

Even though the ten-man game is out of favor at the highest levels, it's an effective strategy used by club teams all over the world and deserves inclusion in your array of tactical considerations.

Running from everywhere

At the opposite end of the spectrum from the ten-man game is the concept of *running from everywhere,* which involves an all-out, attack-at-all-costs style of play. The goal of this stratagem is to run the ball to gain territory from every situation. Teams that are best suited to this tactic usually have very talented backs and may lack a dominant tight five.

The attempt to run from everywhere on the pitch has to be accompanied by mobile loosies (the two flankers and the number 8) who can support their backs wherever they're stopped by the opposition. The forwards must also be excellent ruckers and ready to run for the full 80 minutes.

In club rugby, you're likely to find that competing back lines can be severely mismatched based on speed, attacking acumen, experience, and combinational dynamics. This is the ideal time to unleash your backs, who can build their confidence by thrashing inferior opposition.

The most successful rugby teams are the ones that take elements from each of these two contrasting game styles — the ten-man game and running from everywhere — striking a balance that allows them to best utilize the talent on offer. The most respected coaches are the ones who aren't married to a particular strategy and can guide their teams based on an evaluation of how their players can be most successful.

Analyzing the opponent

In addition to having basic skills, a successful coach makes a point of assessing the opposition's strengths and weaknesses in advance and then works on devising a strategy to beat that team.

At the professional level, coaches watch videotapes and prepare detailed scouting reports. At the club level, you can at least get an idea of your next opponent's playing style by sending someone from your club out to watch the team play. If the person knows what to look for, he or she can provide a wealth of information on strengths and weaknesses, general tendencies, and any outstanding players or unusual tactics.

Exploiting weaknesses

The first order of business for taking down an opponent is to note any obvious chinks in their armor and take advantage of them. For example, you may notice that the opposition fullback or wings are nervous when the ball is kicked high into the air. If they've struggled with the high ball, test them repeatedly until either they perform successfully or you've gained lots of possession from their miscues. (The same goes for players who are hesitant in the tackle. Target them with strong runners to see if this can give you an advantage in attack.)

A fantastic area for exploitation is in the set pieces. If the other side is having trouble winning their scrums or producing good ball, have your team concentrate on the *eight-man push* (where all eight forwards use coordinated strength to drive the opposition back) and direct your scrumhalf to heighten her aggressiveness in pressuring her opposite.

Anywhere on the rugby pitch where you think your team can legally get the upper hand is a legitimate area to exploit, but be careful in doing so. Sticking to the game plan is more important than trying too many spontaneous tactics in the heat of battle. Of course, if your strategy calls for taking advantage of predetermined opposition inadequacies, by all means, exploit away!

Containing the stars

In any rugby competition, certain players stand head and shoulders above everyone else by dint of their exceptional talent or skills. Even though rugby is a team game, sometimes putting in place special measures to stop a certain rampaging opponent becomes necessary. Most of the time, this means either denying that player the ball or applying additional pressure on him whenever he touches it.

Don't rearrange your whole game plan to cope with the speed or power of one individual. What works best is to emphasize basics in tackling and review your defensive goals prior to the match. Contain the stars within the context of your established defensive pattern only, and definitely without resorting to cheap shots or illegal tactics.

Sometimes the best strategies for defeating star players are simple. If one of the opposition's jumpers is poaching all your throw-ins, try throwing the ball to a different spot in the lineout. Kicking the ball away from a particular player, or cheating a little in spacing to reduce gaps for stars to run through can also be simple but effective tactics. The best overall strategy is to minimize the impact by denying them opportunities to make big plays.

Selecting horses for courses

Selecting horses for courses is an old-time rugby saying that means the players chosen for a certain match should be determined by the nature of that particular contest. If the opposition has a mammoth pack and you're worried about losing set piece ball, this is a good time to bulk up your own pack, even if it costs you some mobility. Similarly, if the opponent is loaded with pace in the back line, you may want to choose quicker, more mobile players in your team to counteract their advantage.

The adage also applies to strategic concerns. When your team is forced to use a style of game it's not used to (either because of weather conditions or the strength of the opposition), certain players may be better suited for the revised game plan than your regular starters. For example, a flyhalf who specializes in kicking may be a more suitable selection than an attack-oriented flyhalf on a wet, windy day.

The emergence of impact players as substitutes has added another dimension to the "horses for courses" axiom. Some players are great at coming off the bench and making their presence felt but struggle if they have to play the full 80 minutes. Others can play solid rugby over the course of a match but are very ordinary when they come on as replacements. Recognizing these traits and filling your reserve bench with the appropriate performers is a coaching necessity.

Weathering the Conditions

Rugby is a game meant to be played outside in all types of conditions. Gale-force winds, sleeting rain, oppressive heat, or freezing temperatures usually won't keep a match from happening but will alter its character. In most cases, the conditions on the pitch are the same for both sides. One team may have the wind in one half, but the other gets it in the second stanza. Rain stopping and starting affects both teams equally, and humidity drains everyone's energy.

Depending on where your club is located, playing in rainstorms or on excessively hot days may be normal. The difficulty emerges when you have to play in conditions that are completely foreign or that you're unprepared for. Good coaches do everything possible to have their teams ready to perform, no matter how the elements may intervene.

Altitude is one case where the home team does have a distinct advantage over the visitors. The body takes at least a couple of weeks to fully adjust to changes in altitude, so unless a visiting side prepares for a fortnight in the opposition's backyard, they will feel the stress of reduced oxygen content sooner than their hosts.

Adapting to inclement weather

Rain is the great equalizer in rugby because it makes the ball difficult to handle and it slows everyone down when the ground gets waterlogged. When it's wet out, keeping the ball in hand as much as possible and avoiding throwing it around like a giant oval-shaped bar of soap is a good idea. This strategy calls for more mauling and working the pick-and-go (refer to Chapter 7 for more details), as opposed to passing incessantly (which is likely to produce a multitude of turnovers and scrums).

Many teams opt for a kicking-oriented, positional strategy (the ten-man game) when rain becomes a factor. If the weather dictates a radical change in tactics, put them into place right away, not after an attempt to use your regular style has failed.

A windy day calls for testing the opposition with the high ball, so be prepared for them to do the same thing to you. A strong breeze can also wreak havoc with lineout throws, so stay away from long ones to the back that will end up being blown not straight or away from your jumpers.

Playing the pitch

Rugby pitches in North America vary from plush carpets of immaculate green grass to concrete-like dirt interspersed with weeds. You have to be able to play on different surfaces from week to week depending on your league. Here are a few tips for being able to play on any pitch:

- ✔ Always arrive early to inspect the ground by walking around the pitch before the match begins. This includes looking for safety hazards and any noticeable slopes or abnormalities in the field of play or tryzones.

- ✔ Make sure your players always have a couple of different lengths of studs for their boots so they can swap them if necessary. On a very hard surface, wearing boots with long studs can be like running on an ice rink, but they provide better traction on a soft track.

- ✔ Figure out in advance where the sun and wind are headed so your captain can make an informed choice during the coin toss. If your defensive confidence is high, playing against the wind in the first half can provide a psychological boost to your team, knowing that you'll have the advantage of the wind in the second half.

Adaptation

Growing up and going to college in Southern California shielded me from ever having to participate in sports during inclement weather (unless you count smog alerts). My first years of rugby were played in idyllic conditions, with heat being the only real climatic factor.

That all changed when I moved to Missoula, Montana, and began playing for the Maggots. Suddenly, I had to be able to adapt on a weekly basis. Late-summer snowstorms weren't uncommon, and a blizzard in October was considered normal. The idea of not playing just because a foot of snow was falling was anathema to the hardy denizens of the Montana Rugby Union, so the games went on as scheduled regardless of the conditions.

My atmospheric education continued in Riga, Latvia, where it seemed that only one match out of every ten wasn't played in the rain, and dirt was the surface of necessity until May 1. It was in Riga that I was also introduced to Winter 10s, played in subzero temperatures on a sheet of ice covered in snow for padding. Playing in these conditions, I learned that you get cold only when you're standing around, so to avoid freezing to death you had to keep moving.

The biggest shock was when I went to play for Vail, Colorado, in 1999. I had heard about altitude affecting physical fitness, but because I was out of shape anyway I didn't think I'd be a victim. About a minute into my first match in Aspen, I was gasping for breath and looking to the sideline for a replacement, but none was forthcoming. By the end of the summer, I had acclimated and was warning the newcomers to the Colorado mountains.

Finally, back in Los Angeles after experiencing chilly climes all over the rugby universe, I now actually prefer playing in cold, rainy weather and reserve my complaining for when the mercury rises above 75 degrees. Adapting to unfamiliar conditions forced me to focus on basic skills and mental toughness to overcome challenging circumstances.

Deciding On a Game Plan

Before the first match, a coach decides which style of play best suits the talents of her assembled charges. As the season unfolds and players begin to jell, injuries take their toll, and what works and what doesn't becomes obvious, the coach needs to adapt. She should employ a dynamic approach to preparing each week's game plan that takes into account the present state of her side and the opposition.

When trying to determine what type of play will lead your team to victory, organizing your thoughts by asking yourself a series of questions may be useful. Do you expect to win the contest for possession in the forwards? Are your backs superior to theirs? Where along the continuum, from playing the ten-man game to running from everywhere, takes best advantage of your team's comparative strengths? After you've settled upon an overall strategy that's calculated for your opponent, you then shift to specifics.

The initial area of concern is *first-phase possession*, which refers to a team gaining possession of the ball from set pieces (scrums, lineouts, restarts, and so on) instead of stealing possession from a ball-carrier from the opposing team. Do you expect to win the set pieces, or will you struggle to get the ball from restarts? For example, if you think you'll have a clear advantage in the lineouts, you'll feel more comfortable kicking the ball for touch to keep your opponent pinned in their own end. On the other hand, if the other team is full of dominant lineout jumpers, your team is better off with a plan that keeps the ball in play through several phases and avoids putting it out of bounds.

The next area to look at is how you match up at the breakdown. On attack, do you expect your loosies to get there first in support of your ball-carriers, or will they be beaten to the spot and have difficulty recycling the ball? If you have the upper hand in maintaining possession, you can implement a more expansive attacking style. If you think the enemy has better ball-ferreting skills, avoid the tackle situation by passing before contact and use kicks to advance the ball.

Preparing a game plan is rarely a simple matter of deciding you have better forwards or backs and therefore you should adopt one style or another. More often, you'll identify areas where you expect to hold an advantage, others that will be even, and some where the opposition will be better. The best game plan uses these observations to accentuate your strengths and minimize your weaknesses.

Don't write your game plan in stone. You need to be able to adjust your strategy as the game unfolds. Watching and analyzing your opponents during a game is critical. The first 40 minutes of a match can give a quick-thinking coach plenty of material to rapidly digest and then make changes for the second half.

Attacking Artistically

A successful attacking game plan relies on predetermined patterns and collective goals. Before a team goes into a game, the players should have practiced a variety of attacking moves during training, with everyone clear on their roles and responsibilities.

Attack plans don't have to be overly innovative or elaborate, but they do have to be precisely executed and not easily read by the defense. When the defenders don't know what's going to happen next, they're more likely to hesitate, which creates gaps for your side to exploit. Intricate moves that confuse your own side do more harm than good, so keep it simple at first.

Launching an effective attack

Offensive attacks, where your team has the ball, can be initiated from set pieces, general play, or turnover ball. The starting point for every move is how the ball is presented before the attack begins. If the ball is made available from a controlled platform, it's called *quality possession.* When your attack begins with quality possession, your back line's timing and coordination aren't disrupted, which increases their chances of success.

Quality possession at scrumtime means the ball is delivered cleanly, quickly, and accurately to the backs. Sloppy ball from a scrum that's moving backward is nearly impossible for a scrumhalf to use positively. Likewise, if you're struggling to win clean ball at the lineout, your scrumhalf will be under tremendous pressure distributing the ball. Because scoring a try directly off first-phase possession is rare, launching an effective attack more often depends on how efficiently you can reset your attacking pattern through multiple phases.

The most dangerous attacking opportunities come from turnover balls that are used quickly. Immediately after turnovers (when possession of the ball moves from one team to the other), the team that loses the ball will be ill-prepared to defend because the players will still be in an attacking formation. The key here is that the team with possession launches its attack before the opposition can assume a defensive posture. Rucks and mauls are the most common launching pads for attacking movements because they provide an excellent base for unleashing your back line. This is because defenders tend to get sucked into the fray at the breakdown, creating space and potential mismatches out wide.

If you can't run through or around the other team, you can integrate attacking with the boot into your game plan. You can kick into open space with the goal of regathering the ball, or boot it high to put pressure on the receiver.

Breaking through

Breaching the opponent's line requires a targeted point of attack. If you can beat them out wide, use your speed. If they have a particularly weak tackler, run repeatedly right at him. If they're coming up hard and flat, use deception to draw them out of position. When you can't find a way through, kick it behind them to turn 'em around.

Successful attacking moves rely on correct alignment, running proper angles, and hitting the gain line at pace using a coordinated sequence of movements. Positioning your back line flat and close makes passing easier but provides less time and space to operate in. Placing them deeper and wider gives them more room to move but allows defenders to cover multiple attackers and diminishes the space out wide.

Practice a new move over and over, first in slow motion and then gradually increasing the speed until everyone knows exactly where to be and what to do. Attacking artistically relies on good communication, with your playmaker calling the play and the rest of the team getting into position to run it.

You can usually tell when a set move is about to happen, because the playmaker starts talking and gesticulating to his back line.

Defending Devilishly

The ultimate goal of playing defense is to regain possession of the ball. The effectiveness of any defense is dependent on the structure used and the attitude of the players. The objective is to employ an aggressive, pressure-oriented scheme that focuses on stopping the offense and stealing the ball.

The most important defensive attribute is commitment. Half-hearted attempts to tackle have no place in rugby, because the likely result is that you'll miss the runner and hurt yourself in the process.

Coordinating the defense

The keys to team defense are communication, structure, and execution. Playing defense is a fluid activity where you need to constantly react to an ever-changing situation. Communication is vital, because as the attack changes you need to talk to each other to maintain your pattern. The defensive structure relies upon every player knowing where to cover, making good tackles, and understanding what everyone else is doing.

An effective defensive team plan requires working together as a unit, communicating well, and backing each other up when necessary. Walking and talking your team through their defensive system is every bit as important as hours and hours of tackling drills. Be sure your players understand the concepts behind what's expected of them.

Blocking the advance: Defensive systems

Pressure, width, and depth are the three main principles of team defense. Pressure takes time and space away from the attacking team. Width prevents them from running around the outside of the defense. Depth provides additional levels of defenders who can step up and make tackles.

Two basic approaches to applying defensive pressure, ensuring width, and maintaining depth are man-on-man and drift.

- ✔ **The man-on-man defense:** Defenders are responsible for tackling their opposites.
- ✔ **The drift or one-out defense:** Defenders drift sideways to cover the next attacker outside them.

Man-on-man defense

In *man-on-man* defense, each tackler's assignment is to contain his or her opposite.

Figure 11-1 shows the defensive formation at a scrum, with the defenders *marking*, or matching up against, the attacking team (as shown by the arrows). For example, the defending flyhalf marks the attacking team's number 10. To cover the last player in the formation, the defending fullback moves toward the sideline to cover the attacking team's left wing.

Drift defense

The *drift defense* involves the defenders all sliding outside in unison to take away the attacking team's ability to outflank them. This defense is often used after a lineout or a scrum, and it provides increased width and depth but lacks the pressure element of the man-on-man defense.

Figure 11-2 illustrates a scrum with the defenders setting up a drift defense. The normal progression is that the openside flanker takes the attacking flyhalf while the defending flyhalf pursues the inside center, followed by the inside center being responsible for the outside center, and so forth down the line. The defense drifts across the field, cutting off any attempt to come back inside while forcing the ball-carriers toward the sidelines.

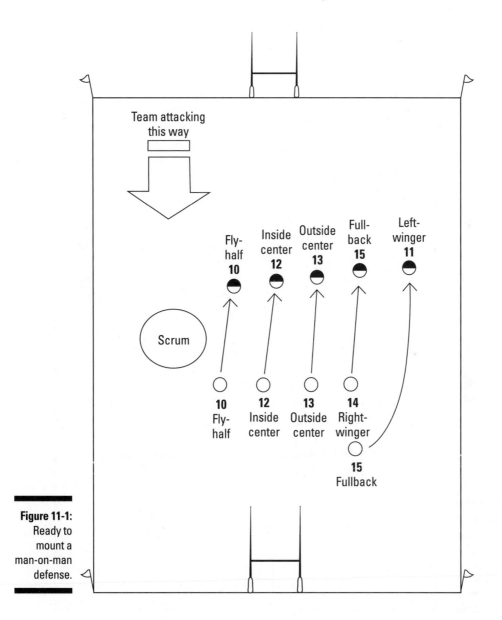

Team attacking
this way

Fly-
half
10

Inside
center
12

Outside
center
13

Full-
back
15

Left-
winger
11

Scrum

10
Fly-
half

12
Inside
center

13
Outside
center

14
Right-
winger

15
Fullback

Figure 11-1:
Ready to
mount a
man-on-man
defense.

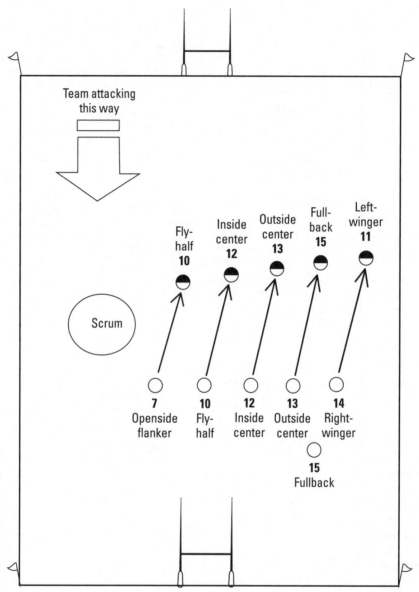

Figure 11-2:
Lining up
to launch a
drift defense
against the
attackers.

When executed properly, the drift defense accounts for an extra attacker being brought into the line. For example, if the extra attacker enters the line between the inside center and the outside center, that player will be tackled by the defending inside center.

Developing commitment and trust

The best defending sides all share a common trait — trust. Developing mutual trust among your players is essential when it comes to team defense. Confidence in your fellow defenders' ability and commitment to tackling builds the trust required to stay focused on your individual defensive responsibilities.

The Crusaders

The Crusaders have won five Super 12 titles and two Super 14 titles because they excel on defense. They have an enormous capacity to defend over long periods of time against multiple-phase attack without losing their defensive pattern or conceding penalties at the breakdown or being offside. The Crusaders take great pride in their defense, and it's the cornerstone of their entire game plan. They have incredible defensive discipline and trust — they trust the team defensive system and they trust their teammates to do their jobs within the team system. They relish the opportunity to make a tackle, always trying to meet the runner behind the gain line and knock him back so that the ball can be turned over. At the fringes of rucks, you'll see Crusader players pointing and calling out to each other while getting ready to make the next tackle so everyone knows their role well before the ball comes out. As soon as the scrumhalf touches the ball, they become an attacking force on defense, charging up the field to crush the infidels for daring to challenge the men from Christchurch.

By sharing self-belief in their collective strength, the Crusaders prevent the attacking side from creating confusion and hesitation among the faithful defenders. They all know their mission and believe wholeheartedly in each other's desire to get the job done. Establishing trust is a fundamental part of developing the resolve necessary to maintain defensive solidarity and a critical element in creating a championship culture. After that trust is established, there's no limit to what your team will endure to achieve its collective goals.

Chapter 12

Talented Training

For most of its history, rugby was largely an amateur sport where even at the highest levels players had to have careers outside the game to support themselves. Training was usually done after the end of the workday. That all changed with the advent of professionalism in 1995, when modern training regimens were introduced and the fitness required to excel in the game shot up accordingly. Rugby players at the international level are now the same as professional athletes in other contact sports, but the approaches to conditioning vary from country to country.

A typical rugby match involves roughly 6 miles of running interspersed with hundreds of bursts of energy when encountering the enemy. To survive and pass this grueling test of cardiovascular and muscular endurance, you need to be strong and extremely fit. As the game has become less stop/start and more fluid in recent years, the fitness level required to keep pace has increased commensurately. This shift requires a more focused approach to physical preparation that develops both baseline conditioning and position-specific fitness.

In this chapter, we describe what you need to do to attain a basic level of fitness, how to mentally prepare for matches, and what to eat for peak performance.

Getting Match Fit

Fitness is acquired in the hours spent running or working out on your own in the gym, not at training. For non-professionals, the limited amount of practice time necessitates a focus on skills and drills and leaves very little room for conditioning. All rugby players should be physically prepared for battle before the season begins instead of following the old method of playing their way into shape. Nothing takes the place of hard work.

Before rashly starting any exercise program, think carefully about the physical demands made on you in a match. You need to build and maintain a level of fitness that ensures you have plenty of the following:

- **Stamina:** Because a match is played over 80 minutes, you need to develop both aerobic and anaerobic fitness. *Aerobic capacity* gives you the endurance needed to roam the pitch for the entire match. *Anaerobic capacity* provides energy for repetitive bursts of high exertion over the course of the game.

- **Strength and power:** Because you constantly encounter opposing forces who want to run over the top of you, you need to be strong enough to stop them and reply in kind. You also need muscular endurance to be as tough in the last minute of play as you are in the first.

- **Flexibility:** When you have the ball in your hands, or are trying to take it away from the opposition in all phases of play, you need flexibility to be effective and prevent injury.

Even in the final minutes of the game, you should still be breathing easily. Sprawling face-down in the turf suffering from exhaustion or cramps does nothing to help your side and is not a good look.

Focus on exercises that target the parts of your body you want to strengthen, but be careful not to overdo it — we don't want legions of *Rugby For Dummies* readers turning up at their doctors' offices tomorrow with strains, sprains, and broken bones. Do only as much as you feel comfortable with, and increase the intensity of your workout gradually. Fitness can't be acquired in a few days or even weeks, so don't try to speed up the timetable — it will only lead to disappointment.

Warming up and having a good stretch

Before every practice or fitness session, start with a well-planned warm-up. Establishing a routine that prepares the body for the higher level of exertion to follow is very important. Jogging a couple of laps, riding an exercise bike, jumping rope, or doing light calisthenics are all acceptable methods of breaking a sweat and warming up.

A good warm-up followed by a stretching routine minimizes the risk of injury. Improving your flexibility can help prevent ligament, joint, and muscle injuries on the big day. Devote at least 10 to 15 minutes to stretching before you start the more strenuous activities. All the stretches that are described in this chapter will help increase your flexibility and get you ready for action.

Perform stretching only if you're absolutely sure you can manage it. Check with your coach and your doctor to determine whether a new program is right for you. This is especially important if you've been injured before or have any health problems.

Stretching for performance

Stretching is an important part of any training program and should be performed with as much care and enthusiasm as the active part of any training session. Prepare your stretching program before training starts, and have goals and objectives already in place.

Obviously, different training regimens require the use of different muscle groups. The stretching that comes after training is targeted toward those groups that have carried the biggest workload.

For example, if the session will feature sprint training, focus on stretching the hamstrings, calves, glutes, and hip flexors. If the workout involves upper-body weight training, stretch the chest, back, and shoulders. Other areas still get stretched, but place more emphasis on these target areas. Any stretching session should have goals and guidelines in place.

Set your stretching goals as follows:

✔ Preparing for training (dynamic stretching in warm-up)

✔ Maintaining flexibility (static stretching in cool-down)

✔ Increasing flexibility (developmental)

✔ Helping recover from injury (which may include all of the preceding points)

Stretching can have many benefits, including these:

✔ Helping to reduce muscle tension

✔ Helping to clear metabolic waste (lactic acid) from muscles

✔ Straightening and increasing the length of muscle fibers

✔ Improving body awareness

✔ Increasing the quality of muscle movement

✔ Helping with muscle firing patterns

All of these elements together increase the quality of recovery, thereby allowing players to train with a higher intensity and have less time in the rest/recovery phase (or on the physiotherapist's table with an injury). Many a promising player has had his or her career cut short because of a preventable injury.

Use dynamic stretching before activity because it takes the muscles through a range of movement and stretches them in the same way they will be used during a practice or game. It also helps establish firing patterns within the muscles' stretch reflex and proprioceptors (sensory receptors found in muscles that detect motion or the position of the body or a limb by responding to stimuli arising within the organism) so the correct signals are being relayed at the appropriate time, thus preparing them to go from a slow jog to an explosive sprint without tearing.

Dynamic stretch routine

After you get warmed up, you can start dynamic stretching. After you start stretching dynamically, don't use static stretching until the cool-down session. Remember, static stretching slows the muscles down, and dynamic stretching wakes them up.

Perform the following exercises across 20 meters (22 yards) of field space. Remember, when stretching dynamically, technique is much more important than speed and the goal is to start slow and gradually increase the tempo. Doing 2 to 4 repetitions of each of the following dynamic stretches is recommended, but on a cold day more may be necessary.:

- ✔ **Groin:** Walking sideways squats and carry-over side-steps
- ✔ **Hamstrings and quads:** Walking lunges and high-knee jogging
- ✔ **Waist and lower back:** Rotating trunk while bending at waist
- ✔ **Back and hamstrings:** Burpees and butt kicks
- ✔ **Waist and adductors:** Placing and picking up the ball
- ✔ **Calves:** Jumping up and down on the toes
- ✔ **Shoulders and upper back:** Rotating arms and ups and downs

Static stretching after training

Finish with a static stretch cool-down period following your training session. Static stretching returns the muscles to the length they were when they started and is most effective when the stretching is focused on the muscles most heavily used in the session. Work for 5 to 15 minutes, and hold the stretches for 15 to 30 seconds each.

Keep track of all your stretches in a stretching diary. It is very helpful in staying focused on the task at hand and keeping some form of order to your stretch routine.

Developing a fitness program

To prepare yourself properly for rugby, you need a fitness program that develops speed, muscular strength, agility, and cardiovascular endurance. To improve your *cardiovascular endurance* — that is, to increase the fitness of your heart and lung system — you need a series of exercises that enhances the body's ability to take in oxygen and circulate it throughout the body to your muscles, which will be screaming for more O2. If you have plenty of stamina, you won't run out of gas or tire excessively while playing or training.

Improving your stamina

When your heart is pumping fast and you're sweating bullets, whether you know it or not you're working on your stamina. One of the best ways to increase stamina is to run varying distances. A good combination is to do distance work and then finish with some sprinting (which we cover in the next section). For distance work, your ultimate goal is to be able to run nonstop for 6 miles (because this is roughly the ground you cover during an average match). To start off, try running around the pitch for about 20 minutes at a slow but steady rate and see how you feel.

If you're unaccustomed to running, increase the distance slowly. Stay within your comfort zone until you can hold a conversation or sing to yourself while jogging effortlessly. When you can do that, increase the distance in small increments. After you reach the 6-mile plateau, gradually increase your speed, lowering your total running time.

When beginning a running program, don't do too much too early, otherwise you may cause muscle damage. Run well within your own limits, and stop if you suddenly find yourself struggling. Your distance and speed will improve over time, but not overnight!

Running at full tilt: Sprint training

Rugby involves periods of jogging mixed with flat-out sprinting. So, after you're comfortable jogging, you need to work on your speed by sprinting shorter distances. Try running at a brisker pace from one end of the field to the other, take a 30-second break, and then run back the other way followed by another break. Do this three or four times. You may struggle early on, but within days you will discover that the number of sprints you can make before collapsing in a heap rises remarkably.

Sprint training is an important element in building up speed. During a game, a player often has to accelerate from a standing start and hit top speed within a couple of seconds. To simulate this activity and improve your speed, include in your training schedule a series of sprints punctuated by prescribed rest periods, which is called *interval training*.

An effective sequence is to run ten 10-meter sprints with a 15-second rest between each one, move up to ten 20-meter sprints with a 30-second rest between them, follow with ten 30-meter sprints with 45 seconds of rest, and then finish with ten 40-meter sprints with 60 seconds of rest between each. Over time, work to decrease the time spent resting between periods of full exertion.

As your cardiovascular fitness increases, you'll find that it progressively takes less time to recover during the resting intervals. Interval training mimics the type of exertion required in a match, so give it your full effort on every repetition — visualize yourself running toward the tryline for the game winner with an opponent hot on your heels.

Sprint training is demanding fitness work and should be done only after you've warmed up properly. If you begin your fitness program without stretching or warming up first, you can cause some serious muscle injuries.

Working on your agility

To improve your agility, construct an obstacle course with cones placed at intervals of 4 to 5 meters (4.4 to 5.5 yards). With a rugby ball in your hands, weave through the markers and practice bounding off first your left foot and then your right foot, as if trying to get past a defender with the side-step or swerve (Chapter 10 gives full details about these moves). Begin slowly, but challenge yourself by trying to move quicker each time.

You can try this in your own backyard or at a neighborhood park. You'll not only improve your agility, you'll also keep the neighbors entertained. Watch out for small dogs yapping at your heels and local kids trying to figure out what on earth you're doing.

Another good drill is to run at speed through the same obstacle course, throwing the ball up and regathering it. Let the ball bounce occasionally, so you get accustomed to playing the ball off the bounce up from the ground while on the run.

Building up your strength

Increased competition among professionals has raised the physical demands of the sport. The lucky few who play for money have become reliant on lifting weights to improve their strength and power. Although weight lifting is mandatory preparation for the advanced player, it isn't essential for prepubescent youngsters, who can build up their strength by going down a different, perhaps safer, path.

A heavy weight-lifting program can cause permanent damage to bones and muscles if the body isn't ready to accept heavy weights. If you want to lift weights, ask your coach for advice about an appropriate, safe, and effective weight-lifting program.

Good, old-fashioned push-ups, sit-ups, dips, and chin-ups are perfect for toning the body and increasing upper body strength. If you begin slowly and gradually build up the number of repetitions, your strength is sure to improve.

Varying your routines

Variation is an important aspect of training. Change your regimen regularly, and don't be afraid to attempt different ways to get fit. If you get bored while training, you eventually won't bother, which won't do much to develop your conditioning. Training with a partner is also very effective, because you'll take turns motivating each other to get into the gym or out onto the track and push yourselves to achieve more than you may on your own.

Get adventurous: Invent your own drills that involve a rugby ball. The more times you have a ball in your hands, the more comfortable you'll become with it. Before long, the ball feels like a natural extension of your hands.

A simple, fun activity for two people is a kicking game. Start just outside the 22-meter lines on opposite sides of the pitch, and try to kick the ball as far as you can over the other player's head. Then your partner has to kick it back to you from wherever it was caught. The goal is to gain ground and drive the other player back toward the tryline. If you're by yourself, kick and chase the ball up and down the field, trying out various styles of kicks and working on regathering. The constant kicking and running will improve your kicking accuracy, catching skills, and overall fitness.

Good coaches use a balanced approach to developing each player's individual fitness and the team's collective fitness. They create a plan that addresses their particular and team deficiencies, monitors their progress, and adjusts as needed over the course of the season.

Because approaches often vary widely within a single country from international down to provincial and club levels, you'll find plenty of different schools of thought on virtually every aspect of getting match fit. The key is to welcome new ideas and make them your own.

Psyching Up for a Stellar Performance

Although looking good and being able to run effortlessly for 80 minutes is terrific, if you lack the right mentality your physical prowess won't translate into effective play. Getting mentally prepared doesn't mean spending days on a psychologist's couch, or calling the psychic hotline to find out what the stars say about your team's chances in the match tomorrow.

Being mentally prepared means you're totally focused on the task at hand and can instantly sum up a situation and work out the best way to handle it on the fly. Rugby is often like a chess game, revolving around intricate strategies with the best players responding instinctively to the variations as they unfold in front of them.

Before each game, take some quiet time to ask yourself these questions:

✔ What are my responsibilities in the game plan?

✔ What's likely to happen in the game?

✔ What do I want to accomplish, and what am I expected to achieve?

✔ How can I best take advantage of any opportunities that present themselves?

Get motivated by visualizing yourself scoring the winning try, kicking the winning goal, or leading your team to a memorable victory. Most great players find this an effective way to build their confidence. If it works for them, it can work for you.

Good mental preparation means you're less likely to shy away when a big, intimidating second-rower runs straight at you. Fear is important so long as it doesn't hinder your performance. All players, at some stage of their playing careers, experience the fear of failure or the fear of injury. It's a natural emotion in a contact sport, but you can use it to your advantage by re-channelling the adrenaline flow into controlled aggression.

For more information about developing a winner's mentality, check out *Sports Psychology For Dummies* by Leif H. Smith and Todd M. Kays (Wiley).

The Zone

Former All Black Murray Mexted, who played in every international match for New Zealand from 1979 to 1986, had a unique way to mentally switch on prior to tests. In the changing room before each match, he would imagine reaching up with both arms to pull down a huge light switch that would put him into what he calls "The Zone." When the switch was thrown, he became totally focused on the task at hand, completely destroying his opposite and contributing in every way possible to an All Blacks victory. He cleared his mind of everything else so he could focus all his mental energy on the game.

Mental toughness separates the good from the great rugby players. While Murray's light switch method may not turn you on, you can develop your own technique to get mentally focused before each kickoff and stay that way throughout the match.

Eating Your Way to Victory

Gone are the days when rugby players believed that loading up their break-fast plates with steak, eggs, and hash browns was the only way to win. A star-vation diet that allows you only one celery stick a day isn't the answer either. If you want to be a successful rugby player, common sense has to prevail — eating and drinking in moderation is the right way to go.

Choosing a balanced diet

Nowadays most professional rugby teams have a nutritionist hovering some-where in the shadows, someone who's counting calories and monitoring milkshakes all under the guise of recommending the optimal diet for rugby fitness. For the elite athlete, dietary modification is a proven method of marginally increasing performance.

For the club player, your diet should be dictated by your general level of fitness. Although no one single food is likely to make you a superstar, as a rugby player you have more energy requirements than the average Joe walk-ing down the street. Common sense should lead you away from fast food and bingeing on too many pints of Ben & Jerry's.

Eat a balanced diet that includes proteins, carbohydrates, fats, and fiber, and foods that provide nutrients, vitamins, and minerals. This means taking in measured amounts of food from each of the four food groups. For peak perfor-mance, more than half of your daily caloric intake should come from carbohy-drates, with no less than 15 percent from protein and no more than 15 percent from fats. Eating more frequently also helps, because six smaller meals per day are better than three big meals.

Clearly, the best thing a rugby player in training can drink isn't the amber fluid — it's water. Dehydration causes fatigue more than any other dietary factor. Contrary to the prevailing wisdom contained in the Oxy Olde Boys training manual, beer does not, in fact, help you take on water to play the game. So drink plenty of water all week long to replace the water you've lost during training. Drinking two tall glasses of water at least two hours before kickoff is a good idea to pre-hydrate before a match, and don't forget to take periodic drinks during activity, every 10 to 15 minutes. Remember that thirst isn't a good indicator of dehydration — by the time you're thirsty, it's already too late.

Taking in fuel

Never eat too close to game time. Consume your pre-game meal about four hours before kickoff, allowing enough time for food to settle in your stomach. The most effective pre-game fuel is high in carbohydrates, low in fat, and low in protein. Loading up on a couple of double cheeseburgers and a giant bag of fries is definitely not recommended before you play. Instead, opt for a bowl of meatless pasta with lots of vegetables and tomato sauce.

At all costs, avoid eating foods high in fat on the way to a game or just before kickoff. Nothing is guaranteed to make a player more sluggish than running on a full stomach of greasy food.

After you finish punishing your body at training, you need fuel to recover, so eat some proteins and carbohydrates within an hour following practice. Milk and yogurt are very good for recovery purposes because they contain about 50 percent carbohydrates and 50 percent proteins. And if your club assembles for a post-practice chat, it certainly helps to drink a pint of water before each pint of ale.

Choosing your supplements carefully

Professional players who use supplements to maximize performance do so under the guidance of dieticians and doctors. In these circumstances, supplements can have a safe and beneficial impact on your play.

If you're a club player and are considering taking supplements, schedule a doctor's appointment and discuss whether they're safe and appropriate for you. Eating right, training smart, and getting plenty of rest are the tried-and-tested ways to improve performance. Don't be tricked into thinking that supplements can provide a shortcut to success.

Avoid caffeinated energy drinks. If they contain heaps of stimulants, they aren't appropriate for use because they lead to an elevated heart rate and dehydration. Also, don't share drinking bottles with your teammates, because doing so tends to increase the spread of the flu or other infections.

Part III
Welcome to the Oval Planet

In this part . . .

This part of the book explores the various rugby competitions around the globe. We start our tour of planet rugby with a look at the Rugby World Cup, the sport's crowning jewel, where we offer up all you need to know about the quadrennial tournament, including its history and format, plus some of the most memorable moments dating back to 1987.

Then we explain how the game is controlled worldwide and take you on a tour of the world's annual international tournaments, including the Six Nations and the Tri Nations Series. The interprovincial scene is next, with a glance at Super Rugby, the Heineken Cup, and the Magners League. We conclude our international sojourn with a peek at the leading domestic leagues in New Zealand, South Africa, and Europe.

Closer to home, we discuss the North American international picture and then focus on the heart and soul of the game, the local club. We finish with a survey of the collegiate, high school, and youth rugby scene.

Chapter 13

The World Cup

For most of its history, rugby has been an insular game. Developing and expanding the sport was seen as despoiling its traditions and uniqueness. With the exception of a few poorly attended inclusions in various Olympic games, until 1987 determining a world champion was always an unofficial bit of guesswork, open to interpretation and argument. That all changed in the mid-1980s when the International Rugby Board (IRB) was dragged kicking and screaming into the modern era.

In this chapter, we give you an overview of what the Rugby World Cup has become in just 20-odd years, explain how the changes came about, provide qualification details, and look at some other components of the World Cup system.

The Crown Jewel of Rugby

The Rugby World Cup is the pinnacle of achievement for players and coaches around the oval planet. Every four years, touring fans converge on the tournament to display their national pride and revel in historical rivalries while attending a multitude of social events and enjoying plenty of rugby camaraderie. The pool matches are like the NCAA Basketball Tournament, where long shots get a chance to topple the favorites and pretenders emerge as contenders. The knockout stages culminate with the Cup final, producing a Super Bowl–like atmosphere with the world's collective focus on one single match. In fact, only the Soccer World Cup and the Olympics command a larger worldwide television audience!

From the first hastily organized 16-team tournament in Australia and New Zealand in 1987, the Rugby World Cup has grown into to a quadrennial spectacle that's watched by more than 3 billion people around the globe. Staging the tournament has become an immense undertaking that involves the resources of an entire nation or region, worldwide corporate sponsorship, and an army of volunteers and paid administrators.

The prize awarded to the winner of the Rugby World Cup is the William Webb Ellis Cup, named after the legendary founder of the game. Lifting the cup in triumph has become the primary goal of the world's leading rugby-playing nations, more important than any other rivalry or competition. For years prior to each edition, national unions and their coaches focus on developing players and strategies to bring Bill (as the trophy has come to be known) back to their shores.

In its current format, which is determined individually during the bidding process to host the next event, the World Cup brings together 20 teams that have qualified either by their performance in the previous Cup or through regional elimination. The participants are seeded according to world ranking and placed in four pools of five teams. Every pool member plays each other, and the top two teams advance to the quarterfinals. The eventual finals victor gets the title of World Champion for the next four years.

The Origins and History of the Rugby World Cup

The World Cup was born out of a desire by the Southern Hemisphere nations to increase the visibility of the game around the world. From its beginnings, rugby was mostly amateur and all aspects of commercialization were tightly controlled by each national union and the IRB. The more tradition-bound members from the Northern Hemisphere feared that commercialization would lead to the encroachment of professionalism — which is indeed what happened, albeit a few years later.

In the early 1980s Australia and New Zealand both proposed the idea of holding a World Cup, and by 1985, after much study and committee work, they were finally able to force a vote on the issue in the IRB Executive Committee. With backing from France, which had always been inclined toward moving the game into the professional ranks, and a late decision by South Africa to support the idea, the measure passed and the world's third great sporting competition came into being.

In less than a quarter of a century, the World Cup evolved from an idea that met stiff resistance to a colossus on the world's sporting stage. In the process, the game changed from an exclusive, clubby activity to a professional game with a worldwide audience. Such is the power of creating an international competition that determines ultimate bragging rights for an entire sport.

1987 World Cup — Australia and New Zealand

The first World Cup in 1987 involved 16 invited teams and was held in Australia and New Zealand. The tournament was a moderate commercial success, but it achieved much more in the area of exposure, with more than half a million fans attending matches and some 300 million supporters following the game on television.

France, Australia, Wales, and New Zealand made the semifinals, giving the tournament an even north-south distribution. The New Zealand All Blacks were the eventual champs, winning at home in Auckland's Eden Park over the French Tricolors 29–9. Direct competition in a tournament format showed that the Southern Hemisphere teams had surpassed their northern rivals.

1991 World Cup — Great Britain, Ireland, and France

The 1991 Rugby World Cup took place in Great Britain, Ireland, and France and was again a 16-team affair, but this time the IRB implemented a qualification process whereby eight sides had qualified through a regional formula to join the eight quarterfinalists from 1987. The surprise of the tournament involved eventual champions Australia upsetting the defending titleholders New Zealand in the semifinals. Australia went on to beat England 12–6 at Twickenham in the final. The World Cup audience also grew substantially, with more than 1 million in-stadium attendees and nearly 2 billion watching over the airwaves.

1995 World Cup — South Africa

In 1995 the World Cup moved to South Africa, whose Springboks competed for the first time. President Nelson Mandela opened the tournament wearing a Springbok jersey, long a symbol of the apartheid era, and appealed for the Rainbow Nation to come together through sport. The tournament was a smashing success from the opening match to the tense final, when in a near fairy-tale ending the Boks beat the All Blacks 15–12 in extra time on a Joel Stransky drop goal.

Their victory at Ellis Park in Johannesburg was the third consecutive triumph of a Southern Hemisphere team. It also marked the end of the amateur era in rugby. With the sport's governing body no longer able to stem the tide of professionalism, the IRB had been forced to acquiesce and allow the game to become a marketable commodity, with paid players and commercial opportunities galore.

The worldwide television audience shocked even the most biased rugby optimists, with more than 3.1 billion viewers around the oval planet tuning in. Rugby had arrived as a worldwide television product just as professionalism was about to take hold.

1999 World Cup — Wales, England, Scotland, Ireland, and France

The 1999 tourney moved once again to Britain, France, and Ireland, with Wales taking the lead role as hosts. The finals tournament was expanded from 16 to 20 teams, and for the first time included quarterfinal playoffs.

The semifinals were thrilling affairs, with South Africa and Australia going into overtime and France shocking the world by knocking off a heavily favored All Blacks side in one of the most exciting Rugby World Cup games ever played. The Wallabies then comprehensively defeated the French 35–12 in the final, becoming the first country to win the Rugby World Cup twice. The 1999 tournament broke all previous records for attendance, TV audience, and revenue.

2003 World Cup — Australia

The 2003 Rugby World Cup was originally scheduled to be co-hosted by Australia and New Zealand, but after a commercial dispute over advertising in stadiums Australia ended up staging the entire tournament alone. Building on the success of the 2000 Olympic games in Sydney, the Australian Rugby Union set a new standard for hosting excellence.

The tournament returned to a four-pool format where the top two nations advanced to the quarterfinals. Australians of all backgrounds embraced the tourney and set new attendance marks while showing their true colors in a unprecedented display of international sporting camaraderie.

The final pitted the pre-tournament favorite, England, against the host Wallabies. In the most riveting World Cup final to date, Jonny Wilkinson booted England to victory at the end of extra time, becoming the first Northern Hemisphere team to hoist the William Webb Ellis Cup overhead. It was a fairy-tale ending for the Men in White and a fitting conclusion to the best World Cup ever.

2007 World Cup — France, Wales, and Scotland

After a particularly contentious host-nation bidding process that pitted old rivals England and France as the two finalists, the 2007 Rugby World Cup was ultimately awarded to France. In a political move to gain the support of the Welsh and Scottish Rugby Unions, four World Cup fixtures were awarded to Wales and two to Scotland, with the remaining 42 matches scheduled for play in France.

The 2007 Finals Tournament was played under the now standard, four-pool, 20-team format, with each pool producing two teams for the quarterfinals. The tournament opened with a shock win by Argentina over France and produced further upsets and excitement for the next six weeks. The biggest shockers came in the quarterfinals when France knocked off New Zealand in Cardiff and England defeated Australia in Marseille. Host France then fell to the defending champions, England, in the first semifinal, and South Africa eliminated Argentina in the second semifinal. The final saw South Africa earn their second world title by beating England 15–6 at a packed Stade de France.

2011 World Cup — New Zealand

Bidding for the 2011 Rugby World Cup was fierce and politically charged as underdog New Zealand surprisingly beat out both South Africa and Japan to play host to their second tourney — their first since the inaugural one in 1987. Pre-bidding favorites Japan were later placated by being awarded the 2019 Cup, with England getting the tourney in 2015. This is the first time that the IRB has officially granted hosting rights to consecutive tournaments.

Getting the country ready to host the 2011 Rugby World Cup has been a tremendous undertaking for New Zealand. Constructing and renovating stadiums, making other infrastructure improvements, and finding accommodation for nearly 100,000 visitors have been awesome challenges, but the rugby-loving people of New Zealand have met them with aplomb. The tournament begins with New Zealand taking on Tonga in Auckland and concludes at Eden Park, the same venue that hosted the very first World Cup final back in 1987.

Canada will play in Pool A against New Zealand, France, Tonga, and Japan. The United States find themselves in Pool C with matches versus Australia, Ireland, Italy, and Russia.

Qualification and Finals Tournaments

Originally, the World Cup was by invite only. In 1991, the IRB instituted a qualification structure, which enabled teams from all over the globe to aspire to compete on the rugby world's premier stage. That structure has been altered over the years. For the 2011 tourney, 12 teams gained entry from their finish in the 2007 Cup and 8 had to earn their places through regional qualifying.

Qualifying for the 2011 Cup was spread out over two and a half years and involved 80 different countries playing a total of 184 matches. The first qualifier was Canada, and the last was Romania. Russia is the only team making its debut on the world's biggest rugby stage in 2011.

Qualifying began with the lowest-ranked nations playing in a regionalized pool system to eliminate the less competitive countries and minimize travel costs. Winning a pool allowed that country to advance to the next level, where they faced stiffer competition from more established international teams. Teams from the Americas, Asia, Europe, and Africa that lost the finals for their regions' automatic qualifying spots still had a final chance for qualification through the final-place playoff.

In 2011, the qualifying teams were Canada and the United States from the Americas, Russia and Georgia from Europe, Samoa from Oceania, Namibia from Africa, Japan from Asia, and Romania, the final-place playoff winner.

North Americans in the World Cup

North American teams have been a part of every Rugby World Cup since its inception in 1987, with Canada competing in all six tournaments and the United States missing out just once. And though the North American teams haven't exactly been powerhouse performers, they have had their moments at the pinnacle of the sport.

Fighting Eagles

Since the U.S.'s back-to-back Olympic triumphs 80 years ago, the Eagles have struggled to field a competitive international side. After winning their opener against Japan in 1987, the U.S. was shut out in 1991 and failed to qualify for the World Cup in 1995. In 1999, the Eagles lost a heartbreaker to Romania and went 0–3 for the second time. In 2003 they qualified at the last possible opportunity and managed their second win in pool play, also against Japan.

How I earned a cap for Latvia

The first qualifying match for the 1999 Rugby World Cup was in September 1996 between Latvia and Norway in Riga. Because it was the kickoff match of a tournament that would eventually culminate in a world champion being crowned in Cardiff, the fixture drew journalists from the rugby capitals of Europe and the post-match function was a lively affair. I lived right across the street from the University Stadium, and Uldis Bautris, my club coach for Rigas Miesnieks, was in charge of the national team squad also, so naturally I attended the game and the following festivities. After chatting with various Norwegian team members, I realized that very few of them were actually Norwegian. Most were expatriates from rugby-playing nations who were living and working in Oslo and who gained eligibility for Norway on residency grounds.

That night, at the suggestion of Latvian lock Wilmars Sokolovs, the notion was born that I could become the first foreigner to play for Latvia. What transpired over the next seven months was a personal odyssey involving a never-before-seen devotion to fitness, twice-weekly training sessions in the snow and rain on dirt pitches, bewildering eligibility paperwork for the Latvian sports ministry, a stint at hooker in both a possibles-versus-probables match and a friendly against Lithuania, and, finally, selection to the Latvian team. Listening to the national anthem with my teammates before we crushed Bulgaria 89–0 in a World Cup qualifier was the proudest moment of my life. Unfortunately our hopes of progressing out of our pool to the next level were dashed by Croatia the following week, and my dream of playing in a World Cup was officially over.

The Eagles had a chance for an enormous upset in their 2007 World Cup opener when they played a very competitive game against England before eventually losing in Lens, France. They then lost back-to-back heartbreakers against Tonga and Samoa before getting crushed by the eventual champions, South Africa.

In 2011, the United States have a real chance to get a third victory in pool play because they've been placed in Pool C with Australia, Ireland, Italy, and Russia. While wins against the first three are highly improbable, the Eagles have convincingly beaten the Bears as recently as June 2010 when they met in the Churchill Cup at Infinity Park in Glendale, Colorado.

Competing Canadians

Canada has been competitive in all six Rugby World Cups. The Canadians have won 6, lost 14, and drawn once in finals matches, including wins over Tonga, Fiji, Romania, and Namibia. Their best showing was in 1991, when they advanced to the quarterfinals where they lost by a very respectable 13–29 score against New Zealand. In 2007, Canada went into the tourney with thoughts of making another quarterfinal appearance but ended up losing to Australia, Wales, and Fiji before finishing with a draw against Japan.

For the 2011 Cup, Canada will be in Pool A where they'll have a realistic shot at winning a couple of matches, and maybe even more. A victory over host New Zealand would rock the tournament, and is thus unlikely, but an upset over sometimes lackadaisical France isn't out of the question. And Coach Kieran Crowley's team will definitely be targeting wins over Tonga and Japan.

Mammoths and Minnows

For countries that have very little chance of ever hoisting the Webb Ellis trophy (which we discuss earlier in this chapter), the tournament is an opportunity to measure themselves against the best in the world. Winning a match, or even just playing well against a major power, is a source of intense pride and a reason for commendation.

Rugby is a sport where there's no such thing as letting up on an overmatched opponent. The way you show respect for the other side is to continue to play as hard as possible against them, no matter how large the lead. This "no letup for 80 minutes" ethos results in some awfully lopsided scorelines. Even so, a 100-point loss isn't a source of embarrassment in the rugby community; it's a measuring stick of how much needs to be done to become more competitive. So, although some of the results may be a bit lopsided, the overall effect is to lift the game of the up-and-coming nations by exposing them to a higher level of play.

The upside of the relative disparity between nations occurs when a country is able to move up the international pecking order. In 1999, Argentina beat Ireland in a quarterfinal playoff match, an unlikely victory that lifted rugby's profile within a soccer-mad country and has since led to steady improvement for the Pumas. Although they failed to make the quarterfinals again in 2003, in 2007 they shocked France in the tournament opener, made it all the way to the semifinals, and eventually won the third-place playoff, beating France easily. In 2011 the Pumas are favorites to once again make it into the knockout stage of the tournament, and are currently seventh in the world rankings.

In 2003 Georgia made it to its first World Cup by beating rival Russia in Tbilisi in front of a crowd estimated at over 80,000. Making it to Australia was a dream come true for the mostly amateur Lelos, and even though they were serious underdogs in every match, they played their hearts out all four times they took the pitch. They opened the tourney with a heavy loss to England, got crushed by Samoa, played a little better against South Africa, and were at least in the match versus Uruguay. Four years later, in 2007, Georgia gave Ireland a real scare before losing 14–10 and then got their first-ever pool win by beating Namibia 30–0. In 2011, the Lelos are in Pool B and will be looking to beat Romania and hoping to do some damage against Argentina, England, and Scotland.

Great World Cup Moments

Some World Cup matches become part of history because of the moment in time when they took place, and others for the pure drama of the battle joined. Over the 185 finals matches played from 1987 to 2003, there have been several contests that rise above the rest.

Australia versus England — 2003 final

The 2003 Rugby World Cup final pitted host Australia against the pre-tournament favorites, England. The home nation against the former colony, the best of the north against the best of the Southern Hemisphere, this match had a story line longer than the queues waiting to catch a train after the match at Homebush station. The stadium was half full of English and half full of Aussie supporters, as white and gold jerseys dominated the jam-packed venue. The match started well for the home side when Lote Tuqiri hauled in a cross-field bomb by Stephen Larkham and the Wallabies took a five-point lead.

England kept their composure as Jonny Wilkinson converted three shots at goal to put England in front 9–5. Then, just before halftime, Wilko put Jason Robinson into the clear down the right sideline, and England went into the changing rooms with a well-deserved 14–5 halftime lead.

The second half settled into a contest of wills: The Wallabies scratched their way back into the match with two penalty goals, but England still led 14–11 as fulltime approached. On the Wallabies' final possession in injury time, a penalty gave Elton Flatley his chance to level the scores and force extra time. With ice water coursing through his veins and the rugby world holding its breath, he calmly slotted the goal and the fulltime whistle was blown, leaving the world's two best teams even at 14–all.

In extra time, the teams continued the pattern. England took the lead on a penalty, and then Australia leveled the scores with 30 seconds left in the second of the two ten-minute periods. With just seconds remaining and the commentators speculating about a third ten-minute sudden death period, England's scrumhalf Matt Dawson somehow broke through the Wallaby defense and got close enough to the line for Jonny Wilkinson to line up a final drop goal attempt. Everyone in the stadium knew what was coming: Jonny stroked the drop, and history was made when the ball sailed through the uprights and England became the first Northern Hemisphere nation to ever win the World Cup. All hail Sir Clive Woodward (the English coach) and England!

South Africa versus New Zealand — 1995 final

The most incredible moment happened after the 1995 World Cup final when New Zealand faced an inspired South Africa. With the score tied at the end of regulation the match went into extra time, and was eventually won 15–12 on a drop goal by South Africa. Without at all minimizing the monumental effort put in by the players on the pitch, what we'll never forget took place at the trophy presentation.

At a time when South Africa was struggling to reunite a nation divided by generations of apartheid, the sight of Nelson Mandela up on the podium in a Springbok jersey, pumping his fists in the air, as Bok Captain Francois Pienaar lifted the Webb Ellis Cup was truly inspirational. It was a moment when sport transcended politics and a divided nation took a brief respite from the enormous task of nation-building to celebrate as one.

Australia versus South Africa — 1999 semifinal #1

The 1999 semifinals both stand out because of what happened on the field of play. In the first semi, South Africa faced Australia after drop kicking England out of the quarterfinals. The game went into extra time and was won by a drop goal from the Wallabies' Stephen Larkham. The game had all the elements of a classic, smash-mouth encounter, punctuated by patches of enterprising play throughout a seesaw affair that sapped the collective energy from the capacity crowd at Twickenham. After the match, supporters from both sides were so exhausted and emotionally drained from the twists and turns of the match that you couldn't tell which team had won. Everyone in attendance knew they had witnessed something special that would be remembered for years to come and were gracious in victory and defeat.

After the drama of the first semifinal, we all chatted over a few beers and came to the well-reasoned conclusion that Sunday's semifinal couldn't possibly match the drama and excitement of the Wallabies' win over the Springboks. The next day, in observing the procession from Twickenham station to the stadium, the All Black fans were relaxed and cocky in contemplating the destruction to come, while the French supporters looked to be on a death march, with heads down and nary a smile among them.

Walking Twickenham

Every now and then, being a rugby TV producer has its perks. After being sequestered by my boss to the windowless edit bay in the basement of Fox Sports World for the round-robin stages of the 1999 Rugby World Cup, my boss approved a classic junket as a reward for my dedication. Being a licensed broadcaster, Fox received a few semifinals and finals tickets as part of the deal. When the top brass passed on them, I played the advantage and asked whether I might be released from my underground dungeon to pop over to London for the semis and then immediately return to L.A. before we taped our studio show.

My "job" was to make sure the pay-per-view signal was all sorted out so the folks back home in the U.S. and Canada could watch live. With a few minutes to spare before kickoff, inspiration struck. It occurred to me that Brown and I had been issued all-access media passes and that we were entitled to walk out onto the hallowed Twickenham turf if we so desired. So, just before the teams took the field, we marched out of the tunnel and past an array of security guards stationed to keep out the riffraff.

Before we knew it, we were walking the perimeter of the pitch, being careful not to step on the field and stopping periodically to feign a purpose for our perambulation, by pointing up at some imaginary friends that were seated among the 50,000-plus who anxiously awaited the impending kickoff. The atmosphere at pitch level was totally and completely awesome. Before we finished our walk around, Brown ran into a photographer he knew from Latvia who asked what possible business we might have walking out on the field before such a huge match. We explained that we had to perform a safety check of the ground just to make sure everything was ready for the match to proceed! Finding everything in order, we marched back up the tunnel and took up our positions in the TV truck. Of course, after our pre-game blessing ritual set the stage, the French team shocked the world with an awesome display of attacking rugby that left the heavily favored All Blacks in tatters. I still get chills thinking about the feeling of looking up at that crowd and the spectacle that followed.

New Zealand versus France — 1999 semifinal #2

The game that followed gets our vote as the most exciting World Cup match ever played. At a time when a beef row had elevated tensions in the Anglo-French relationship, a curious thing happened within the mostly British crowd when the French began their second-half comeback. The crowd suddenly realized that the French had a chance after all, and virtually every non–New Zealander in the stands started pulling for the French to win. The Tricolors, displaying all their Gallic flair, scored 26 unanswered points playing vintage champagne rugby that left the Kiwis dazed and confused. By the end of the match, a Stade de France crowd couldn't have cheered any louder for Les Blues. Their 43–31 victory proved the old adage that any team can win on the day, and on October 31, 1999, that day belonged to the French.

Other Cups on the World Stage

As the popularity of the Rugby World Cup grew from very modest beginnings, the IRB slowly realized that nothing fired the imagination like the possibility of being crowned a world champion. In subsequent years, the IRB sanctioned competitions that provided the opportunity for sevens devotees, women, and age-grade players to earn that coveted title.

Rugby World Cup Sevens

The sevens game — so named because it's played with only seven on each team and characterized by lots of scoring (see Chapter 15 for more info on the abbreviated version of the sport) — has long been a fixture on the international scene, but the first IRB Rugby World Cup Sevens wasn't played until 1993 in Edinburgh. The participants play for the Melrose Cup, named after the city in Scotland where the seven-a-side game developed in the 1880s. In the inaugural final, England defeated Australia 21–17.

The second Rugby World Cup Sevens moved to Hong Kong, to the venue responsible for popularizing the game and bringing it international attention. The tournament delivered a multitude of exciting games and plenty of local color. Fiji, led by their legendary sevens magician Waisale Serevi, defeated South Africa in the final 24–21.

The Rugby World Cup Sevens, following the pattern of almost all sevens events, features consolation brackets. The USA Eagles made an impressive showing in the consolation games, beating a very capable Japanese side 40–28 in the Bowl final to take home some hardware.

In 2001, the third edition of the Rugby World Cup Sevens moved across the Pacific to Mar Del Plata, Argentina. Sevens is a unique game that allows smaller nations to become competitive at a much faster rate than is possible in the 15-a-side game. Qualifying tournaments for the event were held all over the globe, and a total of 91 countries took part. New Zealand totally dominated the tournament, scoring 251 points while giving up only 40 points over eight matches, including their 31–12 victory over Australia to win the Melrose Cup.

Fiji captured their second Rugby World Cup Sevens crown in Hong Kong in 2005. With the old master Waisale Serevi once again calling the shots and scoring a try in the final, the fabulous Fijians defeated the defending champions from New Zealand 29–19 to reestablish their dominance of the seven-a-side game.

Wales won the Melrose Cup in Dubai in 2009, making it a year for upsets. Traditional sevens powers New Zealand, South Africa, Fiji, and England were all knocked out of the competition at the quarterfinal stage, opening the door for a Wales versus Argentina final.

2009 was also the first year for the Women's Rugby World Cup Sevens. Sixteen teams competed in the inaugural event, which was won by Australia over New Zealand on an extra-time try by Shelly Matcham.

The next Rugby World Cup Sevens will be held in Moscow, Russia, in 2013.

Women's Rugby World Cup

The Women's Rugby World Cup was not sanctioned as an official IRB championship until 1998, but the first competition took place in Wales in 1991. Twelve countries participated, and the surprise winner was the United States, beating England 19–6 in the final to become the first modern-day U.S. rugby team to be crowned World Champions! (See Figure 13-1.)

Figure 13-1: U.S.A. Women team photo after winning the World Cup, 1991.

After the first women's World Cup, it was decided to alter the timing so that the event wouldn't be held in the same year as the men's World Cup. Thus, the next tourney was scheduled for 1994 in Holland. Various problems in the lead-up prevented the IRB from giving its approval to the competition in the Netherlands, and as a result most national unions pulled funding from their squads. An alternative tournament was organized in Scotland, and it was attended by 12 sides. The U.S. faced England again in the final. This time, however, England knocked them off their perch as World Champions, winning 38–23 in an exciting affair. With scant support from their national union, the Eagle women soared high on the strength of their individual ability and team spirit.

In 1998 the IRB made it official, and 16 teams competed in Amsterdam. The Canadian women reached their first World Cup semifinal but lost 46–6 to the United States. The Black Ferns from New Zealand rampaged through the tournament and ended up easily winning the final 46–12 over the Eagles.

Barcelona, Spain, was the site for the Women's Rugby World Cup in 2002. England and New Zealand met in the final, and the Black Ferns won their second consecutive title 19–9, firmly establishing themselves as the dominant force in the women's game. New Zealand and England have clearly created a gap between themselves and the rest of the world as a direct result of their unions' vision and investment in developing the women's game.

The 2006 Women's Rugby World Cup was the first IRB World Cup event contested in North America; Rugby Canada hosted the tournament. But despite the new continent, the Black Ferns of New Zealand solidified their position at the top of the world pecking order, completing the three-peat of women's World Cup titles with a 25–17 victory over England.

In 2010 the Cup moved back across the pond to England, but playing at home still didn't give the English women enough of an edge to overcome New Zealand. The Black Ferns battled their way to a fourth-straight crown in a hard-fought 13–10 final win at the Twickenham Stoop.

In pool play, the Canadian women smashed both Scotland and Sweden before losing to France. They rebounded by trouncing Scotland again in the fifth-place semifinal before eventually losing to the United States in the fifth-place playoff to take sixth place overall. After walloping Kazakhstan in their pool opener, the American women fell to both Ireland and England. They got some revenge against the Irish with a convincing victory in the other fifth-place semifinal and finished strong with a win over Canada to earn fifth place.

Junior World Championship

The Junior World Championship grew out of the SANZAR/UAR Under-21 tournament that began in 1995, involving Argentina, Australia, New Zealand, and South Africa, and steadily added other countries in following years. The cup exposes promising youngsters to a high level of international competition, and numerous alumni of the annual event are among today's brightest stars.

The inaugural IRB Under-21 World Cup was held in South Africa in 2002 and was won by the hosts. New Zealand won in 2003 and 2004, in England and Scotland. South Africa won again in 2005 in Argentina, and France won in 2006 at home in the tourney's final year before it became the Under-20 Junior World Championship in 2008. The inaugural event was held in Wales in 2008 and won by New Zealand, who repeated their success in 2009 in Japan and 2010 in Argentina. The next Junior World Championship will be held in June 2011 in Italy.

This change in age eligibility eliminated the Under-19 tournament, reflecting the fact that young players are entering the professional ranks earlier and earlier. Instead of holding a separate Under-19 championship, the IRB created a second tournament for lower-ranked teams that were more evenly matched and called it the Junior World Rugby Trophy. The 2008 tournament was held in Chile and was won by Uruguay. In 2009 it moved to Kenya and was won by Romania, and in 2010 Russia hosted and Italy took the title. The next IRB Junior World Rugby Trophy is scheduled for May 2011 in Georgia.

In the span of just over 20 years, the IRB has created four distinct World Cup competitions, giving men, women, sevens specialists, and future stars their own championship to aspire to, where they can test themselves against the best in the world. The challenge for the IRB is to raise the standard of play of the lower-level nations, which will inevitably lead to rugby becoming a truly global game.

Chapter 14

The International Calendar

Rugby fans around the world enjoy a plethora of international and provincial competitions that run year-round. For more than 130 years, until the first Rugby World Cup in 1987, international test matches served as the highest level of the game. Over that period, leagues gradually developed on a regional basis.

In 1996 the rugby calendar changed forever when the three leading Southern Hemisphere powers, South Africa, New Zealand, and Australia, joined together and created the Tri Nations Series and the Super 12 (since 2011, the Super 15). This established an annual schedule of international matches for each nation and included an interprovincial competition where the leading regional sides from the big three would play a full season of matches leading to a winner. The 1995–96 season also saw the Six Nations unions launch the European Cup, the north's version of the Super 15.

Despite these international developments, the heart and soul of rugby is the game that is still played at the domestic, provincial level. All of the leading rugby nations have their own leagues where future stars are cultivated amid deep-running local passions. In this chapter, we give you a tour of rugby's annual calendar, looking first at the international order, then dropping down to the interprovincial scene, and finishing off with a dab of local provincial color.

How the Game Is Organized

As an entirely amateur sport for most of its history, rugby was controlled by volunteer administrators in individual countries. Each rugby-playing country had its own organizational structure and was responsible for internal decisions regarding finances, eligibility, competitions, and development. Interaction among different nations was managed on a union-to-union basis. In the last quarter of the 20th century, however, the growth of the game led to the strengthening of an existing but limited governing body, the International Rugby Board (IRB).

Rugby's rulers — the IRB

The IRB was founded in 1886, but it didn't attain its all-powerful status until nearly a century later. Headquartered in Dublin, the IRB is the world-governing and law-making body for the game of rugby. The day-to-day business of the board is conducted by a professional staff of more than 50 people. The IRB has 97 member unions, 19 associates, and 6 regional associations.

The Executive Council, made up of representatives from the eight foundation unions, meets twice a year. The eight foundation unions — Scotland, Ireland, Wales, England, Australia, New Zealand, South Africa, and France — each have two seats. Argentina, Canada, Italy, and Japan each have one seat on the council, as does FIRA–AER (the International Amateur Rugby Federation–European Rugby Association). The full membership meets every two years at the association's general meeting; regional meetings are held at regular intervals.

The IRB is now responsible for setting the international test schedule, maintaining the world rankings, developing the game worldwide, running the World Cup through a subsidiary organization, Rugby World Cup Limited, and generally acting as overlord to the sport.

The IRB controls the following tournaments: Rugby World Cup, Women's Rugby World Cup, Rugby World Cup Sevens, IRB Sevens, IRB Junior World Championship, IRB Junior World Rugby Trophy, IRB Nations Cup, and the Americas Rugby Championship. They earn most of their income from holding the Rugby World Cup every four years.

National unions

The first national union was formed in England in 1871 and called, appropriately enough, the Rugby Football Union (RFU). The union came about in response to the need for order and uniformity in the rapidly expanding game. Before the standardization of rules created by the RFU, matches varied significantly in rules and length, depending upon where they were played.

A national union is usually a large, professional organization that has a multitude of responsibilities. The union's composition and role depends on the size of the rugby-playing population and the popularity of the game in a particular country.

In a country like New Zealand, for example, the New Zealand Rugby Union (NZRU) negotiates with sponsors, staffs and runs the various national teams, hires coaches, and contracts professional players for their services. The staff at the NZRU are full-time employees engaged in developing and promoting New Zealand rugby in all its forms, from youth to international competitions.

In a small country like Latvia, with only seven rugby clubs, it's a much different story. The national officials are usually either volunteers or they're paid a small stipend for their work. The responsibilities are often the same as in a large union, but the scale is much smaller.

The United States Rugby Football Union (USA Rugby) and Rugby Canada are somewhere in between New Zealand and Latvia. They both have paid professionals running the organizations, but they also rely heavily on volunteers from both countries to ensure the smooth functioning of the game in all its aspects.

Provincial unions

In countries like South Africa, where rugby is entrenched in the nation's sporting landscape, provincial unions are powerful champions of their regional interests. In addition to training referees and coaches, running youth programs and academies, and selecting and funding teams for competition in national events, provincial unions have a say in how the game is run at the national level. North American equivalents are the territorial or provincial unions like the Southern California Rugby Football Union and the British Columbia Rugby Union.

Local unions

Local unions are concerned with administering the game within a certain geographical area. In the U.S. these are called local area unions, and in Canada they're referred to as sub-unions. These unions are staffed by volunteers and are responsible for scheduling matches, providing referees, organizing play-offs, and resolving disputes between clubs.

The Powers That Be

The first international, or *test match*, was played between England and Scotland in 1871. A test match is a game where caps are awarded by the respective national unions to signify that the players are representing their country. In the early days, caps were made of wool with fancy embroidery and served as a keepsake for those who were lucky enough to earn one. In the modern game, with a few notable exceptions among the smaller amateur unions, this practice of actually awarding a cap has fallen by the wayside, and the term "cap" simply means that a player has appeared on the pitch in a full international match for his or her country.

In the 1880s, England and Scotland were joined by Wales and Ireland, and the International Championship began. These four home unions were joined by France in 1910 to form the Five Nations. Although France was thrown out of the competition from 1931 to 1939, the Five Nations served as the world's first and most prominent annual international competition from the early 1900s to 1999, when it expanded to include Italy and become the Six Nations.

While Europe focused on the Five (and then Six) Nations, the southern powerhouses of Australia, New Zealand, and South Africa had to be content with organizing periodic tours, because they lacked an annual international set of fixtures. Although New Zealand's first recorded test match was against Australia in 1893, it took the southern giants more than 100 years to organize their own yearly international competition.

Where tradition is king — the Six Nations

The Six Nations is the world's oldest rugby tournament, possessing a rich and colorful history that tracks the regional rivalries and the tumultuous times that Northern Europe has endured over the past 125 years. During that period, England and Scotland have played 124 tests, each one a microcosm of the unique political and social circumstances prevailing at the time.

Over the course of 12 decades, two historically distinct terms, the Triple Crown and the Grand Slam, have developed in the Six Nations. To take the *Triple Crown,* which was first contested only among the four original home unions of England, Scotland, Wales, and Ireland, you had to win all three games against those teams. The *Grand Slam* was added into the mix after the French joined. To win the Grand Slam, you must make a clean sweep and defeat every other country. England has won the most Grand Slams and Triple Crowns.

From February to April of each year, the Six Nations occupies the attention of rugby fans around the world. Each nation plays all five of the other teams, and the winner is determined by a scoring system that takes into account wins, draws, and points differential for tie-breaking purposes. The fans bring with them all the attendant historical regional rivalries that have colored the Anglo-French, Anglo-Welsh, and Anglo-Irish relationships (plus all the other national permutations) over several generations. The Welsh team can lose all their other games, but if they beat England that makes their entire campaign a success. Such is the nature of the rivalries in the Six Nations.

After beginning as the home nations in 1996 and expanding to the Five Nations in 1999, the Six Nations has also been contested by women's teams as an official part of the championship since 2007. England has been crowned champs every year since then.

South versus north — the SANZAR home tests

When the Southern Hemisphere unions of South Africa, New Zealand, and Australia joined forces to create SANZAR (SA, NZ, AR) in 1996, professionalism was ushered in with the force of a cosmic Big Bang. Suddenly, the three juggernauts were charged with producing a series of annual rugby events to satisfy the requirements of a mammoth $550 million U.S. television contract.

To fulfill SANZAR's television broadcast agreement, the union periodically hosts touring sides inbound from Europe, the Pacific Islands, and Argentina each June. The IRB sets the fixtures on a rotating basis, where England, Ireland, Wales, Scotland, France, Italy, Argentina, Samoa, Fiji, and Tonga make tours to the SANZAR countries. For example, in 2010 England played two matches in Australia and Wales played two in New Zealand. The IRB schedules the games so all of the teams play each other on a rotating basis and the smaller unions get a chance to periodically measure themselves against the best.

The battle of the Big Three — the Tri Nations

Since its inception in 1996, The Tri Nations Series has delivered some of the world's most exciting and tense rugby action every year. The series features New Zealand, South Africa, and Australia (the three countries that won the first four Rugby World Cups) in a home-and-away extravaganza. In 2006 the series was expanded from six to nine tests, with each team hosting three of them, but in World Cup years like 2007 and 2011 it returns to its traditional format where each country holds just two tests on home soil. The Tri Nations Series has consistently produced some of the finest international matches ever played — including the 2000 Australia versus New Zealand encounter, which is regarded by many as the best test match of all time (see Chapter 25 for details).

Like the Six Nations, the Tri Nations is a natural outgrowth of the traditional rugby rivalries that exist among these three rugby-mad behemoths. New Zealand and South Africa's rivalry on the pitch is well established in each nation's collective consciousness, going back to South Africa's first tour of New Zealand in 1921. Since their first meeting in Dunedin, the All Blacks and Springboks have battled each other with a fierce intensity that is rarely matched in any sport. New Zealand holds a very narrow lead in the all-time series, which serves as a testament to how evenly matched these nations have been throughout the years on the pitch.

Since the inaugural campaign in 1996, New Zealand has dominated the Tri Nations Series, winning 10 of 15 titles, with South Africa taking 3 titles and Australia taking 2.

The *Bledisloe Cup,* which is awarded to the winner of the annual test series between New Zealand and Australia, is the most coveted piece of hardware on offer between these two antipodean nations. The cup is named for the governor general of New Zealand who donated it in 1931. Under the current Tri Nations Series format, the three All Blacks versus Wallabies games double as Tri Nations and Bledisloe Cup encounters. Recently, though, Australia and New Zealand attempted to introduce their brands to the Asian rugby market by playing an extra Bledisloe fixture — in 2009 in Tokyo and in 2010 in Hong Kong. The importance of the Bledisloe Cup to Kiwis was emphatically demonstrated at Eden Park in 2003 when the crowd politely clapped as Captain Rueben Thorne lifted the Tri Nations Cup — then roared with approval when he hoisted the Bledisloe Cup for the first time in more than five years. Since that night in Auckland, New Zealand has yet to relinquish the trophy. The Cup is by far the biggest prize in any sport within the trans-Tasman rivalry.

North versus south — the fall tests

In October and November of each year, the Southern Hemisphere teams head north to face the European powers. Similar to the SANZAR tests in June, these matches afford an opportunity to see how the best of the north shape up against the south. Australia, New Zealand, and South Africa, plus occasionally Argentina, and the Pacific Island nations of Fiji, Samoa, and Tonga, make the journey to play against some combination of England, Scotland, Wales, Ireland, Italy, and France. The inbound sides generally play two or three European nations over a three- to four-week tour.

The British & Irish Lions

The British & Irish Lions are an all-star team composed of the best national team players from England, Scotland, Wales, and Ireland. The Lions assemble every four years and have a long and storied tradition dating back to 1888, when the first representative side from Great Britain made a mammoth five-month tour of New Zealand and Australia, playing an incredible 35 matches. Since that first tour, the Lions (or a derivative side from the U.K.) have played 585 matches around the world.

One of the main features of a Lions tour is that they make a point of playing numerous games against the smaller provincial or club sides in the country they visit. This brings world-class rugby out to the people around the country and gives local players the chance to get a game against some of the world's best rugby players.

A Lions tour is a huge party for legions of British & Irish fans who take leave from work for a month-long rugby celebration that, in many cases, takes about four years to recover from.

The Lions have been hugely successful both on the field and, more recently, as a commercial enterprise. They have dominated the Wallabies, winning 15 and losing only 5 games; trailed the Springboks with 23 losses, 17 wins, and 6 draws; and struggled against the All Blacks, winning just 6 while losing 29, with 3 ties. The Lions teams of 1955 and 1974 earned series victories in South Africa; the 1971 side won their only test series in New Zealand; and the 2001 Lions were the first to lose a series in Australia after four successive triumphs down under.

The Lions' 2009 Tour of South Africa was highly anticipated because South Africa were the reigning World Champions, having taken the Webb Ellis trophy in France in 2007. The side was coached by former Lions and Scotland player and coach Ian McGeechan. The Lions were led on the pitch by Ireland lock Paul O'Connell. The Lions won their first six matches on tour — including a couple of close ones against the Free State Cheetahs and Western Province — before losing the first test versus the Springboks in Durban. They then drew their next fixture against the Emerging Springboks and lost the second test in Pretoria. They managed to salvage some pride with a solid test win in Johannesburg to end the campaign. The next Lions Tour is set for Australia in 2013.

The Nations Cup

The Nations Cup is an IRB-organized annual tournament that seeks to create better competition for a variety of rugby nations. The lineup of teams involved has changed over the years, but generally they're national teams from Tier 2 countries like Romania, Portugal, Georgia, Namibia, Uruguay, and Russia, along with A level teams from South Africa, Italy, and Argentina. The Cup began in 2006 in Portugal but has since been held every year in Romania.

The tournament is part of the IRB's strategic investment plan to improve the game outside of the traditionally strongest countries. The Nations Cup does more than just allow players to test themselves against competitors of like or better abilities; it also provides a way for newer coaches and referees to experience higher levels of action than they can in their own domestic competitions.

The Pacific Nations Cup

The Pacific Nations Cup began in 2006 as part of the IRB's investment program to bolster rugby competition amongst the Pacific Island nations and Japan. At various times in the tourney's short history the Junior All Blacks, Australia A, and New Zealand Maori have all been involved, but its most recent lineup in 2010 included just Tonga, Samoa, Fiji, and Japan — the four countries that were originally intended to be the recipients of the IRB's development help.

The 2010 Pacific Nations Cup was held exclusively in Fiji and was won by Samoa, the first of the Pacific Island nations to win the title. Previous editions of the tourney had been held in several different nations each year, including Australia, New Zealand, Samoa, Tonga, and Japan. The matches are always crowd pleasing and free-flowing, with lots of scoring and exciting action.

The Barbarian Football Club

The Barbarian Football Club was created in England in 1890 to foster goodwill and fellowship among rugby players around the world. The Barbarians' (also known as the Baa-Baas) creed is "Rugby Football is a game for gentlemen in all classes, but for no bad sportsman in any class." The club is unique in that they are a touring-only side that doesn't have a home field, clubhouse, or membership fees. Players are selected by invitation only, and the Barbarians' list of rugby luminaries is loaded with legendary names.

When the Australians toured the U.K. in 1948, the Barbarians played them in a fundraiser to finance the Wallabies' desire to play a match against Canada on their way home. Since that watershed moment, the Baa-Baas have been a regular fixture at the tail end of U.K. tours, promoting a wide-open style of attacking rugby designed to entertain without the pressure of having to win. As a result, the scorelines are normally well above test averages and provide value for money to the paying customers, whose hard-earned money goes to a variety of charitable causes.

The most famous Barbarians victory is the 1973 win over New Zealand. In that match, the rugby world's all-time greatest scrumhalf, Wales's Gareth Edwards, scored "The Try" — regarded by many as the best try ever scored. The Baa-Baas went on to win 23–11 before a hysterical Cardiff Arms Park crowd. In typical Barbarians camaraderie, the moment of the match came after the fulltime blast when the teams gathered at midfield and joined together to sing "Now Is the Hour" and "Auld Lang Syne." At least nine Barbarian clubs have formed around the world to emulate the unique ethos of the original club, including the New Zealand, French, South African, and South American Barbarians.

The Sevens World Series

The IRB's Sevens World Series was launched in 1999 and serves as the annual international competition for the seven-a-side game. While several events had long been a fixture on the annual sevens calendar, including the oval planet's weeklong party each March in Hong Kong, the advent of the series instituted a points system to crown a Sevens World Series Champion. Series points are tallied over the course of the year to determine a winner.

The IRB Sevens World Series consists of eight individual tournaments. In 2009–10 the schedule included stops in Dubai, South Africa, New Zealand, the United States, Hong Kong, Australia, England, and Scotland, and the series was won by Samoa. Not surprisingly, New Zealand has been the dominant team in the official series, winning eight overall titles. Fiji and South Africa have also each notched a Series crown.

Since 2004 the United States has hosted a stop in the Series. For the first three years the venue was the Home Depot Center in Carson, California, but in 2007 it switched to PETCO Park in San Diego, and finally in 2010 it moved to Sam Boyd Stadium in Las Vegas, where it seems to have found a permanent home.

Sevens rugby in the Olympics

Rugby has been played in only four Olympic Games (1900, 1908, 1920, and 1924), and always in its traditional 15-a-side format. This is set to change in 2016 in Rio de Janeiro when sevens rugby will be both a men's and a women's sport at the 32nd Olympiad. The road to rugby's return to the Olympics was a long and bumpy one, but when the International Olympic Committee (IOC) voted in 2009 to include rugby in the Rio Games it marked a huge step forward for the game worldwide.

In many countries, including the United States and Canada, not being an Olympic sport held back the development of the game. Now that rugby is officially part of the Olympic movement, many more resources are being devoted to the game in all parts of the globe. The IRB has been instrumental in encouraging this growth, especially in Africa and Asia.

One of the many reasons that the IOC took the momentous decision to make rugby part of the Olympic family again is that the sport has a well-known reputation for both fair play and camaraderie. In addition, the sport is truly global; as many as 20 nations will be in medal contention in Brazil. An added consideration for the IOC was the success of rugby in the Commonwealth Games since it was added in 1998.

Interprovincial and Provincial Rugby

Positioned just below test rugby in the global rugby pecking order, interprovincial competition pits the best teams against others within their regions. For example, the Tri Nations countries of Australia, New Zealand, and South Africa also compete at the interprovincial level in the Super 15. Likewise, the Six Nations members compete interprovincially in the Heineken Cup. While international, or test, rugby drove the development of the amateur game over its first 125 years, since the dawn of professionalism in 1996 the Super 15 and the Heineken Cup have had an enormous impact on the way the game is played around the world.

The next level is national provincial action, where traditional rivalries abound among the New Zealand, South African, and Irish provincial sides. The heart of rugby will always reside at the provincial level, where local rivals compete within a rich tapestry of historical encounters.

Sensational Super Rugby XV

Super Rugby annually delivers the world's most exciting rugby action. The competition was established in 1996 with 12 sides, then in 2006 it expanded to 14 franchises, and in 2011 to 15. It was previously known as the Super 12 and then the Super 14, but it is now simply called Super Rugby. Five teams hail from New Zealand, five from South Africa, and five from Australia, each playing in their own national conference. The members of each conference play each other home and away and also face off against four teams from the other two conferences. The Kiwi sides are the Blues, Chiefs, Crusaders, Highlanders, and Hurricanes. The Aussie teams are the ACT Brumbies, Reds, Waratahs, Rebels, and the Western Force. The Bulls, Cats, Sharks, Stormers, and Cheetahs are the South African representatives.

The Super Rugby season runs from mid-February to early July and features 18 weeks of regular season play followed by the playoff qualifying round, the semifinals, and the final. In all, there are 125 Super Rugby games each season. The sheer number of games and the length of the season make Super Rugby a fan-friendly tournament, as enthusiasts can follow their teams' progress through the course of a long and difficult season. The relative parity among the teams also makes Super Rugby an exciting competition to follow because the race for playoff berths always comes down to the final regular season weekend.

New Zealand teams have won 10 of the 15 titles since 1996. The Blues won the first two, and again in 2003; the Crusaders have won six times; and the Brumbies in 2001 and 2004. In 2007 the Bulls became the first South African team to win the Super 14, with a victory over the Sharks, and they are currently the two-time defending champions with three overall titles. Super Rugby is the breeding ground for the Southern Hemisphere's stars of tomorrow, because the season directly precedes the selection of the SANZAR countries' national teams for the June tests and Tri Nations.

The Heineken Cup overfloweth

The Heineken Cup is Europe's version of interprovincial competition. The tournament was launched in the fall of 1995 by the then Five Nations committee to provide a new level of cross-border play.

Twelve teams competed in the inaugural season, with Toulouse (from France) lifting the European Cup for the first time. In 1996–97 the league expanded to 20 teams in four pools of five, and after 46 matches the French were singing in the streets of Cardiff (Wales) when Brive were crowned Heineken Cup Champions in front of 41,664 fans at Cardiff Arms Park.

In the 1997–98 season, the format was changed again, with pool matches being played both home and away and the addition of three quarterfinal playoffs, bringing the total number of games to 70. In the final, England's storied Bath club lifted the Heineken Cup after overcoming the defending champs 19–18. Our Man of the Match was none other than USA Eagle Number 8 Dan Lyle, who created Bath's only try of the match.

The politics-driven absence of the English sides in the 1998–99 season prevented Bath from defending their title, opening the door for Ireland's Ulster to defeat Colomiers (France) 21–6 for the first Irish victory on the European interprovincial scene.

In the 1999–2000 season, perennial bridesmaids Northampton (England) pipped Munster (Ireland) by a single point to earn the Saints' first major cup title in the club's long and tortured history of coming up second best in a variety of competitions. The Leicester Tigers (England) pounced on the Cup in 2000–01 and became the first team to defend its title when they repeated the feat in 2001–02. The 2002–03 season saw Toulouse join Leicester as the only teams to hoist the Heineken Cup twice.

In 2003–04 Toulouse made it to the final again but were defeated at Twickenham by a gutsy London Wasps side. The 2004–05 championship game was an all-French affair, with Toulouse notching their third title by beating Stade Francais at Murrayfield (neutral venue in Scotland). The 2005–06 final was played at Millennium Stadium (neutral venue in Wales) and featured Munster versus Biarritz (France). The Munstermen won a close contest by the score of 23–19. The 2006–07 title match was the first to pit two English squads, and was won by Wasps — who beat Leicester in front of a record-setting crowd at Twickenham.

Munster became a two-time winner in 2007–08 with a tight victory over Toulouse in Cardiff. Another Irish side took the crown in 2008–09, as Leinster defeated Leicester in Edinburgh. Toulouse became the tournament's first four-time winner in 2009–10, beating Biarritz in Paris.

The Celtic scene

With the success of the Aviva Premiership in England making a British league impossible, the Celtic nations of Ireland, Scotland, and Wales launched the Celtic League in 2001 to raise the standard of their domestic competitions and to provide additional income. In 2006–07 the competition got a new sponsor and is now known as the Magners League. Currently there are 12 Celtic League teams: four from the Welsh regions, four Irish provinces, two Scottish franchises, and two Italian sides.

The first-ever Celtic League fixture was held on August 17, 2001. Over the course of the inaugural campaign, Irish sides earned three of the four semifinal berths. The final was staged at Lansdowne Road in Dublin, with Leinster defeating Munster for the hardware. In 2002–03, Munster erased the memory of the previous final, with a comprehensive 37–12 victory over Welsh side Neath.

From 2003–04 to 2008–09 the Magners League champion was decided strictly by league competition points, but in 2009–10 they returned to a playoff system to determine an overall winner. In the first Magners League Grand Final, Ospreys (Wales) beat Leinster (Ireland) in Dublin for their third championship.

The proliferation of interprovincial competitions like Super Rugby, the Heineken Cup, and the Magners League all serve to create an intermediate step in the professional era from provincial to national team play. Not surprisingly, Australia, New Zealand, South Africa, England, France, Ireland, Wales, Scotland, and Italy have all consistently improved since these competitions were created. The challenge facing the Americas is to develop its own framework of provincial and interprovincial leagues to stop losing ground.

The ITM Cup

The ITM Cup came into being in 2006, replacing the National Provincial Championship (NPC). From 2006 to 2009, it was called the Air New Zealand Cup. New Zealand is divided into 26 provincial unions that all field representative teams. Although the format has evolved somewhat since the NPC was established in 1976, the current ITM setup has 14 teams, with the top seven competing in the ITM Premiership and the bottom seven doing battle in the ITM Championship. The teams in each flight play each other once, and also play four of the teams from the other division, with all matches counting equally for league points. In 2011, to make schedule room for the Rugby World Cup (refer to Chapter 13), which is in New Zealand, teams will play midweek matches and the semifinals will be eliminated. The remaining 12 teams compete in the Heartland Championship for the Meads and Lochore Cups.

The ITM Cup features a rich wealth of talent throughout the 14 first-division teams. With the recent expansion of the competition, teams that used to be in the lower echelon are now getting a chance to play their larger neighbors, giving fans in all areas the opportunity to see the best rugby players New Zealand has to offer. Many of the provinces play a unique style of rugby that developed through adaptation to particular local conditions and coaching styles. Even though the availability of the All Blacks to participate in the ITM Cup is limited, the tournament is still loaded with outstanding performers — a testament to the incredible depth of the talent pool in the Land of the Long White Cloud!

The Ranfurly Shield

The Ranfurly Shield is the most coveted piece of domestic hardware in New Zealand sports. It's contested on a challenge basis, with the holders usually defending the Log of Wood (the nickname for the Shield) at selected home matches. The trophy was presented to Auckland in 1902 by the Governor General of New Zealand, the fifth Earl of Ranfurly. Since then, the Ranfurly Shield has dominated the thoughts of all New Zealand rugby players and inspired the dreams of countless Kiwi youngsters, imagining themselves making the critical play to win the Shield. One of the things that makes the tournament so special is that even the smallest provinces periodically get a shot at lifting the Shield. When Marlborough upset Canterbury in 1973, the entire town broke into a delirious celebration that will always be remembered as the high point for local pride.

For the challenger's fans, Shield week is a glorious time of eternal hope when numerous receptions and prefatory events focus on the upcoming encounter and culminate with a mandatory road trip to the holder's venue for the game. For the holders, each defense comes complete with a defense song and a full complement of hospitality and shield fervor. For the few players who get the chance to play for the Shield, it's the highlight of their careers and they leave everything on the pitch in pursuit of their place in New Zealand's rugby folklore.

The South African ABSA Currie Cup

Even though rugby-mad South Africans think it's delicious, the Currie Cup is not in fact a hot Asian dish served over rice, but rather South Africa's premier domestic rugby competition. The Holy Grail of South African rugby is named after Sir Donald Currie, who first presented the cup in 1891 to Griqualand West. The inaugural Currie Cup Tournament was held in Kimberly in 1892. In subsequent years, the trophy was awarded periodically using various tournament- and log-style formats. In 1939 the first Currie Cup final was played at Newlands in Cape Town, and after Transvaal beat Western Province the trophy was on offer only occasionally until the return of the annual finals system in 1946.

The Currie Cup format is currently broken into an eight-team Premier Division and six-team First Division. The top four sides from the Premier Division meet in semifinals and then a final to determine a Currie Cup champion. The top two finishers in the First Division have a shot at promotion to the top group if they can beat the lowest two finishers in a home-and-away series.

Western Province has dominated the Currie Cup, winning 32 times, while the Blue Bulls have taken top honors 23 times. Together, the two teams account for 55 of the 71 times the Currie Cup has been officially awarded.

The English domestic scene

Until recently, the English domestic game was contested through knockout play for various cups. Under this model, teams from all divisions would compete in a single elimination tournament leading to an annual English Cup Champion. The establishment of an English League is a recent invention since the launch of the Courage Leagues. With multiple changes in corporate backing, the Courage League became the Allied Dunbar Premiership in the 1997–98 season, the Zurich Premiership in 2000–01, the Guinness Premiership in 2006–07, and the Aviva Premiership in 2010–11.

The process of playing a league season with points tables leading to a playoff and a champion is now an integral part of the English club game. The Aviva Premiership, more than any other domestic league on the planet, contains a huge contingent of foreign players from New Zealand, South Africa, Australia, Ireland, Wales, Scotland, France, and other leading rugby nations. Leicester has historically dominated the competition, winning ten titles since 1987.

The Top 14

The Top 14 is France's premier domestic competition and has been in existence in various formats since 1892. The annual round-robin tournament is run by the Ligue Nationale de Rugby. The season runs from August until June and features relegation for the two lowest finishers and promotion for the two highest from Professional Division Two. The champion is determined by a semifinal and final playoff featuring the top four teams on the ladder after 26 rounds of action.

This competition is hugely popular in France and regularly attracts enormous crowds, with the last six finals drawing nearly 80,000 people each. Over the years Stade Toulousain and Stade Français have won the most championships, the former garnering 17 titles and the latter 13. The current champions are Clermont Auvergne, who beat Perpignan 19–6 in the 2010 final in Paris.

Chapter 15

North American Rugby

Unbeknown to all but the most die-hard fans, rugby in North America has a long and storied history. From hazy beginnings at the collegiate level, the United States managed to win two Olympic gold medals in the 1920s before the game all but vanished from the American sporting consciousness. In Canada, the game developed mostly on both coasts and was able to sustain a continuous if low-key presence for the entire 20th century.

In this chapter we give you an overview of the somewhat nebulous history of rugby in North America, including the formation of the two national governing bodies, detail the significant accomplishments of both American and Canadian representative teams on the world stage, and look at their current involvement in two key international tournaments.

Checking Out Rugby in the United States

Knowledgeable rugby commentators from around the globe often remark that the United States is a sleeping giant. The theory is postulated that as soon as the U.S. is properly exposed to the game, a vast supply of superior athletes will take the world by storm. Unfortunately, this school of thought totally misses the mark on two key points. The first assumption is that superior athleticism will make Americans world-beaters. This ignores the critical role that learning the game from a young age serves in developing players with rugby vision. Knowledge of the game and finely honed skills are more significant than physical attributes in separating the good from the great players. If the NFL Pro Bowl team lined up against the All Blacks, even with a solid year of rugby-specific coaching the NFLers would get a massive lesson in tactics and would struggle to compete at all.

The second misperception is the notion that American expertise in the business of sports will be able to transform shortcomings on the field with a magic bullet of slick marketing and boatloads of cash. This notion is false for two reasons:

- The U.S. sporting marketplace is incredibly crowded with well-established sports all competing for a finite pool of television time and sponsorship dollars. This situation is further complicated by the emergence of made-for-TV sports like the X Games, which are created and backed by the networks themselves.

- Rugby is viewed by most Americans as a foreign game and therefore is ignored by mainstream media companies and sports marketers. Americans are notoriously parochial and inward-looking when it comes to sports.

The good news is that rugby in the United States is now taking off at the grassroots level (see Chapter 17), and the inclusion of sevens rugby in the Olympics in Rio in 2016 (refer to Chapter 14) has increased the amount of television coverage and overall exposure for the game. With increased TV coverage and surging growth in youth participation, the game is poised for rapid development during the next ten years.

Origins and Olympic gold

In this age of all-encompassing media coverage of sports you can easily forget that in earlier times people primarily played games for fun. Many different kinds of ball sports emerged and flourished on a regional basis throughout the United States without benefit of central governing bodies to codify every rule and legitimize each individual competition. Rugby was one such game that was played in various forms across the country. The origin of the game of rugby in England was deliberately obscured by those who wanted to promote it as an exclusive endeavor. In America, the beginnings are murky because rugby's roots are intertwined with those of American football — and for a while they were one game before splitting into completely separate sports.

Rugby historians generally agree that the first rugby match in the United States of which a written record exists occurred in May 1874 when Harvard University played host to Montreal's McGill University. This contest led to attempts at determining a definite set of rules and inspired collegians in various parts of the country to take up the game. For the next 30 years, rugby was the primary form of football competition in the United States. If you could go back in time to watch, however, the game would bear little resemblance to rugby as we know it today.

The catalyst that split the game into rugby and American football was the attention of President Theodore Roosevelt. Following an outcry over numerous deaths and injuries caused by the then violent nature of the game, reform was demanded and Roosevelt led the charge to modify the more extreme parts of the sport. The end result was that most of the leading colleges latched on to the reconstituted game, which eventually became gridiron football, while in certain areas, notably the West Coast, rugby continued to be the dominant version of the sport.

In the years before World War I, teams like the All Blacks and the Waratahs, the precursor to the Wallabies, toured from Los Angeles to Vancouver on their way to Britain. Thus, it was no surprise that when the U.S. Olympic committee authorized a team to compete at the 1920 Games in Antwerp almost all of the players were from Northern and Southern California. The rugby competition at the seventh Olympiad was really just a match between the United States and France, which the Americans won 8–0 to earn the gold medal.

The 1924 Games in Paris were far more dramatic but still featured only the United States, France, and Romania. After the Americans and the French both dispatched the Romanians, who were awarded the bronze medal, the two sides met in front of a 50,000-strong, heavily partisan crowd at Colombes Stadium. The French in the stands had come to see their countrymen win a gold medal — and when the match swung decisively in the visitors' favor, the audience took on the characteristics of a mob. A 17–3 triumph by the Americans only inflamed the assembled spectators (see Figure 15-1 for a look at the victors).

The poor behavior in the stands of that 1924 match is sometimes pointed to as one of the reasons why rugby was never again contested in the Olympic games. Any momentum for the sport gained by winning two consecutive gold medals quickly ebbed when subsequent Olympiads failed to include rugby in their program of events.

Formation and reformation of USA Rugby

In response to the need for a centralized national structure, the United States of America Rugby Football Union (USARFU, later renamed USA Rugby) was formed in 1975 to serve as the game's governing body. The formation of the national union was essential to coordinate test matches with the International Rugby Board (IRB) and its member unions. The Eagles' first test under the USARFU banner was played against Australia on January 31, 1976, in Anaheim, California.

Figure 15-1:
1924 U.S.
Olympic
gold medal
team.

Although the Eagles lost 24–12 in their inaugural flight, they played the Wallabies close and landed quite respectably on the world stage. Later that summer, a bicentennial-inspired group of Eagles pushed the then Five Nations runners-up France to the limit, scoring two fabulous tries before finally being vanquished 33–14. The early Eagles sides were renowned for their fearless and aggressive American football–style tackling technique. What they lacked in skills they made up for in commitment. From 1976 to November 2010, the Eagles played 123 test matches, amassing 40 wins, 82 losses, and 1 draw. Although they've yet to beat a founding IRB country (England, Ireland, Wales, Scotland, France, New Zealand, Australia, or South Africa), over the years they've defeated Canada, Fiji, Samoa, Tonga, Portugal, Georgia, Uruguay, Chile, and Japan.

After 30 years of amateur administration by well-meaning but essentially unqualified personnel, in June 2006 the USA Rugby Board of Directors voted to make itself redundant. (Patrick knows, because he was one of the board members who raised a hand in that historic vote.) The 27-member constituent board was unwieldy and incapable of leading the union into the future. So, after a comprehensive review of the governing structure by Atlantic Sports Management and Training, a new governance model was proposed for USA Rugby. The new board was reduced from 27 to 9 members. The makeup of the board of directors was truly revolutionary — six independent directors, two international athlete representatives, and only one member appointed by the USA Rugby membership. The committee members were all relegated to participate in the newly created USA Rugby Congress, which serves to bridge the gap between the membership at the grassroots level and the executive staff and new board of directors. The real power in USA Rugby was given to a new board that would be dominated by independent directors.

With the improved governance model in place, an impressive new board was recruited — with Kevin Roberts, the flamboyant, rugby-loving global CEO of Saatchi & Saatchi Worldwide, selected as the new chairman of USA Rugby. The new board's first order of business was finding a new chief executive, and after a worldwide search Nigel Melville was hired as both the CEO and president of rugby operations for USA Rugby (see Figure 15-2).

Since 2006 the results have been mixed in the boardroom and on the pitch. Although notable success stories exist, such as the Olympic inclusion of sevens rugby and the Rookie Rugby program (which we discuss in Chapter 17), the jury is still out on whether USA Rugby is any closer today than it was in 2006 to a breakthrough performance at the Rugby World Cup.

The National Office is located in Boulder, Colorado, and oversees the seven Territorial Unions and 37 Local Area Unions that compete for regional and national championships. This organizational structure will soon be replaced by a yet-to-be-defined number of Geographic Unions across the country. This restructuring tracks the move to state-based rugby organizations that has worked so well at the youth level.

Figure 15-2:
USA Rugby
CEO and
President
of Rugby
Operations
Nigel
Melville.

Nigel Melville: USA Rugby's chief executive

Nigel Melville is a former captain and scrumhalf of the English national team. Despite a playing career that was plagued with injuries, he represented his country in 13 tests over four years. After his playing days were over, Mr. Melville moved on to become Director of Rugby for Wasps RFC and later for Gloucester RFC, leading both professional teams to win their league and national challenge cup competitions. Nigel left Gloucester in 2005 and started as CEO of USA Rugby in October 2006. Since then, he has had to adjust to work within the extraordinarily competitive sports marketplace in the U.S., where rugby is only a minor sport, as opposed to the U.K., where rugby is a big deal.

Being CEO of a national rugby union is a very difficult commercial and political balancing act, where you are responsible for driving the entire country forward, but in Tier 2 countries like the U.S. you lack the internal financial resources to get the job done alone. The key skill is being able to deftly negotiate your way through the backroom politics and business challenges of working with the IRB, the United States Olympic Committee, U.S. TV networks, sponsors, commercial partners, and others whose resources are critical to help the game grow. Recently Melville confided to us that he hopes his legacy will be that USA Rugby will be better off when his time is done, and he is particularly satisfied with the progress made over the last five years at the youth level. According to Melville real progress comes from the bottom up, and on that point we wholeheartedly agree.

Soaring with the Eagles

The Eagles represent the United States around the world in international play. USA Rugby fields ten national representative teams. In addition to the Men's and Women's Fifteens, Sevens, Collegiate All-Americans, and Junior All-American teams, the men's national team also has a developmental team called the Men's Select XV, and USA Rugby has recently added the Boys' High School All-Americans to the mix. Being chosen to play for one of the U.S.'s representative sides is an honor bestowed upon only a select few players each year.

The aspiring male or female player can become an Eagle by following one of a variety of pathways. Those fortunate enough to get started early in high school or college can compete to make the High School All-Americans (males only), Junior All-Americans, or Collegiate All-Americans teams. For the club-side player, being a standout performer in the national club playoffs will give you exposure to the national coaching staff who attend these events. For senior men, starring for one of the Rugby Super League teams can provide a fast track to the national team.

The good news for youngsters who aspire to someday play for the Eagles in the Olympics or the Rugby World Cup is that the once murky pathway to the elite level is now much clearer, and the majority of players recently chosen for the men's national team now come directly from the All-American teams.

Players who soar high enough on the international stage in the Eagle jersey can earn professional rugby contracts overseas. In 2010, 19 Eagles were contracted as fully professional players who ply their trade in the U.K., Ireland, France, Italy, Japan, South Africa, and New Zealand.

Eagles atop the world: Women's rugby

Unlike men's international rugby, which started 132 years ago when England first played Scotland, women's tests are a relatively new phenomenon. Because the United States was one of the first nations to play women's rugby, female players have been able to compete at the highest level right from the beginning, without having to play catch-up like the men.

Todd Clever: Captain America

Two of the greatest aspects of rugby are the places you get to go and the people you get to meet while playing against them. By that standard, Todd Clever is a rugby traveler of the highest order. The current Eagles captain and former Men's Sevens standout has been playing international rugby since 2003, but his appearances for the United States are not the only tours that have filled up his passport. Clever has also played professional rugby overseas for several years in some of the world's toughest competitions.

Clever began playing rugby while in high school in San Jose, California. His play earned him a slot on the United States Under-19 team in 2000. From there, he took his burgeoning skills to the University of Nevada, Reno, where he was a three-time Collegiate All-American. The next stop on his rugby journey was a spot on the Eagles. He earned the first of his 33 international fifteens caps against Argentina in 2003 at the age of just 20. In 2004, Clever made his first appearance for the Eagles in the abbreviated form of the game at the Hong Kong Sevens. He traveled the globe with the U.S. team on the IRB Sevens World Series circuit, playing in 23 tournaments over six seasons. He also became a regular starter at flanker for the Eagles XV, and was eventually named captain.

One of the truisms of rugby is that to get better you have to play against better competition, and it was this element of Clever's career that saw him fly where no Eagle had flown before. In 2006, he played for North Harbour in the first division of what is now the ITM Cup in New Zealand. In 2009 he went overseas again, this time to South Africa to play for the Lions in the Super 14, now known as Super Rugby. He was the first American to play there and to score a try in that competition. He even got the opportunity to play against the British and Irish Lions on their 2009 tour of South Africa, and was named Man of the Match. But he wasn't done with his rugby travels yet. In 2010 he made the move to Japan to play for Suntory Sungoliath in the Japanese Top League, and led them to the championship in 2011.

Clever will certainly earn many more caps for the United States, and will again captain the side at the 2011 Rugby World Cup in New Zealand, adding to his already long list of rugby experiences.

The United States women's national team program was very successful right from the outset. Since their first match in 1987 against Canada, the American women have amassed an impressive 45–30–3 record, winning 58 percent of their tests. The Eagles won the first unofficial Women's Rugby World Cup (WRWC) in 1991 over a heavily favored England 19–6. The Eagles continued to be one of the world's top teams throughout the 1990s, making the Women's World Cup final in both 1994 and 1998. Suffering from internal strife going into the 2002 event, they were eliminated at the quarterfinal stage.

In 2006, the Eagles went 4–1 at the IRB Women's Rugby World Cup in Edmonton. Losing only to the beaten finalists from England, the Eagles defeated Ireland, Australia twice, and finished their campaign by shutting out Scotland 24–0 to finish in fifth place in the WRWC rankings.

For the 2010 IRB Women's Rugby World Cup, the Eagles set their sights and expectations high, looking to break back into the world's top four. But after crushing Kazakhstan 51–0, they lost to Ireland 12–22 and England 37–10, which knocked them out of the semifinals. They finished strong, however, avenging their loss to Ireland with a convincing 40–3 victory and then defeating Canada 23–20 to finish the tournament in fifth place once again (see Figure 15-3).

The Eagles' early success was the result of an increased emphasis on women's sport within the United States and the established rugby powers' reluctance to get behind the women's game. Women's sporting participation in the U.S. grew dramatically in the 1980s, and with the unique allure of rugby's full-contact action and special camaraderie, the game spread quickly across the country on collegiate campuses. This growth occurred during a time when women's rugby was largely ignored by rugby unions around the world. And so in the early days of women's international rugby, the U.S. had a larger pool of gifted athletes to draw upon and was thus able to compete quite well at the highest level.

Figure 15-3:
U.S. national women's team at WRWC 2010.

U.S. sevens

With only seven players per team playing on the same size pitch as a fifteens match, sevens rugby offers a spectacle of nonstop action where speed, skills, and athleticism rule the day. In contrast to the limited accomplishments of the United States in the 15-a-side game, the Eagles have fared much better in sevens rugby. The Eagles now compete as a core team in the IRB Sevens World Series each year, which means that they attend all eight Sevens World Series events each year and compete against the best teams in the world for the annual series championship. In stark contrast to the 15-a-side version, where the Eagles have yet to beat any of the Tier 1 nations, the Eagles have beaten Fiji, Wales, Australia, England twice, France three times, and Argentina five times in the Sevens World Series. The recent success in sevens has led to the Eagles earning their first-ever spot in a Sevens World Series cup final at the 2010 Adelaide Sevens.

The USA Sevens competition kicked off in February 2003 at the Home Depot Center, marking the first time the United States ever hosted an official IRB-sanctioned international sevens tournament. In 2007, the USA Sevens moved to PETCO Park in downtown San Diego. In 2010 the USA Sevens moved to Las Vegas, and since then it has grown significantly in both attendance and TV exposure. For the first time ever, the USA Sevens was broadcast live on NBC in 2011, exposing the sport of sevens rugby across the country. So far, the move to Las Vegas seems to be a good fit because the party atmosphere of sevens matches well with the vibe of Sin City.

Investigating Rugby in Canada

Rugby in Canada dates back to the 1860s when it was initially played by army and navy personnel in British Columbia and Nova Scotia. The first recorded match was played in Montreal among the members of an artillery unit in 1864.

The early desire for standardized play, always a crucial moment in any burgeoning game, was met by Toronto's Trinity College, which published a set of rules for rugby that same year. In 1868 the Montreal Football Club was formed, making it Canada's first official rugby organization. These identifiable firsts point to a growing interest in the sport in diverse parts of the country.

Over the next two decades, as more and more clubs sprouted across the width of the nation, an administrative structure also developed, beginning with the establishment of the British Columbia Rugby Union in 1889, and followed by the formation of the Maritime Provinces Rugby Union in 1890 and the Manitoba Rugby Football Union in 1892.

Rugby's development in Canada was slowed considerably by both World Wars, but since 1945 it has spread to every province. Rugby is now a permanent fixture on the Canadian sporting landscape.

The birth of Rugby Canada

The first incarnation of a national governing body for the sport took place in 1929 with the creation of the Rugby Union of Canada. The organization functioned for the next ten years before going into hibernation for the duration of World War II and beyond. Following the war, most administrative issues were dealt with on a provincial level until the reformation of the national group in 1965. During the 1960s Canada played test matches only sporadically, so that a mountain of responsibility wasn't placed on the volunteer administrators.

In 1974, the body that is now known as Rugby Canada was incorporated and took over the day-to-day running of the sport at the national level. This was sufficient until the first Rugby World Cup in 1987. The desire to compete in the tournament prompted Canada to become a member of the IRB. (For more details on the IRB, refer to Chapter 5. For more details on the Rugby World Cup, refer to Chapter 13.) Since that momentous decision, Rugby Canada has placed a high priority on regular participation at the international level in men's, women's, under-23s, under-20s, and sevens rugby.

The Canadians played their first recognized international in 1932 against Japan, but it wasn't until the 1970s that they began to play tests on a regular basis. Canada has always been known as a tough team that can't be intimidated on the pitch. Occasionally over the last 15 years the national team has competed successfully with the top teams in the world.

In the 1991 World Cup, Canada opened the tournament by beating Fiji and Romania before losing a close contest to France. The two wins, however, were good enough to advance to the quarterfinals for the first time. On a quagmire of a pitch in Lille, France, Canada hung tough against the All Blacks but came up short, losing 13–29.

In 1993 Canada shocked Wales 26–24 at the Arms Park in Cardiff, and in 1994 they beat France 18–16 in Nepean. In 2000 Canada continued the tradition of battling strongly against quality opposition by drawing a match 27–27 with Ireland in Markham, Ontario. Their most recent triumph over a Six Nations side came in 2002 when the touring Scots were upended 26–23 in Vancouver after flyhalf Jared Barker kicked 16 points. In 2005, the 13th-ranked Canadians upended the 8th-ranked Pumas from Argentina 22–15 at Calgary Rugby Park.

Since the game went professional in 1995, Canada has contributed numerous players to the top leagues in Great Britain and France. Unfortunately, this has prevented the members of the national team from training together in a cohesive fashion before big tournaments and has led to some disappointing results. Canada had high hopes of making its second quarterfinal appearance going into the 2003 Rugby World Cup, but was able to win only one match against Tonga and failed to move on to the knockout stage.

In the 2007 Rugby World Cup in France, Canada failed to win a match, losing 42–17 to Wales and 16–29 to Fiji, drawing 12–all with Japan, and finishing pool play with a loss to Australia 37–6. Looking ahead to the 2011 Rugby World Cup in New Zealand, the Canadians are hopeful that they can improve on their 2007 results and somehow emerge from Pool A (New Zealand, France, Tonga, Japan, and Canada) as one of the top two teams to make the quarterfinals.

Canadian women on the rise

Women's rugby in Canada began in the late 1970s in various parts of the country, but no organized interprovincial competition existed until 1983. Four years later, the women's national team played its inaugural match in Victoria, British Columbia, against the United States.

Canada has competed in all five Women's World Cups beginning in 1991. In the first tournament in Wales, Canada lost to New Zealand in the opener but drew with the hosts to end up 0–1–1. In Scotland, for the 1994 event, the team lost in the quarterfinals to England, beat Japan in the Shield semifinal, and fell 5–11 to the Scottish women in the final for an eighth-place finish.

The 1998 World Cup in Amsterdam was the first to be officially sanctioned by the IRB, and the Canadian women benefited from increased support from Rugby Canada. The national side reached their first World Cup semifinal in the Netherlands but lost 46–6 to the United States.

In 2002 Barcelona was the site for the fourth Women's World Cup, and once again the Canadians were solid contenders. An opening-round 57–0 destruction of Ireland was followed by another shutout, this time 11–0 over Scotland. That victory propelled Canada into the semifinals to face England, where they were thumped 53–10.

Rugby Canada hosted the 2006 IRB Women's Rugby World Cup in Edmonton, Alberta, making it the first-ever IRB-sanctioned World Cup event to be staged in North America. The Canadian women lost heavily to the eventual champions from New Zealand 66–7 in pool play, but still managed to qualify for the Cup semifinals on points differential after beating Spain and Kazakhstan by a combined scoreline of 124–5. England then defeated the Canadian women 20–14 in the Cup semifinal, and France beat the locals 17–8 in the third-place match. Canadian Heather Moyse was the leading tryscorer in the tournament, with seven tries.

In 2010 the Women's Rugby World Cup was staged in England, and Canada got their campaign rolling with a 37–10 victory over Scotland, followed by a 40–10 defeat of Sweden. This set up a pool leaders' clash against France where the winner would advance to the semifinals, but Les Blues were too much for the Canadians, who lost 23–8 to France. The Canadian women next faced Scotland in the fifth-place semifinal where they crushed the Scots 41–0. In the fifth-place final pitting North American rivals,

Canada came up short against the United States 23–20 to finish the 2010 Women's Rugby World Cup in sixth place.

Canadian National Women's League

A central plank in Rugby Canada's long-term development strategy is the evolution of the women's club game. To foster the development of women's clubs across the country, Rugby Canada partnered with the provincial unions to create the National Women's League (NWL) in 2007. Similar to the concept underpinning the formation of the Rugby Canada Super League (which was replaced by the Canadian Rugby Championship in 2009 — we discuss this in Chapter 16), the NWL was formed to provide more high-quality games for women's club players, coaches, and referees as part of the overall high performance plan for women's rugby in Canada.

For 2011, the National Women's League includes teams from six provinces, divided into two tiers: Tier 1 & 2. Tier 1 includes British Columbia, Alberta, Ontario, and Quebec. Tier 2 is comprised of Saskatchewan, Ontario U-23, Nova Scotia, and Alberta U-23. Each team plays all the others in its tier in pool play from May to August, with the divisional winners meeting to determine the annual National Women's League Champions.

Rugby Canada is keen to see the NWL structure of provincial representative play expanded down to the lower-age grades as part of their national elite player development plan in future years.

Canadian sevens

The Canadian sevens team has performed very well in the seven-a-side game. They have regularly collected hardware in the World Sevens Series, and in 2004 they won two Bowl trophies in Dubai, United Arab Emirates, and George, South Africa, and were beaten finalists in the Plate division in Los Angeles. Some of Canada's stars of the future can be seen on their sevens team today.

Going Global: North American Internationals

One key to improving performance on the international scene is to regularly play matches against quality opposition. In the last 20 years, USA Rugby, Rugby Canada, England, and the IRB have made a variety of attempts to provide Canada and the United States with the opportunity to play in annual tournaments to raise their level of competitiveness.

The Churchill Cup, the June inbound tests, the America's Rugby Championship and the November tours are the four annual elite-level competitions for North Americans.

The Churchill Cup

The Churchill Cup is a cooperative alliance among the Rugby Football Union (England), USA Rugby, and Rugby Canada. In 2010, the Churchill Cup featured six teams, including the USA Eagles (see Figure 15-4), Rugby Canada's national team, England Saxons, France A, Uruguay, and Russia. The format included two groups of three teams that played each other to determine the finalists for the Cup, Plate, and Consolation finals.

The England Saxons have dominated the Churchill Cup from the beginning, winning five of the eight Cup finals contested since 2003 (the New Zealand Maori won twice and Ireland A won once).

In 2009 and 2010, the Churchill Cup round robin stages were held at Infinity Park in Glendale, Colorado. The highlight of the 12 matches played in Rugbytown, U.S.A., was an absolutely electric finish between Canada and France A in the final match. With France A expected to win by most, Canada delighted the crowd with two late tries; the last one covered 60 meters and brought the entire stadium to their feet cheering loudly for the underdog Canadians who defeated France A 33–27.

In 2011, the Churchill Cup will be contested entirely in the U.K. And sadly, the Rugby Football Union has announced that they will withdraw from the Cup after 2011, effectively scrapping the competition after nine years of collective investment by the RFU, USA Rugby, and Rugby Canada.

Figure 15-4: USA Rugby national men's team at Infinity Park for the 2010 Churchill Cup.

The June inbound tests

With the end of the Churchill Cup in sight, and in an attempt to mitigate the reduction of tough matches for the North American teams, the IRB has announced that USA Rugby and Rugby Canada will be awarded three inbound test matches each year in the June window starting in 2012. Rugby insiders expect that one of the three tests will be the annual Can-Am match.

Losing the Churchill Cup and replacing it with tests against lower-ranked Tier 2 nations like Russia, Spain, Portugal, Georgia, and Romania will do little to develop the North Americans. The key issue to be determined is whether the IRB will be able to convince Tier 1 nations to travel to North America in the June window each year.

For Canada and the United States, being able to host and compete with the world's best on an annual basis is essential to developing their game.

The November tours

In November each year, the national teams from the Southern Hemisphere typically tour the Northern Hemisphere and play at least three test matches. In recent years, the U.S. and Canadian men's national teams have toured Europe in that November window to play matches against Tier 1 A sides and tests against Tier 2 nations.

In 2010, the Eagles completed a three-match tour that included two tests. They started at Saracens and were beaten 20–6 by the professional club. Next up was a test against Portugal where the Eagles notched an important 22–17 victory over their hosts. The final match of the tour was staged in front of 35,000 partisan fans in Tbilisi where the Eagles lost 17–19 after a botched scrum under the USA posts allowed the Georgians to score the winning try on the last movement of the match.

The Canadian national men's team played four matches on their 2010 November tour of Europe. They got off to a rousing start crushing Belgium 43–12, then they annihilated Spain 60–22 before suffering a tough loss against Georgia 22–15, and then they finished strong against Portugal, winning 23–20 to take three out of four matches on tour.

Americas Rugby Championship

The Americas Rugby Championship is an IRB-sponsored tournament that was created to replace the North America 4. The new competition was designed by the IRB as a developmental tool for the United States, Canada, and Argentina to have annual games scheduled for their pool of developmental players vying for places in their national men's teams.

In 2009, four Canadian provincial teams played for one semifinal berth, with the BC Bears emerging as the victors, while the USA Selects were beaten by the Argentina Jaguars in the other semifinal. The inaugural 2009 ARC final pitted the Jaguars against the BC Bears, and the Argentinean developmental team won 35–11 to take the honors.

In 2010, a new format was introduced that saw Tonga A added to the mix and the number of teams reduced from six to four (USA Selects, Canada A, Argentina Jaguars, and Tonga A). Once again, the Jaguars emerged victorious after they beat Tonga A 28–20 in the final.

Chapter 16

Amateur Rugby in North America

. . . .

In This Chapter

▶ Checking out club rugby throughout the U.S.A.

▶ Getting acquainted with the Canadian club scene

. . . .

*T*he rugby club is the heart and soul of the North American game. It's where new players are introduced to the sport, where lessons are learned, and where rugby's unique camaraderie and love for the game are nurtured. In contrast to the professional game around the world, the North American club scene still embodies the amateur ethos of the game. The local club is the place where anyone can show up and become part of the action. Inclusiveness distinguishes rugby clubs from most other sporting activities. No matter where you come from or when you arrive at a rugby club function, you'll immediately be welcomed into the family as the bonds of the game supersede race, religion, sexual preference, politics, and any of life's myriad trivialities that may otherwise divide us.

North American rugby clubs are all amateur and organized in a series of tiers. At the top of the heap are the Rugby Canada Super League and the USA Rugby Super League. The club structure is further divided into several divisions, which serve to offer meaningful championships for teams of varying size, gender, and skill levels. In this chapter, we focus on the backbone of the North American game: the clubs.

Clubbing with the Yanks

Club rugby in the United States is played solely for the love of the game. The players compete for the joy of the contest, the administrators organize club activities on a volunteer basis, and everyone involved shares the common kinship of commitment to the rugby lifestyle. This participant-based focus, where the main goal is to make sure that next week's game comes off, has resulted in rugby developing very quietly across North America over the past 137 years. More than 92,000 registered players in the United States play for nearly 2,700 clubs, from Alaska to Arkansas and New York to California.

BROWNIE SAYS

Maggotfest

I can proudly say that I'm a Maggot and have been since 1994. No, I'm not a terrible person, I just happen to belong to one of the finest rugby clubs in the world, the Missoula All-Maggots. The Maggots are by charter dedicated to playing hard rugby and having fun, and to that end they have hosted a unique festival on the last weekend of April or the first weekend in May every year since 1977.

The Maggotfest gathers 28 men's and 8 women's sides from throughout the U.S. and Canada for what can only be described as a celebration of the ideals of the sport and a spur to the inclinations of those who choose to play it. The party kicks off on Thursday afternoon, when a specially selected "hosted team" arrives early and plays an opening match against the home side at Maggot Park. A raucous party soon follows and eventually spills into downtown Missoula. Early the next morning, both teams board the Maggot Bus for a long ride into Idaho for a white-water rafting trip down the Lochsa River. Survivors who make it back to town are treated to the Friday-night arrival bash at a local watering hole, where the other 34 teams make their first appearance and begin vying for the weekend's honors.

In a normal rugby tournament, wins and losses are the measure of success. At the Maggotfest, overall team spirit on and off the pitch is the most highly revered quality. A good showing on Friday night can put a team in the running for the most coveted of awards, that of "Most Honored Side." The rugby gets going and the beer starts flowing at 9:00 on Saturday morning. Fixtures are determined with an eye toward producing interesting matchups between sides with similar skill levels and tendencies.

After a long first day of competitive rugby, the Fest really hits its stride with the Saturday night party. Held in a llama barn at the Western Montana Fairgrounds, it's part Mardi Gras, part Halloween, and all rugby camaraderie extraordinaire. Teams dress thematically, or not at all, and 1,000 people infused with the rugby spirit dance to the band, drink beer, throw beer, and generally have a smashingly good time. Sunday features one more match for each club and the awards ceremony. An award is bestowed for "Best Play on the Pitch," but it is wholly secondary to the "Most Honored Side."

The real winner at Maggotfest is the community of rugby devotees who live for the one weekend a year when the game and lifestyle they love and cherish are celebrated with wholehearted devotion.

The development of the game in the United States has been largely driven by initiatives at the club level. Prior to the formation of USA Rugby in 1976, pockets of rugby activity existed on the East and West coasts and a few spots in between. The leading clubs played a critical role in spreading the word about the sport and providing a means for rugby people to enjoy their chosen game.

TECHNICAL STUFF

Traditionally, the United States club model includes an administration consisting of a club president, vice president, secretary, and treasurer, as well as various crucial appointees. The club officers are usually current or former players whose age and leadership skills have cursed them into taking on an organizational role. The *fixtures chair* is responsible for making sure the pitch is ready, and the *social chair* has the all-important job of looking after the third half, the mandatory reception following each home game. Add to that a coach and a slew of willing players, and *voilà* — you've got a rugby club.

The USA Rugby Super League

The USA Rugby Super League (RSL) represents the top tier of club rugby in the United States. The league was launched in 1997 to address the need of the country's top clubs for a higher level of competition week in and week out. Before the Super League was created, the top teams would play only one or two regional rivals of similar standard before the national playoffs each year. The concept behind the Super League was to create a competition where the best teams in the country would play against evenly matched opposition throughout the season, and then compete for the national championship.

Like most good things in that era of USA Rugby, the Super League was started by a group of leading club visionaries who, being unable to persuade the national office to address their need for better regular competition, took matters into their own hands and created the league over the objections of USA Rugby. With leadership from former USA Rugby president Bob Watkins and Keith Engelbrecht of the Dallas Harlequins, the Super League clubs joined together in 1996 and signed up Harp Lager to sponsor their first two seasons of play. The benefits of the league were immediately apparent to all — with the best teams being matched against opponents of similar ability every week, the scorelines were much closer and the standard of play was raised for all involved.

After four successful years of operation outside of USA Rugby's control, the Super League was finally sanctioned in 2001 by the national governing body as the top-level rugby competition in the United States. After several top teams pulled out of the league, the Super League has dropped down from 18 to 11 clubs competing in two divisions for the 2011 season.

Although some limited exceptions exist, most Super League players are unpaid for their services. Most often if a player is being paid, the arrangement usually involves a foreign player who was recruited from overseas to bolster the local talent. Even those being paid are only semi-professionals at best, because the money is barely enough to live on. Most players need a real job to supplement their income from rugby.

The 2010 RSL final pitted the defending champions, San Francisco Golden Gate, against the New York Athletic Club. NYAC scored ten points in the final five minutes to erase a seven-point lead and win 28–25.

Finding the right club to join

The key to finding the right club is to first figure out what kind of rugby experience you want to have. If you're a newbie and don't know what to expect, you're probably better off hooking up with a second- or third-division club. They'll be familiar with taking aboard new players, and you'll have a better chance of getting playing time sooner at lower levels. If you've played a bit of footy already and are looking to improve your skills, focus on first-division clubs, paying special attention to how the coaching staff interacts with the players at training.

Rugby is unique as a team sport in that you're immediately welcome at virtually any club in the world when you say you're a rugby player. Even so, before you join a club, you must go to a training session to meet their players, coaches, and supporters before deciding if the club is right for you. After you go through a practice session and then get a chance to chat with the team after training over a beverage, you'll be ready to make the call.

United States club championships

Whether playing for a local social club or for one the few established national powers, there's a championship for American clubs to aspire to win. The U.S. club structure is multi-tiered, with men's Division I, II, and III all playing off to crown a national champion. The women's club structure includes Division I and II playing to determine annual champions. Sevens rugby has national championships in nearly all the divisions for men and women also. Regardless of division, competing for and winning a National Club Championship is a highlight of any American player's career.

The road to becoming a National Champion isn't easy. First, clubs have to advance out of their local area union competitions, which are basically the teams within their leagues. The next level is to qualify for one of the territorial berths that each of the seven territories have for their respective divisions. Depending on the past year's performance, two or three openings per territory are available in the divisional playoffs.

After a club secures its ticket to the big dance, the journey becomes much more arduous, as team members scramble to get time off from work and to cobble together the money needed for airline tickets and hotel expenses. USA Rugby provides the structure, but the clubs are responsible for all the costs. From regional tournaments, a quartet of winning teams advance from the round of 16 to the final four. The final four teams play off over a long weekend, with the winning team having to play two matches in 72 hours. Despite these challenges, the joy of being a National Champion is something that remains dear forever as the accomplishment grows in stature every time the story is retold.

GUTHRIE SAYS

Rugbytown, U.S.A.

Back in 2005, I took a call from a gentleman named Mike Dunafon. As I soon discovered, he was the mayor pro tem of the City of Glendale, Colorado, and had a revolutionary idea to build North America's first rugby-specific stadium complex and rebrand the city as Rugbytown, U.S.A. After toiling away for 15 years in the slow-moving rugby development business, this was music to my oval ears. Recognizing the importance of the opportunity, I referred Mike to the right folks at Fox Sports in the technical production department, so the Infinity Park planners could make sure the new stadium was built to be broadcast ready to the network's new high-definition standards.

When Infinity Park opened three years later, I flew out to Colorado to take a closer look for myself and was stunned. Everything was spot-on. The stadium was perfectly sized (for American rugby events) with a capacity of 5,000, and the stands were built close to the pitch so the fans would be right on top of the action. The pitch looked like a putting green, held up well to the rigors of scrummaging, was lightning fast, and was very firm underfoot (in fact, Infinity Park won the 2009 National Turf award as the best field in America). But that was only the beginning. The entire stadium was plug and play, meaning that we wouldn't have to run any cables to broadcast matches from there. And the lights were world-class,

exceeding HD standards. The stadium had a huge sports facility for weight training, seven different changing rooms for teams and officials, and a bar overlooking the pitch with floor-to-ceiling windows where you could have a beverage while watching the action from midfield. The next phase of the complex added an IRB-approved artificial turf training pitch, plus a 9,000-square-foot (836-square-meter) Events Center with state-of-the-art production capabilities. The final piece of the puzzle was completed in February 2011, with the addition of the High Altitude Training Center.

Since it opened, Infinity Park has hosted international events, including the Churchill Cup (2009 and 2010) and the North America 4, plus national events, including the USA Rugby Men's National Club Championships, National Collegiate All-Star Championships, and Rugby Super League Finals. In addition to regularly hosting local, regional, and state-based youth rugby events, Infinity Park is the home of the Glendale Raptors RFC. Former Wallaby and Springbok assistant coach Eddie Jones told me in the Try Club that Infinity Park was one of the finest rugby facilities he had seen anywhere in the world, and he's right — Infinity Park is nothing short of a real-world field of dreams for all rugby fans in the United States. (Check out the accompanying figure to see for yourself.)

(continued)

(continued)

Considering the Canadian Club Scene

There are nearly 500 rugby clubs in Canada, serving 35,000 registered players throughout the entire country — from British Columbia to Newfoundland and Labrador. The clubs are governed by the ten provincial unions and play in a variety of championship leagues and formats. The three largest unions — British Columbia, Alberta, and Ontario — also have sub-unions that run the sport on a regional basis. Each provincial union is responsible for selecting its own representatives for competition in the Rugby Canada National Championships.

Like rugby countries the world over, Canada's clubs range from huge organizations fielding numerous teams at different levels to small ones that put out only two men's teams each weekend.

As can be expected, in the past players from provinces where rugby is less ingrained in the sporting environment were often overlooked when it came time for national selection and honors. To help even the playing field and provide nationwide exposure and competition for all, Rugby Canada and its member unions founded the Canadian Rugby Championship.

The Canadian Rugby Championship

The Canadian Rugby Championship (CRC) was launched in 2009 as a replacement competition for the Rugby Canada Super League, which was disbanded by Rugby Canada at the end of the 2008 season. The CRC is comprised of four provincial teams (British Columbia Bears, Ontario Blues, Alberta Prairie Wolf Pack, and Newfoundland and Labrador Rock) that, beginning in 2011, play a five-match schedule from the end of July to early September. The team with the most points in the standings at the end of the regular season is crowned champions.

In 2010, The Rock hosted the final in St. John's. After playing the Prairie Wolf Pack to a 0–all draw after 40 minutes, The Rock took control in the second half with the wind at their backs and won 18–9 to earn the right to lift the MacTier Cup in its inaugural presentation (see Figure 16-1).

To cut travel and accommodation costs, CRC teams usually schedule one match on Saturday, followed by another in the same area the following Tuesday, so the traveling clubs can play two away matches in five days' time. Having to play on only two full days of rest means that depth is more important than ever for CRC squads.

Figure 16-1: The Rock with the MacTier Cup — 2010 Canadian Rugby champions.

Canadian national championships

Rugby Canada holds national championships in six age categories across three annual competitions. The Canadian Rugby Championship is the highest level of club play for senior men who aspire to be national champions and be exposed to the national team selectors.

The National Women's League has an annual two-tiered provincial competition where the country's top women play to crown national champions at the senior and under-23 levels. In 2010, British Columbia defeated Ontario 34–22 to take the Tier 1 title, while Ontario U-23 crushed Alberta U-23 79–0 to win the Tier 2 championship.

For younger players, the National Championship Festival is the place where you can earn a national title and get yourself on the high-performance radar. In 2010, the National Championship festival had three different age groups, with under-18 and under-16 for men and under-19 for women. In the U-19 final, Quebec upset Ontario 15–14 to win the province's first women's age-grade national title. The U-18 champions were Ontario, who beat their perennial finals rival British Columbia 43–13. Ontario picked up the provincial double when their U-16 side beat B.C. 29–26 in a pulsating match to win the national U-16 crown.

Combining the championships into one festival setting made the event into a major happening on the Canadian sporting landscape. In addition to family members and enthusiastic rugby spectators, the festival drew national selectors, executive board members from participating unions, and staff from Rugby Canada. The future stars of Canadian rugby had a chance to strut their stuff in front of the very people they wanted to impress and work closely with in the future.

Chapter 17

Collegiate, High School, and Youth Rugby in North America

College campuses were the first home of organized rugby competitions in North America. From the first game in 1874, through rugby's dark years at the end of World War I, to the early 1960s, the collegiate game was the only consistent presence keeping rugby's torch lit in the United States. Even today, for many North American participants, playing in college is their first exposure to the game and remains the primary developmental arena for local clubs to stock their teams.

Recently, however, the sport has enjoyed unprecedented growth in high school and youth programs across the United States and Canada. In this chapter, we focus on the three areas that are the future of the North American game: collegiate, high school, and youth rugby.

Playing the American Collegiate Game

On May 5, 1874, Harvard University hosted Montreal's McGill University in the first recorded match of rugby played on U.S. soil. Over the next 30 years, the game evolved through the process of rules codification and modification. These changes culminated in the 1906 legalization of the forward pass, the final deviation that forever divided rugby from American football. By 1906, most colleges across the country had switched from playing rugby to playing American football.

Bucking the national trend, the West Coast held firm and the University of California at Berkeley and Stanford University actually dropped American football in 1906, setting the stage for later Olympic glory (refer to Chapter 15 for more details).

In 1910, an All-Star team comprising primarily Cal and Stanford players toured Australia and New Zealand under the banner of the American Universities team. Rugby had become the contact game of choice out West and regularly drew up to 20,000 fans for the annual showdown between Cal and Stanford. In 1912, 1913, and 1914, the New South Wales Waratahs, New Zealand All Blacks, and an All-Britain side toured the West Coast to play the All-Americans.

By the end of World War I, however, American football took center stage on collegiate campuses throughout the country, and rugby suffered through a period of stagnation that would last until its revival in the mid-1960s.

Today, rugby is the most popular club sport on U.S. college campuses. With approximately 500 men's teams and 350 women's programs competing in 2010, collegiate rugby is once again flourishing on campuses across the United States. During the past five years, collegiate participation within all categories of USA Rugby increased by 29 percent.

USA Rugby awards five national collegiate titles for men and women in Divisions I and II, and for men only in the USA Rugby Collegiate Premier League. For the Division I and II colleges, each territory produces a predetermined number of teams to compete in regional playoffs, leading to a national final-four tournament to crown the annual USA Rugby National Collegiate Champions.

The National Collegiate Athletic Association (NCAA) has women's rugby on its list of emerging sports. Because of Title IX fairness concerns (a law that requires there be relative parity in the number of men and women who participate in NCAA-sanctioned sports), we may see the NCAA install women's rugby as an intercollegiate sport under its control. If the NCAA opts to include women's rugby, the result will be a substantial increase in coaching and administrative support for the women's game on campus.

Even so, most people's initial impression of collegiate rugby is of a bunch of rowdy, beer-swilling frat boys getting naked and having a good old time. And while that reputation isn't entirely unearned, USA Rugby is working hard to turn it around by offering heaps of best-practices advice for the administrators and coaches of collegiate programs who are determined to lift the standard of play and rehabilitate collegiate rugby's image on campuses nationwide (see www.usarugby.org for more information).

On the paddock in 2010, the University of California at Berkeley won their 25th Men's Division I National Collegiate Championship when they defeated Brigham Young University 19–7. Penn State University took the women's Division I title by defeating Stanford 24–7 (see Figure 17-1).

Figure 17-1:
Penn State
University,
USA Rugby
women's
collegiate
champs,
2010.

Starting in 2011, USA Rugby has a new top-tier national competition for the best men's collegiate teams called the Collegiate Premier League. The CPL is comprised of 32 teams in two divisions that compete over seven matches from March through April each year. The quarterfinals, semifinals, and final are in May. The CPL was created to provide the best possible competition for the country's leading collegiate teams, week in and week out.

Another sign of rugby's growth in the U.S. is that more and more colleges are offering scholarships, loans, and other financial benefits to recruit stand-out high school rugby players. (Go to www.usarugby.org and click on the College option in the left navigation bar for more on scholarships and other financial aid available to skilled rugby players across the country.)

Starting Young: High School and Youth Rugby in the U.S.A.

The bad news for the rest of the rugby world is that more Americans than ever before are playing rugby, which means it's only a matter of time until the U.S.A. becomes competitive at the highest level. The good news for all those fans from rugby powerhouse nations around the world who are shaking in their boots right about now is that USA Rugby still needs at least another five to ten years to translate this growth into substantial success on the international stage.

In the six-year span from 2005 through 2010, every sector within USA Rugby experienced substantial growth and the number of participants increased by nearly 50 percent! The most significant trend is that the single largest segment (34 percent) within USA Rugby is players under 18 years old — the result of unprecedented expansion in the high school and youth segments.

The doubling of youth participation from 2005 through 2010 presents a double-edged sword to USA Rugby. How can the national governing body best use its very limited financial and other resources to serve a growing constituency? And how should those resources be allocated and prioritized going forward? We believe the key to making the United States truly competitive around the world is to nurture an ever-increasing crop of younger players in order to produce individuals who have the instincts to compete with those who have been playing barefoot since they were 5 years old.

High school championships

The rapid growth of high school rugby is one of the least well-known but nevertheless biggest success stories in the advancement of the oval game in the United States. In the past five years, the number of high school rugby players in America increased by 84 percent. More than 650 high school rugby programs across the country support approximately 28,000 players. If these high school students stick with the game through college and then join the top clubs over the next several years, USA Rugby's representative sides will improve by having a much larger pool of more experienced talent to choose from.

USA Rugby introduced the National High School Championship in 1985. The tournament now involves the top eight nationally ranked high school teams. In 2010, Xavier High School (New York City) defeated Gonzaga College High School (Washington, D.C.) 32–10 to earn the single-school national championship.

Beginning in 2008, USA Rugby created a new national championship category for high school teams that draw players from more than one school: the USA Rugby Boys' and Girls' Under-19 national championships. The 2010 Boys' U-19 National Champions were Utah United after they beat local rivals and perennial national powerhouse Highland 22–17. In the 2010 USA Rugby Girls' U-19 final, the Sacramento Amazons defeated Fallbrook 32–10 to become National Champions.

Youth rugby

Developing youth rugby is the biggest long-term challenge for the sport in the United States. The good news for American rugby fans is that youth rugby is finally starting to roll out as a sports activity in primary and middle schools. In the United States, the median age that players begin participating in rugby is 18 years old. By the time most Americans have figured out the nuances of the game, they're approaching 30 and are beyond their athletic prime.

To lower the age of introduction, USA Rugby is targeting youth development as a key area for growth. With support from the International Rugby Board (IRB), USA Rugby has implemented a Rugby for All development program. This plan involves using state-based rugby organizations, which are now operating in 28 states to provide expertise, materials, and other support needed to launch, maintain, and nurture new youth teams. The program contains physical education curriculum lessons, a youth development guide, a coaching guide, and videos and other helpful aids. The plan advocates including rugby in statewide youth sports programs because kids are four times more likely to play a sport if it is first introduced to them through their physical education classes at school. To find out more about youth development, visit www.usarugby.org and click on Youth/High School in the left-hand navigation bar.

For children too young for full-contact rugby, *non-contact* or *touch rugby* is used as an introductory tool. This version of the game eliminates tackling and other contact, minimizing parents' safety concerns. The main advantage of non-contact rugby is that all players still get to run with the ball and play both offense and defense. Because no tackling, rucking, or mauling is allowed, the collisions are replaced with a two-handed tag of the ball-carrier. The non-contact game is ideal for boys and girls from 6 to 10 years old. When their bodies are ready for the stress of the tackle game, they can move on to playing rugby with a local youth side.

Rookie Rugby

The most successful initiative of USA Rugby in recent years has been the development and rollout of the Rookie Rugby program. As the starting point for USA Rugby's Rugby for All development plan, Rookie Rugby is very basic, and that is the main reason the program has been so effective. Instead of attempting to introduce scrums, lineouts, rucks, and mauls (which can be very difficult to grasp), Rookie Rugby focuses on fun and simple games that can be

(continued)

(continued)

played by groups of varying numbers in relatively small spaces. In essence, Rookie Rugby puts rugby balls into the hands of primary and middle school boys and girls and challenges them to run around, pass the ball, and have fun (see the accompanying figure).

Because the program uses such simple, non-contact games, coaches don't need to be rugby experts, and the program curriculum is designed to be run by teachers and coaches with no rugby experience at all. Participants get to know the importance of teamwork, fair play, and respect for opponents, coaches, and referees. USA Rugby estimates that 150,000 children participated in Rookie Rugby in 2010. The curriculum materials include a Rookie Rugby resource CD, plus a 25-page program guide that includes a continuum, honor code, and introduction, as well as info on the object of the game, how to play, the rules of the game, how to coach and referee, and other helpful reference points. Rookie Rugby is available online from the USA Rugby website (www. usarugby.org). USA Rugby estimates that more than 250,000 kids will be exposed to Rookie Rugby in 2011.

Canadian Collegiate Championships

No formal national collegiate championship exists in men's rugby in Canada. Individual provincial unions hold their own competitions to determine their divisional winners. For Canadian men of collegiate age, the Rugby Canada National Junior Championship is the competition that determines a national champion each year. The National Junior Championship is comprised of 12 teams divided further into four regional conferences (Atlantic,

Central, Prairie, and Pacific). In 2010, the Newfoundland and Labrador Rock defeated the Vancouver Wave 13–10 to win the Rugby Canada National Junior Championship.

The women's collegiate rugby national championship is played under the auspices of Canadian Interuniversity Sport (CIS). The CIS is the national governing body for 19 different sports at the university level, including track and field, basketball, and hockey. In women's rugby, 35 teams compete in the Canada West, Ontario, Quebec, and Atlantic divisions for six playoff spots. In the 2010 CIS final, the St. Francis Xavier X-Women defeated the Concordia Stingers 17–10 in the gold medal match to earn the right to hoist the Monilex Trophy overhead for the second time.

High School and Youth Rugby in Canada

In the most competitive rugby-playing nations around the world, by the time kids reach high school age they're already steeped in rugby skills and culture because they've been playing and watching since they were very young. In a place like Canada, where rugby is well down the national sporting ladder, many players have their first introduction to the game at the high school level, although youth rugby is growing in popularity.

High school rugby

Rugby at the secondary level in Canadian schools is organized and run by high school athletic associations in each province, with assistance from the provincial unions. Every province has its own organizational structures to fit its specific needs.

According to Rugby Canada, there are approximately 500 boys' and girls' high school programs in the Greater Toronto Area alone, with an estimated 350 more in British Columbia. Although high school players aren't required to register directly with the national office, approximately 15,000 boys and girls play at the high school level across Canada. Throughout the country, high school rugby is a valuable introductory component of the sport — its continued growth is essential to the long-term health of Rugby Canada.

Youth rugby

Youth rugby (or mini rugby, as we call it) is a catchall term that includes players between the ages 5 and 15. In Canada, the development of young players is handled mostly through individual clubs as part of an overall provincial strategy.

The advantages of starting players from as young an age as possible are borne out by the success of rugby-playing nations where youth rugby is taken as the natural order of things. The sooner players begin to amass the basic skills of passing, running, and kicking, the easier it is to develop critical thinking and strategic skills at the high school level.

Mini rugby players start without boots, and because the game is initially non-contact they don't engage in tackling. An appropriately sized ball is also used, the better to be passed by smaller hands. The fundamentals are introduced in a nonthreatening environment where the emphasis is on having fun and developing sportsmanship, rather than serious competition. Girls and boys play on the same team, usually until about age 10. Like the sport at the highest level, mini rugby is great for all kids because, regardless of size or development, everyone has a place in the team. (Refer to Chapter 2 for details on player positions and characteristics.)

The goal of mini rugby is to acclimate kids to the essentials of the sport and then slowly introduce the finer points of the game. Along the way, they grasp the beginnings of teamwork, physical fitness, and social skills. A rugby club with a mini rugby program is by definition a family-friendly place.

Part IV
Coaching and Refereeing

The 5th Wave   By Rich Tennant

"I've got a ruck in aisle 5. I'm going to call a scrum unless I see that veil pretty soon."

In this part . . .

This part addresses the two areas key to developing the game in North America: coaching and refereeing. We start with the basic requirements needed to become a rugby coach. Next, we examine the false assumptions about injuries in rugby and discuss how coaches can make the game safer for their charges, and follow it up with the steps coaches need to take to become certified in the United States and Canada.

To round off this part, we concentrate on refereeing. We start with a discussion of what it takes to become a referee and then explain the certification process on both sides of the border.

Chapter 18

Coaching

Coaching isn't really a profession — rather, it's an obsession, attracting some of the strongest individuals in the game. In North America, because only a handful of lucky ones actually make a decent living from the job, your motivation to coach has to come from reasons other than financial gain.

The hard work that coaching requires is rewarded by the warm feeling of being an integral part of a team. You get an enormous amount of satisfaction when your team achieves greatness, or when a player you've nurtured is selected for a representative side and goes on to be successful. Numerous people rely on you and look to you for guidance. Their success is your success.

The effectiveness of the coach is paramount, because good players without a good coach make a mediocre team. Although rugby players often get all the kudos for strong performances, much of the credit should really go to the coach.

In this chapter, we explain the abilities and talents required of a coach. If you decide that the hot seat is just a little too hot for you, you can choose from a range of other jobs that give vital support to the team.

Grand Obsession: The Making of a Good Coach

Picture the scene: It's the end of the tournament, and the winning captain stands there clutching the trophy with a smile as wide as the Grand Canyon. An interviewer pushes through the crowd and shoves a microphone under the captain's nose, asking him to explain just how his team managed to do it. The inevitable response is, "I'd just like to thank our coach for getting us to where we are today." Cue to rapturous applause, hugs, and kisses all 'round.

Natural talent and a strong work ethic can take you a long way, but to make it to the very top in any sport you need the trained eye, dedication, and cajoling of a coach. Someone who cares enough about you to coax, nag, bully, and pester the very best out of you. Someone who's there to monitor your progress at that 5 a.m. training run, or to demand you do another 30 minutes on the tackle bag when all you want to do is have a shower and go home. Although sometimes you love to hate them, coaches can make all the difference between being good and being great.

You can figure out who the coach is at a rugby game pretty easily — it's the person patrolling the sideline, gesticulating at the players on the pitch, and shouting advice. He or she is invariably the most emotionally involved person at the ground.

A coach has three main areas of responsibility:

- ✔ Improving a team's skill level
- ✔ Improving the fitness, strength, and power of a team
- ✔ Motivating players so that the team reaches its potential

Improving skill levels

A coach should do everything possible to ensure the skill levels of all players improve as the season progresses. Obviously, skill levels vary from individual to individual, so you need to adjust your training program to make allowances for these variations. Your main aim, though, is to improve the overall skill level of the team as a unit.

To improve your team's skills, implement a challenging and mixed training schedule that maintains the interest of all the players. For example, you can mix it up by incorporating both skill drills and weight training into the regimen. Refer to Chapter 12 for some ideas on how to do this.

Getting your team fighting fit

A good team is a fit team, so incorporating fitness routines into your schedule in order to build up stamina is important (refer to Chapter 12 for details on how to devise the best exercise program for your team).

For your team to succeed, you need to develop a good, simple, and effective training program. When you have your training program set, stick to it. You also need to balance the amount of time you devote to fitness work at training with the need to teach skills and strategy. The best approach is to ask your players to do their primary fitness work on their own, so you can reserve session time for teaching technique and strategy.

Motivating your team

Motivating players depends largely on trust — and trust comes through openness and honesty. When you have to drop a player, don't make up feeble excuses or blame your decision on someone or something else. Players will quickly find out if you're bending the truth, so always be honest and upfront.

The members of any team talk to each other and look after each other's interests, both on and off the pitch. If you lose the trust of your players, your future with the team is limited because the players won't be motivated to listen to your advice or instruction. But if you earn the trust of your players, they'll do anything for you.

Motivation also involves saying the right words at the right time. You don't have to memorize the speeches of Winston Churchill; being positive during training and in the dressing room gets your players in the right frame of mind to get on the pitch and defeat the competition.

Never underestimate the importance of encouragement. As long as it's not overdone, praise can cure many ills. Guide your players and give them direction and purpose. When they finally master a particularly difficult drill, offer them praise, saying, "Well done!" Whatever support you give them will be returned to you on the rugby pitch. The art is to keep things simple without insulting the intelligence of your players.

A smart coach has to be prepared to mix the message up a bit to prevent the problem of players getting sick and tired of just one person ranting at them. Calling in experts from other fields, guest specialist coaches, or other authoritative voices, often inspires weary players.

Coaching Safety

Safety is a principal concern to everyone involved in rugby. It resonates throughout the laws of the game and directly affects coaches and players. Two very good reasons for this preoccupation with safety exist.

First, rugby is a team game where players repeatedly assemble in set formations. Scrums and lineouts require careful coordination and specific binding of several players to accomplish a collective goal. The combined force of several working together as one is much greater than a single player, and the laws of the game reflect this. Coaches are responsible for understanding, explaining, and enforcing the rules of the game.

Second, rugby is a full-contact sport where players must repeatedly tackle each other. A typical international match may have 150 tackles over 80 minutes of play. Being able to make tackles over and over again without injuring oneself is essential to playing the game. As such, defenders must develop proper tackling techniques, and ball-carriers have to know how to engage the tackler in contact and fall correctly. As the coach, ensuring that your players can perform the correct techniques so they can safely play the game is your job.

Keeping your players safe

The most important factor in preventing rugby injuries is coaching. Injuries often occur when new players are thrust into situations they're not prepared to handle. For example, coaches must avoid placing beginners in the front row of a scrum without first making certain they're ready for that particular position. A good coach needs to withstand the temptation to allow new players to participate in matches until they're sufficiently trained in all the skills required in a live game.

For North American coaches, special attention should be paid to teaching your players how to safely tackle in rugby. You can be sure that many of your players will arrive with bad habits picked up from playing gridiron. These bad habits are very difficult to overcome, which is why reviewing safe tackling in training on a regular basis is vital.

Former footballers will be keen to mix it up but are likely to approach the point of contact with their heads in dangerous positions. They will have been taught to use their helmets as a weapon and to get their heads across the face of the ball-carrier when making contact. This exposes the head, neck, and spine to serious injury. In rugby, the tackler is instructed to place her head alongside either hip of the ball-carrier (i.e., 'cheek-to-cheek') to prevent frontal collision with the head and neck. The shoulder is used as the main point of contact.

Another factor in preventing injuries is conditioning. Rugby is a demanding aerobic and anaerobic activity that requires short bursts of energy over long periods of sustained exertion. Football players aren't rugby fit, and without getting their one-minute rest breaks after every five seconds of action they falter quickly under the strain of continuous play. When players get fatigued, the first thing to suffer is mental concentration, which makes them more prone to fall inappropriately or enter contact situations with poor technique and get injured.

As a coach, your responsibility is to ensure that all your players are sufficiently experienced at their particular position, have a solid command of how to safely manage contact, and are in good physical condition before they take the pitch.

False assumptions and the truth about injuries in rugby

Parents often shy away from rugby at the thought of subjecting their children to the rigors of "football without pads." To understand the fundamental difference between rugby and football, a crucial distinction must be drawn here — rugby is a contact sport, whereas football is a collision sport.

Avoiding false security

Something curious happens when a player suits up in the protective armor worn by football players. With a helmet, shoulder pads, and hip, leg, knee, and other assorted pads covering nearly every inch of football players' bodies, a false sense of invulnerability results and is only heightened by gridiron coaches encouraging youngsters to throw their bodies around with reckless abandon. This is further reinforced by the football tackling technique, which places a premium on either stopping the ball-carrier cold in his tracks or driving him backward. All the padding and the emphasis placed on impacting the runner head-on combine to produce football collisions that are extremely forceful, violent, and unpredictable.

In rugby, players don't have a false sense of security brought on by being encased in body armor. Moreover, and especially at the youth level, safety in contact is a central teaching concern. Not having 10-pound crash helmets to hide within, rugby players are *not* taught to "put their head in there and smash the ball-carrier" like in football, but rather are specifically warned to keep their heads out of harm's way in the tackle situation.

Practicing how to tackle

The point of contact for the tackle in rugby is lower than in football, with the knees to thighs as the target, so the ball-carrier's head and shoulders are avoided by the tackler on impact. The goal of the tackle in rugby is also significantly different. In stark contrast to the football objective of not surrendering even an inch lest the offense make a first down, in rugby tacklers are taught to opt instead for the sure tackle rather than the big collision.

Also, new players are carefully introduced to tackling, starting first on their knees and then progressing to walking, jogging, and finally running only after they've demonstrated proper technique and are comfortable enough to advance to the next stage.

In football, all 22 players can hit each other at any time and from almost any direction, which encourages players to make huge "blindside hits" where the victim never sees it coming before getting absolutely smashed. In rugby, unless you're carrying the ball, about to receive it, or directly involved in contesting possession, players on the opposing team are prohibited from hitting you. This means that in rugby you have a much better sense of when and where the contact is coming from.

Knowing when you're at risk usually allows you to brace before impact and then fall in a manner so as to absorb the kinetic energy through the thick muscles of the back, buttocks, legs, or hips (as opposed to bouncing off the turf, as happens when you're taken by surprise). For these reasons, contact in rugby is much more controlled, predictable, and safe than in football.

Tackling a Tough Job

The coach has the onerous task of successfully putting together the most bewildering of jigsaw puzzles. He or she has to mold 15 very different, often diverse, and sometimes uncooperative individuals into one perfectly interlocking unit.

The coach has to be an adviser, mentor, psychologist, teacher, diplomat, comrade, leader in arms, master of subterfuge, butcher, baker, and candlestick maker. If you aspire to be a coach, you need to have

- **A superior understanding of the game:** Coaching skills are best gleaned from practical experience, because players soon figure you out if you don't know what you're talking about. Being a former player also helps, though you don't have to have reached superstar level! Many of the best rugby coaches were mediocre players who, during their playing days, developed a good grasp of the game, especially the laws, tactics, and strategies required to win matches.

- **A genuine love of the game:** You need to love the game and be fascinated by all its subtleties. Like your players, you must constantly add to your knowledge, because you'll never find yourself knowing everything about the sport. Rugby is a game that is continually evolving and throwing up quandaries that confound even the most brilliant of rugby minds.

- **A democratic approach:** As a coach, you need to be firm without being a dictator and have the ability to get along with and get the best out of a diverse array of characters. Many coaches fall into the trap of taking all the praise after a victory, or blaming everyone but themselves for a loss. Good coaches don't go on about how their team won because the players followed instructions, or lost because they didn't.

Coaching skills can't be acquired entirely from textbooks. Coaching is a mind game, a skill, and an art. You need initiative, creativity, intuition, and a vast amount of personal get-up-and-go. When you encounter 20 different problems at once, you'll soon discover whether coaching is for you.

The art of communication

One day at training, Welsh coach John Dawes told his players that if the blindside flanker was to break quickly from the scrum, the halfback would shout a code word beginning with the letter *p*. If the openside flanker was to break early, the code word would begin with the letter *s*. A scrum was set. Suddenly halfback Gareth Edwards screamed, "Psychology!"

Neither flanker moved.

Bob Dwyer, who coached Australia's national team in the '80s and '90s, described what is required to be a successful coach. According to Dwyer, a winning coach requires not the intellect of a nuclear physicist, but experience, common sense, imagination, and a very, very good memory. As far as Dwyer is concerned, if coaching is approached in the right vein, it's "an honorable profession."

If you want to become the coach of a winning team, the simplest approach is the best. Taking Bob Dwyer's criteria one by one, a successful coach has

- ✔ **Experience:** To know what to do when under pressure.

- ✔ **Common sense:** To stay levelheaded and calm no matter what the circumstances.

- ✔ **Imagination:** To come up with innovative moves and tactics.

- ✔ **An excellent memory:** To remember the weaknesses and strengths of the opposition so that tactics and strategies to exploit or counter them can be devised.

No one criterion is more important than the others. The key is finding the right balance that suits your individual style of coaching.

Deciding Whether Coaching Is for You

You won't really know if you have the capabilities to be a coach until you try it. You'll know you have the right temperament for the job when you find yourself on a muddy pitch on a Saturday morning teaching a bunch of children, juniors, young men, or young women — and enjoying it.

Deciding whether coaching is for you requires a bit of self-assessment. The first thing to consider is whether you enjoy being around other people — this is a vital characteristic of a rugby coach. In addition, you must

- ✔ Relate well and get along with just about everyone

- ✔ Know how to communicate with the many people relying on you to provide them with the right information

- ✔ Be even-tempered and able to handle the pressures of being in charge of up to 20 children (or adults who act like children)

Also ask yourself these questions: Do you love rugby? Do you like offering advice and helping other people? Are you prepared to work hard? Do you excel when under pressure? If the answer to all these is yes, then give coaching a go.

After you've been involved in a few games, you'll know whether coaching suits you — and whether you suit coaching. If you can successfully get the message across to teams that are difficult to organize and motivate, you just may have the coaching touch! (See Chapter 19 for information that will help you get into the coaching game and details about the different coaching opportunities that are available.)

You're Not Alone: Support Staff

A coach may sometimes feel like a rock, solitary and endlessly battered by the elements. At the bottom rung you find yourself doing all the jobs necessary to make a team run, but as you progress more help is available.

At higher levels, a strong network of support staff surrounds the head coach in order to spread the stress and responsibilities more evenly and to help the team reach its full potential. Such support occurs not just in the professional ranks but also at the top amateur clubs that are well organized and well funded.

For those who don't want the full-blown responsibility of being head coach, numerous other jobs are available that can be perfect for you. A support role can be just as important to the running of a rugby team as that of the head coach.

At the lower levels of the game, support staff are relatively few and no one gets paid. You usually find a head coach and maybe an assistant coach and a volunteer trainer. At the higher echelons of rugby, however, teams from the representative level and up are usually professional in their approach and the support staff can involve a cast of many.

Kieran Crowley: Kiwi-Canadian coach

Kieran Crowley (see figure) is part of a world-wide Kiwi coaching diaspora. New Zealand is a relatively small country (population 4.3 million), but they produce as much top rugby playing and coaching talent as any other nation on earth because they regard the sport as their national game; it's deeply embedded in the overall culture and psyche of the country. The problem is that since the game has gone professional, a severely limited number of head coaching jobs are available in New Zealand. Advancement up the ladder from ITM Cup to Super Rugby to national team coach is difficult to accomplish with so many viable applicants all looking to fill the same positions. So what's the solution for highly qualified men like Crowley? Head overseas.

Crowley has an outstanding resume, both as a player and as a coach. He played over 200 times for his province (Taranaki), played 19 tests as fullback for the All Blacks, was part of New Zealand's 1987 World Cup–winning team and the 1991 World Cup squad, and was also an excellent cricketer. He was an assistant coach for Taranaki for four years before holding the top job for five, during which time he kept an under-resourced province in the thick of the then National Provincial Championship hunt every year and made New Plymouth a daunting place to play for even the biggest provincial opponents. He also led the New Zealand Under-19 team to a world title in Belfast and served as an All Blacks selector. Unfortunately, there are numerous coaches in New Zealand who can claim similar laurels and have similar ambitions, so in order to advance his career and get some fresh rugby experiences, Crowley did what many other talented Kiwi coaches have had to do. After the 2007 Rugby World Cup, he took a head coaching job abroad.

Crowley has been a good fit for Canada. He's a relentless ambassador for the game and works hard at his job. He understands the nature of Canadian rugby because it's similar to what he faced at Taranaki — a strong and competitive forward pack and a back line that has maybe a little less speed and attacking acumen than their higher-ranked opponents. This lineup brings his teaching skill into play as he develops the Canadians into a team that may do some serious damage at Rugby World Cup 2011 in his homeland of New Zealand.

Coaching: Assistant coach

Most teams from club level upward have at least one assistant to the head coach. At a typical training session, teams eventually break up into two groups: forwards and backs. Because one person can't oversee both, more pairs of eyes and hands are needed.

The best teams usually have a three-person coaching structure, comprising a head coach, a forwards coach, and a backs coach. The forwards coach is usually a specialist at scrums, lineouts, rucks, and mauls. The backs coach has particular expertise in back-line strategies and moves and understands the requirements of all the positions from 9 to 15 (refer to Chapter 2 for details about all player positions). The three coaches work closely together and are usually responsible for selecting the team.

Someone who has played forward doesn't necessarily make a good forwards coach, nor does a former back automatically make the best backs coach. Sometimes an outsider's perspective is refreshing and more thorough because it comes from someone who has had to learn the intricacies of the position from the ground up without benefit of direct playing experience.

Coaching: Defense coach

In recent years, professional teams and international sides have employed coaches who have focused on improving the defensive strategies of the team. Often, these coaches are former *rugby league* players who, because of the tight defensive structure of their game, are able to pass along important tips on tactics that stop opponents. (Rugby league is a rugby derivative played with 13 players, popular only in Australia and northern England.)

Managing the team

Because the coach is primarily focused on the squad's performance on the field, an effective team manager is needed to make sure that everything runs smoothly off the pitch.

The duties of a team manager normally include ensuring that

- Training venues have been reserved and are ready for use.
- Players know exactly where they have to be and at what time.
- Transport for the team and support staff is organized.
- The team has the right playing and training equipment such as rugby balls, tackle bags, and kicking tees.

In addition, team managers need to have all the information that's relevant to their team on match day, including directions to the pitch, kickoff times, where the team will change, and who the match officials are.

The team manager has to attend to the needs of the coach and the players, which means becoming mother, father, nurse, and everyone's best friend. The role also encompasses that of psychotherapist, because the team manager's shoulder is the one players usually cry on when they have been dropped from the team or feel as though they have failed.

The team manager's job is probably the most demanding one within the organization because it requires an abundance of common sense, a tough hide, a willingness to work, and the ability to solve problems logically. Though the job can be a thankless one, many consider it to be very rewarding.

Training the team

At lower levels, a team probably won't have a trainer. At the representative level, however, teams often have their own fitness gurus.

The trainer puts the players through their drills during training and makes certain that when they're off the field they're involved in appropriate weight, exercise, and nutritional programs.

Massaging the players: The physiotherapist

For professional organizations, the physiotherapist works closely with the team doctor and trainer to ensure that injured players receive the right course of treatment. A rugby team's physiotherapist specializes in sports science, injury management, and treatment, and is an important member of the support staff.

When a player is injured on the field, the physiotherapist runs out onto the pitch with the doctor to treat him or her. Between them, they quickly assess the seriousness of the injury and decide whether or not the player should come off the field.

The physiotherapist may also pre-tape players on match day and at training sessions. This involves using bandages, braces, and tape to prevent new injuries from occurring or previous ones from reoccurring.

Calling on the team doctor

At the professional level the team doctor is a paid position, while at club level the doctor is usually a volunteer. In addition to working with the physiotherapist to assess injuries sustained during a match, the team doctor helps players recover from those injuries. The team doctor diagnoses injuries on the field and tracks the progress of the injured players while they recover. The coach relies on the team doctor to advise when an injured player has recovered and is available for selection.

In accordance with the *blood-bin rule* (which dictates that if a player is bleeding, he or she must leave the pitch and may not return until the bleeding stops), the team doctor is usually found doing quick stitch-up work on injured players during matches so they can get back into the game as quickly as possible.

Chapter 19

Coaching Certification and Advancement

*A*fter you make the fateful decision to become a rugby coach, a whole new world of agony and ecstasy awaits. Before you grab your clipboard and start barking orders at your new charges, you need to get properly certified as a coach. USA Rugby and Rugby Canada have similar but slightly different accreditation programs to assist both new and experienced coaches.

In this chapter, we describe the coaching certification process, discuss international resources to continue your training, and focus on issues presented by the various levels of the game.

Coaching Accreditation in the U.S.

USA Rugby's Coach Development Program (CDP) blends input from the International Rugby Board (IRB), Rugby Football Union (RFU), Positive Coaching Alliance (PCA), and the National Center for Sports Safety (NCSS) into one comprehensive system for training coaches. So whether you want to coach youngsters or old boys, the CDP is the place to start for USA-based coaches.

Looking at the Coach Development Program

The Coach Development Program (CDP) mixes study on the Internet with participatory conferences that give coaches the opportunity to tailor their development to the level of the players they're going to be coaching. Coaches first read information and are tested on it in an online environment — then they're checked at the workshops to see if they've fully grasped the material presented to them.

Currently, USA Rugby offers two different coach development workshops:

- **Introducing Rugby:** This two-day course enables coaches to present the game to total newcomers to the sport. Extra stress is placed on getting the basics down before moving on to the more complicated aspects of rugby. The course pays particular attention to safety in the scrum and in the tackle situation.

- **Developing Rugby Skills:** This two-day course is concerned with how to run training sessions, how to teach strategy, and how to formulate drills that give players the skills required to perform in the most rigorous of competitive arenas.

  If you aspire to coach a first-division club, a Super League side, or a representative team, then this is the course for you.

Getting certified

To gain certification, a coach has to be a current member of USA Rugby, complete the IRB's Rugby Ready online module, and complete the Positive Coaching Alliance's Double-Goal Coach online program. The final step is to attend a CDP workshop (see the preceding section for more about workshops). Workshops are held around the country, and if you preregister 15 days in advance, the cost is $180 for a full weekend of instruction.

If you pass all the tests and successfully demonstrate your understanding at a workshop, you get a three-year USA Rugby Coach Certificate. You can then get a three-year extension by attending other seminars, workshops, and forums sponsored by USA Rugby.

The USA Rugby website also has an extensive collection of coaching tools available for download. For more detailed info on all of USA Rugby's coaching programs and a schedule of workshops in your area, go to www.usarugby.org and click on the Coach the Game option in the middle of the left navigation bar.

GUTHRIE SAYS

Why I love coaching rugby

Professional coaches work for money. Amateur coaches like me do it despite the fact that our coaching commitments take us away from family and often result in having to pay out of pocket to meet club expenses. So how do we possibly justify such a drain on time and resources? The answer for me is very simple: I love the feeling I get when I'm standing on the sideline and witnessing my team dominate the opposition.

Domination in this sense doesn't come with any malice or mean-spirited behavior, because the ethos of rugby prevents me from being involved in any of that nonsense. Rather, domination means the ability to control your body movements on the pitch so when you go into contact, you win the physical contest every time. But before a coach can successfully teach those specific technical details, the primary challenge is to teach the concept of controlled aggression. In rugby, with 30 bodies looking for contact, losing your temper after receiving a big hit is very easy, and as soon as you do, your brain stops working. So before I can teach technical details, I have to get the players to master their own minds and be capable of

exercising self-control, no matter how hot the battlefield gets.

The seemingly conflicting notions of going full speed and being under control are the cornerstone of the game and what makes rugby such an effective device to change young people's lives for the better. After your players understand the idea of controlled aggression, then the fun really begins. You can load your players up with technical details, knowing all the while that they are capable of maintaining their composure during the heat of battle and that they will use superior technique to dominate the opposition.

The Oxy Olde Boys recently played a match where we won every single scrum and spoiled 100 percent of the opposition's lineout throws. Even though we won, I wasn't really that concerned about the score because we had completely dominated the other side. I love coaching rugby because it provides an opportunity to give something truly special: the crucial life skill of competing with everything you have while always retaining your sense of purpose and place.

Coach Training in Canada

Rugby Canada has a well-established and successful coach education program that's been in existence for more than 30 years. The National Coaching Certification Program (NCCP) consists of a partnership among Rugby Canada, the Coaching Association of Canada, and the Government of Canada through more than 60 provincial and territorial National Sport Federations.

The NCCP offers three coaching courses based on the different levels of the game:

- ✔ **Community Coach:** This course provides a basic introduction to the principles of play for non-contact rugby, and is designed for new coaches and parents of youth under 12.

- ✔ **Competitive Coach:** This course is for high school, university, and club-level coaches. Full contact is introduced, and the concepts of tactical and technical improvements are brought into focus. This course is for coaches responsible for novice- to intermediate-level players.

- ✔ **High-Performance Coaching:** This course is under development and is meant to serve Super League coaches and provide coaching talent for the Canadian national teams. At this stage, positional play, tactical awareness, and technical skills for the national team level are featured.

Go to www.rugbycanada.ca for more information and to register for the next coaching course in your neighborhood.

The International Rugby Academy

The International Rugby Academy (IRANZ) is based in Wellington, New Zealand, and offers a variety of coaching courses. IRANZ was founded by former All Black number 8 Murray Mexted, former All Black coach Laurie Mains, and legendary All Black hooker Sean Fitzpatrick. The list of course instructors is chock-full of former stars and rugby luminaries unmatched anywhere in the world.

For youth coaches, the Intermediate Coach Course is a five-day course that focuses on how to coach 13- to 15-year-olds. For club-side coaches, the Practical Coaching Course is an outstanding way to discover how the leading coaches in the oval world are preparing their teams. With an all-star staff of former All Blacks and Wallabies, and esteemed experts from other sports, the Practical Coaching Course is well worth the time and money required to attend the program. (We know this firsthand, as we were the first Americans ever to be certified by IRANZ!)

For coaches who aspire to a professional career in coaching, you have three additional course options to consider:

- ✔ Advanced Coaches' Course
- ✔ Club Development Course
- ✔ High-Performance Coaches' Course

All three are considered the gold standard among coaching academies around the world. These courses are held in conjunction with IRANZ's Elite Players Course at the Massey University Sport and Rugby Institute in Palmerston North, so the coaches can work with some of the world's leading talent in a practical setting. With a host of coaching and playing greats on staff, including Laurie Mains, Tony Gilbert, David Nucifora, Nick Mallett, Eddie Jones, Jim Telfer, Nick Farr-Jones, John Kirwan, and Josh Kronfeld providing instruction, these courses are the place to go for those seeking the best training available. See www.internationalrugbyacademy.com for more information on dates and custom courses.

Coaching Hatchlings to Eagles

Before the professional era in rugby began in the mid-1990s, almost all coaches from mini rugby to national teams were volunteers or lightly compensated individuals who served because they loved the game. In those days, nearly every coach began his or her progression up the coaching ladder by working with kids. By the time superior coaches had reached the top level, they had years of experience in dealing with all age groups and situations, cementing their knowledge of the sport in the process.

Sadly, this is no longer the case in many parts of the world, and coaching has become a big-money occupation. The desire for wins and publicity at the highest levels has attracted recently retired international stars to take the reins of professional clubs without the benefit of ever having coached before, while seasoned veterans of the coaching game look for work.

One place where that is not true is in North America. Only a very few coaches make a living running rugby teams, meaning the rest of the multitudes are still in it because they have a passion for the game. However, because rugby is a sport played mostly by collegians and adults in the United States and Canada, relatively few coaches have experience coaching at all levels and can appreciate the distinct demands of each rung on the rugby ladder.

Nurturing the youth

An area of phenomenal growth in North American rugby is the exploding number of children who are being exposed to the game. Unfortunately, more kids want to play than qualified coaches are available to handle them. Coaching youth players (aged 5–15) takes a tremendous amount of patience — not to mention a good rapport with nervous parents.

The key element to coaching youngsters of all ages is to always emphasize the fun aspects of the sport. When introducing the game, never put pressure to win on your juvenile charges. Rather, make the primary message you deliver be the inherent value of competition for its own sake. Instead of striving for victories, encourage players to enjoy themselves while obtaining the skills necessary to play the game at higher levels.

Having an oval ball in high school

The secondary school setting is rapidly becoming an important entry point for young rugby enthusiasts — which means the high school coach has to focus on bringing newcomers up to speed more quickly than does the youth coach, but without neglecting to instill a healthy respect for the sport itself in a competitive environment. Tackling, passing, and ball-handling drills should be supplemented with lectures on sportsmanship and the overall ethos of the game.

Getting the basics right at this stage is still far more important than wins and losses. No competitive person likes to lose, but knowing how to do so is every bit as important for teenagers as is winning with good grace. A coach must always highlight that rugby isn't a sport that tolerates trash-talking, showboating, or disrespectful behavior of any kind toward opponents, officials, spectators, or teammates.

The most beneficial concept that high schoolers can take away from rugby is the value of teamwork. By its very nature, rugby is a game that requires trust, communication, cohesion, and shared desire to achieve results. Practicing how to work with others and how to be selfless while putting the team first is an invaluable lesson for future success in academics, business, and life in general.

Corralling collegians

The collegiate arena is by far the most difficult milieu in which to coach because of the intensity of the participants involved. Most collegians are new to the sport, and many are attracted not just by the game but also by the social atmosphere that surrounds it on many campuses. Rugby at this level is often seen as an outlet for athletes who are no longer playing other organized sports, or as a chance to vent pent-up aggression. Channeling this energy in a positive direction is the duty of all college coaches.

As the game grows in North America, more and more collegiate programs are moving away from the traditional free-wheeling, hard-partying setup to a more structured and better-funded model. Coaches at places where this is the case have a distinct advantage over their colleagues at institutions where the sport is less organized.

Beyond simple instruction in technique and discipline, a critical component of coaching collegians is to impart the necessary information about the game's history, traditions, and worldwide camaraderie. Seeing themselves as part of a bigger picture when they take up the game breeds attention to issues like fairness and situation-specific sociability. A coach shouldn't try to temper the boisterousness and natural experimentation of these burgeoning adults, but rather help them to examine what sorts of behavior are appropriate in the rugby context on and off the pitch.

Catering to the clubs

The requirements for successful club coaches differ depending upon the division in which their teams play.

At lower levels, the coach must be a total club person, dealing with all the elements that affect the entire group. Recruiting players, fundraising, and various other managerial tasks can be a large part of this coach's job description. The ability to teach the basics is also necessary, because new players are the lifeblood of the future. Striking a balance at training between preparing a team to win and developing new talent from scratch is the toughest challenge for a coach at this level. Winning in the present is important, but continuously building and solidifying the entire club, including families and supporters, is the key to any coach's long-term success.

At the upper levels, coaches function more like their professional counterparts, concerned mainly with strategic decision making, training programs, and the upcoming weekend's opponent. A coach in this situation is usually a veteran of the sport who has taken on the challenge of guiding a squad of rugby-enthused individuals with a strong desire to perform and win. Coaches at this level can focus directly on the players because they usually have a support staff to take care of the day-to-day running of the club.

Chapter 20

Managing the Game: The Referee

*T*he most important person at any rugby match is the referee — without the services of this crucial official, the game can't be played. Despite being the whipping boys for the media at the international level, and the victims of ill-informed derision from sideline hecklers on local pitches, referees are almost always unbiased adjudicators and conscientious guardians of the sport they love.

In this chapter, we look at what it takes to be a referee, the responsibilities for those of us who decide to join this honorable society, how to begin refereeing, and how to climb your way up the appointment ladder in North America.

The Responsibility of the Whistle

According to the laws of the game, the referee is the sole judge of fact and law during a rugby match. To properly discharge that awesome portfolio of absolute authority, a referee must be able to fulfill the requirements in five areas of responsibility:

✔ Knowledge

✔ Consistency

✔ Communication

✔ Temperament

✔ Fitness

Knowledge

Referees must know the laws of the game. Now, that doesn't mean they have to memorize the entire law book before ever taking up the whistle, but something more than a passing familiarity with the dictates of the lawmakers is essential when starting out. Knowledge of the most frequently enforced laws and all the potential choices when things go wrong promotes trust in the referee among the players being controlled.

A referee should strive to know more than any player who is subject to his or her decisions for the simple reason that it bolsters confidence in calling the game. Knowledge is indeed power. If referees are uncertain about the law, it makes them hesitant in blowing the whistle (and nothing is worse than an indecisive referee). The process of becoming a referee, which we get to later in this chapter, provides for constant learning and evaluation. All good referees take quiet pride in their knowledge of the law and don't feel the need to lord it over their less-informed rugby brethren.

Consistency

Although it would be ideal if every referee called a match in exactly the same way, inevitably different styles and slightly varying interpretations develop around the world. At the international level, the International Rugby Board (IRB) strives to minimize these deviations as much as possible by careful assessment of all test match whistle-blowers. At the other end of the spectrum, local referees have less supervision and training and are thus more likely to vary in their performance from week to week. The goal for any individual referee is to work toward personal consistency.

By consistency, we mean calling the game in the same fashion from start to finish. A penalty for not releasing the ball in the tackle has to be the same for both teams in all situations, whether it is in the first or 80th minute. Nothing is more frustrating for players than to perform an action at one point in the game and have it be legal, then to be called for a penalty for the same action later on in the match. Consistency breeds respect, because even if a player disagrees with a call, if it is always called that way she can adapt her game to reflect the referee's interpretation.

Communication

Until very recently, the only sound that came out of a referee during a match was the high-pitched blast of the whistle. An occasional chat with a touch judge or a serious offender was basically the extent of their conversational output. In the modern game, however, the referee is expected to manage the game by being a consummate communicator.

In professional and test rugby, almost all referees are wired for sound. Listening in on their chatter for 80 minutes is like hearing a condensed version of what a preschool worker must sound like when talking to young children. The referee constantly identifies phases of play, admonishes potential wrong-doers, gives warnings, and signifies that everything is okay when players follow his or her commands. For example, a common refrain may be, "Ruck formed, no hands, leave it alone 7, that's fine, play on." By communicating what they see happening and calling this out to the players, fewer infractions are likely to be committed and thus fewer stoppages in play occur, which is better for the game. Because players are now coached to actively listen to the ref's directives, smart players are avoiding penalties, which keeps the game flowing.

The referee also has the responsibility of being a teacher for less experienced teams at the lower levels. New players are often more aggressive than they are rugby-smart, and it's always better for a referee to help these players understand the laws than it is for the other team to show them the consequences of their actions in nonverbal ways; this is especially important at the high school and collegiate levels. Players can learn more in one match with a good referee than in a dozen training sessions. No matter how many times a particular concept is taught at practice by a coach, when a referee provides real-time direction during live competition of what players should and shouldn't be doing, understanding is greatly accelerated.

Temperament

Not everyone is cut out for refereeing. A referee must be intelligent, tolerant, calm under pressure, and approachable and have a genuine love for the game. These qualities are needed to maintain a positive relationship with the players without pretending they're your best friends or, alternatively, treating them like naughty schoolchildren. Belligerence and arrogance are the two least becoming qualities in referees — those who have these characteristics in abundance give the rest of their colleagues a bad name.

Referees must always remember their role is to be fair and impartial, to let the players decide the outcome, and to call the game as they see it without resorting to bias based on reputation or previous misconduct. As a player, seeing a certain referee turn up at a match and thinking, "This ref hates us" is horrible. What you want them to feel is, "This ref's fair." By making decisions dispassionately and without personal animosity, a referee builds a reputation for fairness that goes a long way when trying to control 30 agitated rugby players.

The highest compliment that can be paid to any referee is to go unnoticed at the end of a match. The best referees are stewards of the game who don't try to impose themselves or their beliefs on a particular contest.

Fitness

Referees can satisfy all four of the preceding criteria, but if they can't keep up with play enough to see what's going on, it won't do them any good. If they're able to run for 80 minutes without tiring, they're more likely to maintain mental sharpness throughout the entire match.

Because most refs are former players, they have an initial sense of what it takes to run for an hour and a half with very few chances to rest. What they don't realize, at least until they take charge of their first few matches, is how much extra running referees do because they are constantly chasing the ball. As a forward or a back, few moments exist in a match where you continually chase after the ball, but that's exactly what a referee has to do the whole time.

Becoming a Ref in the States

A simple fact in the United States is that more rugby matches are played every week than there are qualified referees to officiate them. The result is that rugby as a whole suffers because usually the younger players (who are most in need of quality refereeing) are the ones who are neglected. Fortunately, though, the upside of this chronic shortage is that anyone who thinks they may want to take up the responsibility of the whistle has ample opportunity to give it a go. If you've ever thought you can do better than the person out there calling the game, our advice is to get started studying your law book and buy yourself a whistle.

Getting started

Before you head out onto the pitch for the first time as a whistle-blower, watching a fair bit of rugby on TV and in person is helpful so that you can at the very least be familiar with how to position yourself at set pieces and breakdowns. The next step is to volunteer to referee a second side game or a scrimmage for your club or a team in your area (very few offers to referee are ever turned down; we think the last one was in 1982). You'll be assigned second side matches, which give players who didn't make it into the first team a chance to play, so that a more experienced referee can watch and help explain any questions afterward.

The first designation you receive is *associate referee,* which is your title until you get some experience and demonstrate a working knowledge of the laws of the game. After you're evaluated a few times by higher-ranking referees, you're assigned to the entry-level C panel at the rank of C-3. This begins a process of evaluation and hopefully progression up the refereeing ladder from the C to the B panel, and all the way up to the A panel.

Dana Teagarden: International referee

Dana Teagarden is America's most recognized international referee. Growing up in rural Kansas, she was an outstanding student and an exceptional athlete who earned an appointment to the United States Air Force Academy, where she discovered the game that would change the course of her life. After breaking her ankle and being cut from the basketball team, she went looking for a new sport to play and found rugby. Her athleticism made her an immediate force, and she was named a Most Valuable Player of the USAFA side that won the first Women's Collegiate National Championship. Early on, she was a student of the laws of the game and admittedly had little patience for referees who weren't up to her standard. As is the story with many referees, her complaining led directly to her to taking up the whistle when a mentor thrust her into a match and challenged her to do better because they were tired of listening to her!

Teagarden is a civil engineer by degree — she's worked on projects ranging from commercial construction to the International Space Station — and her career took her all over the U.S. Wherever she was working, she got involved in rugby, often playing, reffing, and coaching in the same weekend. Her playing ability got her into the National Player Pool, but being tagged as a utility woman — she played number 8, flanker, flyhalf, and fullback — kept her from earning an international cap.

After taking a five-year break from the sport, Dana returned to it in 2005 and focused solely on refereeing. After years of dividing her attention, Dana was able to concentrate on being the best referee she could be and her efforts paid off. She made her international debut at sevens and fifteens in the 2005–06 season, and while in charge of the 11th-place final at the Women's Rugby World Cup 2006, she drew the attention of IRB referee's manager Paddy O'Brien, who asked that she be appointed to the IRB Sevens in San Diego in 2007. She again performed impressively, with her speed and handling of men's matches, and has been on an upward trajectory ever since.

The respect she's earned is reflected in her assignments. She's been one of the busiest women's international referees in the world, and was the first woman to be appointed to referee a full men's test match in 2010, but even that level of accomplishment has only driven her to work harder to improve. Above all, though, Dana truly loves the game. She says, "The reason I love rugby is there's a place for everyone who wants to be part of the rugby family. It doesn't matter how big or small you are, boy or girl, young or old. You can play, coach, referee, or help administrate — if you choose to be part of the family, then you're accepted and respected for what you bring to the table. And you have friends, and friends of friends, the world over."

Another option is to attend a refereeing clinic before picking up a whistle. These clinics are put on by USA Rugby around the country and are a good introduction to the basics of how to manage a match. The introductory-level, or Level 1, referee course Introduction to Officiating is designed for anyone who wants to ref but hasn't had any formal training and hasn't already been around the game for a long time as a player or coach. The Level 1 course costs only $50 U.S., takes one day to complete, and allows you to jump up the ladder and get certification as a C-3 referee.

Moving up

As you gain experience and are assessed, you can be moved up from C-3 all the way to C-1. To move from C-1 to the B-3 designation, you have to take a Level 2 referee course. This course is good preparation for referees who want to control important local matches, or maybe even more.

The Level 2 clinic is called Developing Officiating Skills, takes place over 16 hours across two days, costs $100 U.S., and is a prerequisite before a referee can advance up the ranks to the B-3 classification. The higher you rise, the more likely you are to receive assignments to referee in top matches, usually among the highest divisional teams in your area. If your performance, desire, and fitness warrant the move, you'll eventually be elevated through the B panel.

The progression through the B panel is much more rigorous than the C panel. You'll be required to travel and referee outside your home area, and you have to receive above-grade evaluations from a national evaluator.

Reaching the top

If you have the skills, knowledge, on- and off-field demeanor, *and* you're in good enough physical shape, you'll receive appointments to referee national-level games and show your stuff to the top decision makers. If they like what they see, you may be moved up to the national panel, or A panel, and then be eligible to receive test match appointments.

To reach A-3 or above, you have to take the Level 3 referee course. The Level 3 referee course is called Analysis and Preparation and requires 32 hours of instruction. To receive Level 3 accreditation, attendees need to attend all course modules, get two passing-grade practical assessments, pass an open-book laws exam, and prepare a season plan. This highly sophisticated certification involves studying the theories underpinning the laws and is designed for referees who aspire to rise to the top of the craft. Very few referees ever gain this distinction, and the ones who do seem born for the job. Remember, though, that refereeing at any level is a rewarding experience and provides immeasurable service to the game.

To find a referee course in your area, go to www.usarugby.org and click on the Officiate the Game option in the left navigation bar.

Who's the ref?

On a classic junket to the Rugby World Cup 1999 semifinals with Brown, I ran into Welsh international referee Derek Bevan in the media accreditation area before the first semifinal. We had interviewed him in 1998 in Wales as part of our buildup to the 1999 tournament, and I was impressed by his graciousness and wanted to let him know we really appreciated his taking the time to work with us. He recognized me, and after exchanging pleasantries — oblivious to the fact that he was in charge of the impending match — I asked him which team he was picking to win the first semi.

In typical Welsh fashion, without so much as uttering a word, he smiled almost imperceptibly, and just then the IRB referee liaison thrust himself between us and directly declared, "Of course, *ahem,*" clearing his throat, and continuing, "it would be inappropriate for the match referee to make any comment whatsoever on the outcome of the match." Having realized my gaffe, I immediately retreated from the engagement nodding apologetically, knowing that further exchange of words would only cause greater harm and embarrassment.

Flash forward to one week later at the World Cup final in Cardiff: I was walking through the stands before the game and noticed Mr. Bevan in the stands holding court, telling a rather animated story to a fellow ref. Just then, Derek looked right at me, pointed, and said, "And that's the guy!" Both refs laughed heartily, as I forced an embarrassed smile and waved back, acknowledging my identification as the subject of the story. Ever since then, I've made it a point to check all the referee assignments, which is a good idea if you want to prevent the joke being on you!

Picking Up the Whistle Up North

Taking up the honorable profession in Canada is similar to doing so in the United States, with the main differences being terminology and organizational structure. All ten provincial unions are responsible for developing their own referees, and every effort is made to provide consistency in evaluation.

Referees in Canada are designated as *introductory* until they receive their first evaluation, when they are moved up to C-3. This follows the same international structure that is also employed by the Americans, all the way up to the A panel, or Canada panel. Advancement is by individual assessment, and referees also have the opportunity to enhance their skills at Level 1, 2, and 3 clinics conducted at varying intervals across the country. The point of entry for would-be Canadian match officials is the Level 1 course titled Introducing Officiating, followed by the Level 2 course, Developing Officiating Skills, and the Level 3 course, Coaching of Match Officials.

One area where Rugby Canada differs from its southern neighbors is in its aggressive push to recruit new referees. Referees have tended to come from the ranks of retired players who take up the whistle to stay involved in the game when their playing days are over. Referees' societies throughout Canada are now encouraging virtually any young player who shows the slightest inclination toward refereeing to consider making a career switch at an earlier age, potentially making it to the international level with a whistle in the mouth rather than in the ear.

Part V
Following the Game: The Informed Fan

POLAR LEAGUE RUGBY FANS ARE PARTICULARLY APPRECIATIVE OF A GOOD JUMPER IN A LINEOUT.

©RICHTENNANT

In this part . . .

After you know the basics and where you fit into the rugby food chain, you probably want to know where you can get more rugby information, what media outlets can improve your knowledge of the game, and how to get the most enjoyment out of watching it being played.

In this part we detail the various options for watching the game on television and following it on the Internet and suggest which channels and Web sites to visit if you want to catch all the action from around the world. We also take a look at the media personalities involved in bringing the game to the viewing public and explore some of the jargon unique to the game.

Then it's off to the match itself, where you discover how to find a contest to watch and how to find your place in the crowd. We finish with a survey of all the best sources of rugby information.

Chapter 21

Get Your Game: Rugby on TV

*R*ugby television programming can be difficult to find. But don't worry, because we've got all the details on where and when you can watch on six different TV channels across Canada and the U.S.A. In this chapter, we survey access to rugby programming in North America so you know where to go to get your weekly dose of the game they play in heaven.

Rugby on Television in the U.S.A.

Driven by the explosive growth of rugby and its inclusion in the 2016 Olympics, the sport is now more widely available on TV than ever before. Unfortunately not much free rugby exists on TV yet, but if you're willing to pay a bit every month you can watch plenty of rugby programming:

✔ **Fox Soccer Plus:** This channel was launched in March 2010, and in its first year it showed more than 300 rugby matches from a number of top competitions. Its current lineup includes Aviva Premiership, Heineken Cup, Magners League, Amlin Challenge Cup (the second tier of the European Cup), and LV Cup matches. In addition, the channel airs the magazine show *Rugby World* on a seasonal basis. Fox Soccer Plus is available on most major satellite and cable providers in the United States, and costs per month vary by system. FSP also offers an online subscription component through FoxSoccer.tv, which carries both live and on-demand action from the leagues it covers.

✔ **NBC/Universal Sports:** The network that shows the Olympics has ramped up its coverage recently. NBC has broadcast both live and delayed games from the U.S. leg of the Sevens World Series and also the Collegiate Rugby Sevens. It also plans to offer selected matches from the 2011 Rugby World Cup. The network's cable partner, Universal

Sports, shows the Sevens World Series, the IRB-produced weekly show *Total Rugby*, and select USA Rugby test matches and plans to show the rest of the Rugby World Cup. Episodes of *Total Rugby* and highlights coverage of the Sevens World Series are also available for free online. Universal Sports is part of the standard package on Time Warner Cable, but isn't available on DirecTV or Dish Network.

- **DirecTV:** This satellite giant purchased broadcasting rights to the SANZAR (South Africa, New Zealand, and Australia Rugby) package and is currently offering its customers live 2011 Super Rugby. It also owns the 2011 Tri Nations rights but hasn't yet indicated what its plans are for offering that series to customers.

- **BBC America:** In 2010 and 2011, BBC America showed one match per round from the Six Nations Championship, focusing mainly on England's matches but occasionally showing other important ones. BBC America is available on Time Warner Cable, DirecTV, Verizon FiOS, Dish Network, and AT&T U-verse.

Rugby on Television in Canada

Like in the U.S., rugby on television in Canada is a relatively new product. Beginning with the 1999 Rugby World Cup, Canadian rugby fans have been able to watch weekly rugby programming. Two national cable networks offer rugby programming in Canada on a regular basis:

- **Setanta Sports:** This Dublin-based company offers a wide variety of subscription rugby programming for Canadian viewers. The network covers the Six Nations, the Tri Nations, Super Rugby, the Magners League, the Aviva Premiership, Northern versus Southern Hemisphere tests, the Currie Cup, and the ITM Cup. Setanta Sports is available through most national Canadian satellite and cable providers, as well as through numerous regional providers. The network also offers Setanta-i online on a pay-per-view basis.

- **TV5:** Part of the basic cable package for most Canadians, TV5 delivers programming in French. It covers all France's games in the Six Nations live, plus periodic coverage of the French domestic competition and the Top 14, as well as selected Heineken Cup matches featuring French teams. TV5 also airs a weekly magazine program featuring French domestic club highlights on Saturday mornings.

Because many of the Canadian professionals play for French clubs, the weekly highlights on TV5 allow Canadian fans to follow national team players who ply their trade abroad.

Speaking the Language

Rugby has its own unique language. All the major rugby-playing nations of the world have developed their own lexicon of rugby terminology that is used by fans and the media alike. (Without a domestic rugby vocabulary of our own, North Americans revel in this cornucopia of linguistic diversity.) Because 99 percent of televised rugby originates outside North America, before you can understand and fully enjoy foreign play-by-play, you need a short course in the lingo that's used to describe the game and its traditions.

The history of rugby on TV in North America

In the dark ages prior to 1995, rugby was a very closely held secret in North America. Unless you played the game in college or lived in one of the few pockets of rugby activity around the country, chances are you wouldn't have the slightest clue about the game. ABC's Wide World of Sports broadcast a few rugby snippets in the early 1970s, and ESPN provided limited coverage of the 1987 Rugby World Cup and the Hong Kong Sevens, but other than those isolated instances if you wanted to watch rugby on TV the lack of access left you crying in your beer.

If you wanted to watch a live match, your only option was to go to an English pub that carried closed-circuit viewing of the Five Nations. Other than those ten matches per year, you couldn't watch rugby from the comfort of your own living room. Rugby enthusiasts were forced to have their overseas friends make recordings, ship them to North America, and then get them converted from PAL (European format) to NTSC (North American format). In total, it may have cost you $75 U.S. just to watch a match that was two weeks old by the time it arrived.

That all changed in February 1995 with the launch of *Championship Rugby,* North America's first and only weekly rugby program, which delivered the best rugby from around the world. In 1998, *Championship Rugby* became part of the Fox Sports family of properties and continued as the voice of rugby for more than 500 two-hour programs until its final episode in December 2003, when it was replaced by *The Rugby Club. The Rugby Club* program ran throughout 2004, and when Fox Sports World was rebranded as the Fox Soccer Channel in February 2005, rugby was dropped entirely from the new channel lineup under the soccer-only format. Rugby returned to Fox in 2010 with the creation of Fox Soccer Plus, which currently shows various international competitions plus the weekly magazine show *Rugby World.*

Since becoming televised in North America, rugby has grown by leaps and bounds. Television has been the vehicle, but the reality is that the game has sold itself to North Americans. USA Rugby's membership has grown from 21,000 to nearly 100,000 registered players since rugby has been shown on TV.

Rugby's TV jargon glossary

RUGBY JARGON

The particular dialect of rugby-speak depends on the country of origin and the commentators who are calling the game. And while this list is by no means intended to be exhaustive in its scope, here's a sampling of a few rugby terms and phrases you may hear and what they really mean in plain English:

✔ **"They're going to keep it in tight":** The team in question is going to play a conservative game plan and try to keep the ball in the forwards to maintain possession.

✔ **"It's getting a bit niggly out there":** Some of the players are beginning to lose their discipline and are stamping, punching, or otherwise communicating their unhappiness with each other.

✔ **"She's having trouble finding touch":** The player kicking the ball is having difficulty with her accuracy, and the ball isn't going out of bounds where she wants it to.

✔ **"He launches a huge Garryowen!":** The kicker has punted a high ball in the middle of field for his chasers to pursue and hopefully regather.

✔ **"Monstered in the tackle":** The ball-carrier is flattened by the tackler and loses control of how the ball is presented for the next wave of attack.

✔ **"They're really working hard in the engine room":** A team's locks are putting in a mighty effort.

✔ **"That's a bit one-eyed":** Someone is able to see things only from a single perspective.

The best of the commentators

Having had the distinct pleasure of watching and then rewatching almost every single rugby match that's been on television over the past 16 years, we naturally have our own list of the best rugby commentators:

✔ **Grant Nisbett (Sky, New Zealand):** Nisbo is the world's best play-by-play man. He's cool and impartial under pressure, is technically sound in laws knowledge, and communicates a genuine love for the game. A real class act and consummate professional behind the mic.

✔ **Miles Harrison (British Sky Broadcasting):** Miles is the best of the Northern Hemisphere, but tends toward hyperbole at times. Best when paired with Stuart Barnes.

✔ **Greg Clark (Fox, Australia):** Clarkie is smooth as silk at calling all the action and has a solid command of the finer points of the game. He's the best of the Aussies by a wide margin.

- **Tony Johnson (Sky, New Zealand):** He communicates the excitement of the match without being partial and is extremely well prepared. He gets the hard names right and possesses a wealth of knowledge about the game.

- **Ken Laban (Sky, New Zealand):** Ken has developed a unique approach to play-by-play where he actually describes what the players are trying to do while on attack and in defense, plus he gets all the tough names right and blends his extensive knowledge from league and union.

- **Andy Capostagno (SuperSport, South Africa):** Andy is the most balanced of the South African commentators and delivers the call with a relaxed, friendly demeanor and soothing voice.

- **Joel Stransky (SuperSport, South Africa):** The 1995 Springbok RWC hero is finally coming into his own as an in-studio analyst, but still has a way to go on his color commentary.

- **Justin Marshall (Sky, New Zealand):** A newcomer to broadcasting after an outstanding rugby career, he explains the game from a player's perspective and catches little things that others miss.

- **Phil Kearns (Fox, Australia):** Phil is not afraid to speak his mind, and has plenty of opinions to share. He's a no-nonsense type who relishes the battle up front but tends to be a bit one-eyed if the Wallabies or Waratahs are involved.

- **Hugh Bladen (SuperSport, South Africa):** A true icon in the Republic, Bladen's been around since tries were only worth three points. He has an encyclopedic memory of South African rugby gathered from calling virtually every Springbok test over the past 40 years.

Chapter 22

Spectating and Staying in Touch with Rugby News

Spectating at a rugby match can range from standing on the sideline, cheering on your local club side, to sitting way up at the back of a stadium, rooting your national side to victory. Regardless of the setting, rugby crowds are some of the best behaved and most pleasant in all of sport.

In this chapter, we give you advice on how to get the most from your visit to a rugby match and become the model rugby spectator. For those of you who really want to get into the spirit of things, we offer some tongue-in-cheek tips on how to impress those around you with your incredible rugby knowledge. We also provide a vast array of resources to bring you up to speed with rugby happenings in the U.S., Canada, and around the world.

Finding a Match to Watch

Congratulations — you're about to take the plunge and actually attend a rugby match. Rugby is one of the most user-friendly sports, generally attracting an intelligent, passionate crowd who believe that watching rugby at any level is a wonderful treat.

If you're interested in attending a club match but don't know if a team exists in your area, a little online searching can fill the void. For the United States, go to www.usarugby.org, and in Canada, go to www.rugbycanada.ca to find a club near you.

Another option is to use any of the major search engines to find a local club. Type "local rugby unions in _____," filling in the blank with your state, province, or geographic region. You'll end up with a long list of choices to at least give you a starting point to track down a club. Most union sites have links to their clubs, or contact details for a responsible party who can supply further information. Most club sites provide roughly the same team-specific details.

To find out when and where international and representative matches will be played in Canada and the U.S., check out the above-mentioned Web sites for dates, venues, and how to purchase tickets.

Blending In with the Crowd

Whether you're going to watch a full-blown test match or a local Division II encounter, the spectator areas at rugby games are safe and suitable places for a family outing. Even at 80,000-seat stadiums in rugby hotbeds, the atmosphere in the crowd is still relatively restrained and positive.

In this section, we give you guidance on how to behave so as not to upset other spectators. We also give advice on the right kind of clothes to wear to maximize your comfort.

Following rugby etiquette

Rugby definitely has an unwritten code of conduct for its fans. Remember, players, supporters, and everyone involved with the game are rightly proud of the fact that rugby retains its civilized nature even in the age of professionalism. So that you know what's acceptable and what's not at a rugby match, we've put together a few words of wisdom that may save you from embarrassment:

✔ **Don't be afraid to ask questions:** If you're a novice fan, feel free to query your neighbor about things you don't understand that are happening in the match. Most rugby fans love nothing better than to help out newcomers with the intricacies of the game because it allows them to show off their superior level of expertise. If you feel like making comments of your own, you should at least sound well-informed. You don't need to spout Shakespeare; initially, your immortal lines can include phrases like, "Excellent tackle" and "Great take in the lineout." The section on how to sound like an expert later in this chapter can also give you some ideas for comments that sound deep and meaningful.

✔ **Criticize, but don't denigrate, the referee:** Taking issue with the referee's decisions is okay — but making him or her the target of verbal abuse isn't. Demonstrating regard for the referee shows you're a spectator who understands the traditions that make rugby the noble game it is. In other sports referees are called all sorts of horrible names, but in rugby the referee is a figure of respect, which is why the players always address the person in charge as "Sir" or "Ma'am."

✔ **Show respect for the opposition:** The good rugby fan applauds the opposition when they do something impressive. Friendly, civilized behavior makes the occasion more enjoyable — even if your team is losing.

✔ **Maintain decorum:** When an opposition player is about to take a shot at goal, be silent. Don't imitate the idiots who try to distract the goal kicker. Such antics are frowned upon — most rugby spectators believe rugby is an intellectual pursuit to be treated as a thinker's game, not as an opportunity for hooligans to misbehave.

✔ **Check the allegiances of those around you very carefully:** If you're among fans of the same team, you can get away with a lot more than if you're among supporters of the other team. If you find yourself surrounded by people supporting the opposition, be more circumspect in your comments.

✔ **Buy someone a beer (where available):** If you go off to buy a beer, ask the person next to you if he or she wants one. This gesture will instantly make you a friend. Having friends around you at a rugby match gives you a nice feeling of solidarity and the opportunity to exchange views on the game.

Dressing for the occasion

A good choice at any rugby match is rugby-related gear like jerseys or hats, either purchased from online retailers or obtained from your local club. These items allow you to declare your rooting proclivities without saying a word. Some fans believe that the height of fashion is to deck themselves out in clothes that scream out their rugby allegiances (see Figure 22-1).

Figure 22-1:
Showing their true colors, rugby fans cheer their team on.

The best clothes to wear to a rugby match combine a bit of fashion with a lot of function. You need to be wearing something that can protect you from whatever type of weather a rugby afternoon or evening can bring. Rugby in many parts of the United States and Canada is a spring and fall sport, so you often have to confront chilly or wet weather. Dressing appropriately for the weather conditions usually means more clothes rather than fewer. Don't forget that, as a spectator, taking off layers of clothes if you get too warm is easier than trying to get warm when you haven't got anything else to put on. If in doubt about the weather, at the very least take a waterproof jacket.

Spectating across North America

The best place to watch a game is near the halfway line, because a spot here gives you a good view of the whole field. For test matches, the seats at the halfway line are the most expensive. Another good place that affords a fine view of the action is near the 22-meter lines.

At the club level you can generally follow the ball up and down the sidelines (taking care to stay back far enough to let the touch judge have unfettered access), so you're always in position to see what's going on in every situation.

Going to watch a test match

A *test match* occurs when the top representative teams of two national unions meet in a game sanctioned by the International Rugby Board (IRB). This is the elite level of competition — playing for one's country is a rugby player's highest honor. Various teams around the world may have adopted nicknames like the All Blacks and the Wallabies, but make no mistake — when they meet it's New Zealand versus Australia, direct country-to-country combat.

A test match, or *full international,* is marked by the playing of both national anthems prior to kickoff and the presence of a neutral-country referee. All players who see action in a test are awarded a *cap* for their efforts. Many teams around the world mark the occasion of a player's first appearance for his or her country by actually giving out a ceremonial cap, as was done in years past.

Test matches can be part of a larger competition like World Cup qualifying or the Pan-American tournament, or as part of a tour by the visiting side. In one-off tests, sides meet on an irregular basis as determined by the IRB. This is usually done to bolster the lesser teams by having them play rugby power-houses from around the globe.

Tests in North America are still generally played in smaller stadiums, but in rugby-mad countries they can be held in mammoth venues. The all-time record for a test was set in Sydney in 2000, when an Australia versus New Zealand Tri Nations clash drew 109,874 spectators! Whether a test is attended by that number or several hundred die-hards, the atmosphere is special because the teams are playing first and foremost for national pride.

Enjoying the club experience

If you're geographically challenged and unable to make it to a test in North America, don't fret. Likely plenty of other rugby is being played somewhere near you. The beauty of watching matches at the local level is that crowds are rare and you can follow the game in its purest form.

Getting a close-up view of the action at club level

A great way to familiarize yourself with the game and enjoy rugby in its essence is to attend a local club game. In most divisions it's free, but at the semi-professional level of Super League in the States and Canada a reason-able entrance fee is usually charged. Standing close to the action, you get a better appreciation of the intensity and physicality of the game. This is the ideal way to get to know the referee's signals and discover what the different players actually do, what is required for each position, and how players react to different tactics. Overall, being close to the sideline helps you get a good feel for the game.

Enjoying the camaraderie of local clubs

At a club match, everyone is there because they love rugby or someone play-ing it. This is where you find the really passionate rugby supporters who follow their club through thick and thin. Clubs rely on good community spirit and volunteers for their very existence. Quite apart from the outcome of the game, a successful match day means everyone has enjoyed themselves in a welcoming environment.

The atmosphere at club games is generally amiable, and you quickly feel at home. Faster than you can say "kick for touch," someone is usually selling raffle tickets to help make money for the club. Pitch in and buy a ticket or two — in your own small way you may be helping develop a club champion who can eventually end up representing the United States or Canada on the world stage.

Spectators are almost always welcome at the post-match function, where the two teams and their supporters get together to share a beer or three and talk about the game. This is when you can sense the genuine bonds that develop in this sport.

Sounding like a rugby expert

You really need only a few phrases to sound like a rugby genius. After the first scrum, turn to your neighbor and say, "That tight-head will have to watch himself, because he's pushing in at an illegal angle." We guarantee you that the person next to you will turn, look at you as if you're a sage old hand, and nod her head. You'll get this reaction even if what you say isn't happen-ing, because no one can really tell if the tight-head prop is pushing into the scrum at the wrong angle — it's such a fine line of judgment. (We discuss scrums in detail in Chapter 8.)

Another crucial phrase to remember is, "They're offside." No matter which team you're following, or whether the opposition is offside or not, every person in the crowd *believes* the opposition is offside, and just loves tell-ing the referee about it. If you say "They're offside" at various well-timed moments of the game, you're sure to get knowing nods from those around you. (Refer to Chapter 6 for an explanation of the offside law.)

All kidding aside, if you're in doubt about the kind of reception your com-ments may attract, just applaud when everyone else applauds and you'll be safe.

Touring Overseas

Touring to far-distant places is a great rugby tradition. Due to the strong international flavor of the game, any club, no matter what level, is usually able to find plenty of overseas clubs willing to offer a match. So if someone in your club is up to the task, a fascinating itinerary can be organized, enabling players to discover the delights of playing and watching the game in some of the most unexpected rugby pockets of the world.

A tour can be organized around a major event like the Rugby World Cup or a British and Irish Lions tour, or undertaken for no reason other than that everyone wants to get out of the country and play some rugby. When and where you go is a decision for individual clubs, but certain elements are common to successful touring.

Cost is number one, because unless at least 25 players can go it makes for a lonely and body-battering tour. Itinerary is also crucial. Trying to squeeze too much into a couple of weeks of travel is more taxing than relaxing. Finding the right clubs to play is another necessary component. This can be achieved by being honest about your club's capabilities and skill level. Being beaten by huge margins in every tour match because you're playing teams way above your level is no fun.

For players and fans, rugby tours are the ultimate way of letting their hair down and getting to know each other. Living with your teammates and fellow club members for a couple of weeks in the close quarters of buses and hotel rooms is an ideal way to build spirit and cohesiveness. Of course, one maxim that always has to be followed is that "What goes on tour, stays on tour" — meaning that particularly funny, embarrassing, or debauched moments are for consumption only by the tourists themselves and not casual listeners back home.

Finding Out More about the Game

After you watch some rugby either at club or test level, or anywhere in between, you'll probably want to find out more about this fascinating sport. Although very little coverage is available in most North American newspapers and on broadcast television, a multitude of other resources on the Internet can help you fill in your knowledge gaps about the game played with the oval ball.

Rugby matches on the Web

If you want to watch rugby on the web, you have three subscription options. In the United States, FoxSoccer.tv shows Heineken Cup, Magners League, Aviva Premiership, Amlin Challenge Cup, and LV Cup matches for a monthly fee. Universal Sports offers a pay package for the Sevens World Series and also shows highlights for free, along with episodes of *Total Rugby* on demand. In Canada, Setanta-i offers pay-per-view options of various competitions (Refer to Chapter 21 for more about watching rugby on television).

Rugby Canada and USA Rugby also use the Ustream service (www.ustream.tv) to air various competitions and matches from across North America for free.

Rugby news in cyberspace

Rugby is blessed with some excellent Web sites, so getting a daily fix of information, the latest news, or in-depth detail on any aspect of the game isn't hard for rugby addicts. Most of the leading sites also have excellent archive sections, where you can easily access background information on a wide variety of rugby-relevant subjects. Some Web sites focus on the game in a particular country, while others present broader coverage reflecting rugby's status as a global game.

As Internet and television rugby producers, we rely on several of these Web sites to stay up-to-date on everything that's going on in the competitions.

ESPNScrum

ESPNScrum (www.espnscrum.com) is a U.K.-based Web site. It covers the international game but is particularly strong in the areas of Six Nations, Heineken Cup, Magners League, and Aviva Premiership information. Scrum also features blogs, live scores, podcasts, news feeds, and lots of video.

Pick and Go

Pick and Go (www.lassen.co.nz/pickandgo.php) is a searchable database of rugby results for international and Super Rugby. Want to know how many times the Springboks have beaten the All Blacks at Eden Park? Just type it in to get your answer. It also has a statistical table that focuses on coaching, a list of future fixtures, and a cool RWC section.

Planet Rugby

Planet Rugby (www.planet-rugby.com) is the world's leading rugby Web site. We use this site every single day. Based in the United Kingdom, it gives in-depth coverage on what is going on in the Northern Hemisphere and around the world. Planet Rugby also has a string of international correspondents who report on what's going on in their part of the world. The site has a good balance of news, analysis, and opinions. It also has forums available on almost every conceivable rugby subject.

RugbyDump

RugbyDump (www.rugbydump.com) is the best place to watch rugby video from all over the world. The site has all the biggest hits, best tries, most controversial plays, and best interviews from most of the major rugby competitions. Lots of opportunity exists to comment and join in on the inevitable discussions after seeing the action for yourself.

Rugby Heaven

Rugby Heaven (www.rugbyheaven.smh.com.au) is the leading Australian rugby Web site. The site relies on the resources of the *Sydney Morning Herald,* the *Daily Telegraph* in London, the *Australian Associated Press,* and various other news agencies, enabling Rugby Heaven to provide the latest news from around the globe.

Rugby Heaven boasts numerous interesting sections, such as World Cup, Six Nations, Tri Nations, Super 14, Provincial, and Off the Field. The site also has online competitions, chat rooms, polls, and many interactive services. It's a good starting spot to find out what's going on in the game.

RugbyMag.com

RugbyMag.com (www.rugbymag.com) is the best source for news about American domestic rugby, with plenty of information about the college scene and all levels of fifteens and sevens rugby.

Stuff

Stuff (www.stuff.co.nz) is a useful Web site if you're looking for information about rugby in New Zealand. The sports section of this all-Kiwi site will tell you what's going on in rugby all over New Zealand. Articles from newspapers throughout New Zealand appear alongside original commentary from various luminaries.

SuperSport Rugby

If you want to follow the game in South Africa, SuperSport (www.supersport.co.za/rugby) is the recommended site. It provides plenty of news and commentary on the Currie Cup, Vodacom Cup, and all other domestic issues in the republic. The site also follows the Springboks religiously.

IRB and union Web sites

A good starting point to find out about the game of rugby is the Web site for the worldwide governing body of the sport, the International Rugby Board (www.irb.com). This site gives information on every national union in the world and features sections on all IRB-sponsored competitions, as well as a complete version of the laws of the game and other relevant material. You can also find useful tidbits on refereeing, coaching, and training, or you can look at the current world rankings.

The IRB also hosts an official Web site for Rugby World Cup 2011 at www.rugbyworldcup.com, where you can find all the info you need to follow the rugby world's quadrennial showcase before, during, and after the tournament.

The New Zealand Rugby Union Web site

As one would expect from the official site of the organization in charge of the country's unofficial religion, the New Zealand Rugby Union (NZRU) site (www.allblacks.com) cleverly caters to the passionate rugby fan who's interested in the goings-on in the Land of the Long White Cloud.

The site also offers the latest breaking news, details of upcoming games and results, and extensive information about the New Zealand team. You can find information about the union's leading players and what's happening at all levels of New Zealand rugby.

The England Rugby Football Union Web site

The inventors of the game have an excellent site (www.rfu.com) that gives you all the information you'll ever need about rugby in England, including player profiles for all their representative teams and a comprehensive look at the overall game.

The United States and Canadian rugby union Web sites

USA Rugby's official site (www.usarugby.org) contains a wealth of information on the U.S. national teams plus the various annual national championships, news, coaching, refereeing, and membership data. This site has been recently updated, giving it a sharper look and making it much easier to use.

Rugby Canada's site (www.rugbycanada.ca) offers a full array of information on the game, from youth development programs to the Super League and everything Canadian in between. If it's happening in Canadian rugby, you can find it on this site.

Reading up on rugby books

Rugby books generally fall into three categories: autobiographical or biographical, instructional, and events-related/historical nonfiction. Here are my favorites from each of these classifications.

✔ **Autobiography** — *Anton Oliver Inside with Brian Turner:* Anton Oliver is a former All Blacks captain and Otago stalwart. Regarded as an exceptionally tough player throughout his career, he is also a thoughtful and intelligent man who isn't shy about expressing his opinions in this book. He is a controversial figure in New Zealand rugby, loved and hated. I admired his front row grit long before I ever read this book, and after doing so I count him as one of my favorite players of all time. An entertaining read, especially for those fans with an interest in Kiwi rugby from the beginning of the professional era.

✔ **Instructional** — *Thinking Rugby* by Ken Hodge and Alex McKenzie: Rugby is a thinking game, and this book takes that idea to another level. This was the first book to examine in a clinical way the steps necessary to becoming a better rugby player through psychological skills training. Originally published more than ten years ago, this book is still relevant for anyone who wants to improve their mental approach to the game. Co-author Ken Hodge is also a fellow All-Maggot! (Refer to Chapter 16 for a description of Maggotfest.)

✔ **History/analysis** — *Somebody Stole My Game* by Chris Laidlaw: The author is a former All Blacks captain, Sky Sports commentator, Rhodes Scholar, diplomat, radio host, and syndicated columnist. In this 2010 book Laidlaw examines how rugby has lost its way in attempting to become first and foremost a commercially successful worldwide game at the expense of the amateur ethos and experience. He has keen insights into how the running of the game in the past led to the problems of the present and offers solutions for the future.

Part VI
The Part of Tens

The 5th Wave   By Rich Tennant

PAINTING THE DEAD BALL LINE ON A RUGBY FIELD

© RICHTENNANT

In this part . . .

Every *For Dummies* book includes a Part of Tens, chapters that each contain ten or so interesting pieces of information.

In this part, we offer our list of the ten best male and female North American rugby players as a ploy to get the debate flowing. Then, we list and justify our ten best moments, with five from around the world and five from the American and Canadian experience.

Chapter 23

The Ten Greatest North American Men

*I*n this chapter we profile the ten greatest male players ever to pull on a U.S.A. or Canada national team jersey — the very best to have ever graced our North American fields with their rugby genius.

Compiling a list of the ten best American and Canadian male rugby players of all time was no easy task, considering how many outstanding men have played the game in North America. In making our selections, which we present in no particular order, we considered not only their individual accomplishments but also, more important, how their particular talents helped their teams to succeed. As with any top ten list, some very qualified candidates didn't make the cut. To recognize their accomplishments, we wrap up this chapter with an honorable mention section.

Gareth Rees

Gareth Rees (see Figure 23-1) is the highest profile North American rugby player of all time. He made his debut against the United States in 1986. In an international career that spanned 13 years, he earned 55 caps for Canada. He was the only player to appear in each of the first four World Cups from 1987 to 1999. Rees retired following the 1999 Rugby World Cup as Canada's all-time leading scorer, amassing a career total of 487 points. He played for several leading professional clubs in Europe including Castres (France), Wasps and Harlequins (England), and Newport (Wales).

With outstanding vision and an excellent tactical and goal-kicking boot, Rees stands head and shoulders above all other North American flyhalves. In May 2002 he became the chief executive officer of Rugby Canada and reinstated national team coach David Clark before stepping down on the eve of the 2003 Rugby World Cup.

Figure 23-1:
Gareth
Rees.

Dan Lyle

Dan Lyle is the best rugby player ever to put on an Eagles jersey. He was a talented tight end who played college football at the Virginia Military Institute. Like so many Americans who switch from football to rugby, Lyle was introduced to the sport in his 20s yet still managed to assimilate the finer points of the game using intelligence and hard work. He debuted for the USA Eagles in 1994 against Ireland, then went on to play professionally in England for Bath and Leicester. He became one of Europe's finer players, setting up the only try in Bath's 1997 European Cup triumph. Dan earned 45 caps (24 as captain) before retiring following the 2003 Rugby World Cup — on the heels of a towering performance where he earned our praise as the outstanding number 8 of the tournament.

At 6'5" and 250 pounds, Lyle's solidly built frame was impressive, but his greatest assets were his intelligence and tremendous athleticism. A number 8 with power, speed, and good distribution skills, Lyle was also an imposing defender. Perhaps his greatest skill was claiming restarts and lineouts, where he was one of the world's best players at contesting possession in the air (see Figure 23-2).

Figure 23-2:
Dan Lyle
soars for a
lineout.

Al Charron

Al Charron is an ironman who appeared 72 times for Canada since his debut against Argentina in 1990. A tall and rangy back-row forward, Charron played flanker, the number 8, or lock with equal skill. He was invited to play with the Barbarians RFC five times and was named to a World XV in 1999. Following Rees's lead, Charron's participation in the 2003 Rugby World Cup earned him the distinction of having appeared in four World Cups. He captained Canada 22 times during his career and was a fixture for many years on the Canadian sevens team.

Dave Hodges

Only the second American to earn 50 caps, former USA Eagles Captain Dave Hodges is just the kind of player you want leading your team into battle. At 6'4" and 235 pounds, Hodges was a fierce defender who led by example, putting his body on the line every time he took the field. He was a versatile forward, possessing a full complement of back-row and locking skills. He played professionally in Wales for Llanelli and Bridgend and was named Llanelli's 2001–02 Player of the Year.

A 1989 All-American linebacker at Occidental College, Hodges played professional football in Europe for the Hamburg Blue Devils in 1993–94 before dedicating himself full-time to rugby. Like Lyle, Hodges's intelligence and tremendous work ethic enabled him to smoothly adjust from football to rugby without missing a beat.

Mike James

Mike James is one of Canada's all-time great forwards. The big lock has played 51 times for his country in the second row. Standing almost 2 meters (6'5.6") tall, James has been a lineout force throughout his career. James retired in 2007 from professional club rugby in France after a seven-year stint with Stade Français. Prior to moving to Paris, James played for Perpignan. He made such an impact in the Top 14 and the Heineken Cup that he has been named three times to play with the French Barbarians. The British Columbia native has been counted on to provide the Canadian national team with an extra bit of experience and aggression since he made his debut against the United States in 1994.

Brian Vizard

The Vizman debuted for the Eagles against Japan in 1986 and went on to earn 22 caps for the United States, captaining the team eight times. An imposing figure at 6'6" and 230 pounds, Vizard played the number 8 in the days before lifting in the lineout, when having a tough lineout enforcer was absolutely critical. Foolhardy would-be tacklers encountered an Edward Scissorhands–like fury of razor-sharp elbows and relentlessly churning knees. He made numerous appearances for the Eagles Sevens side in Hong Kong and elsewhere around the world. Viz played the majority of his club rugby for the Old Mission Beach Athletic Club, leading them to six USA Rugby National Club Championships along the way. From what we can gather from tall tales, artifacts, and fossil remains, Viz was the kind of player everyone wanted on their team but dreaded playing against — a big, strong, determined, aggressive, and angry man who wanted to win more than anyone else on the pitch.

Rod Snow

A versatile prop, Snow is a rock of consistency with 62 caps and was named to a World XV in 1999. He had a long professional career before returning home to help his hometown Newfoundland Rock win the Rugby Canada Super League Championship in 2005. At the ripe old age of 40, he's still playing top-level rugby.

Luke Gross

At 6'10", Gross was a monster in the lineout. When he retired from international play, he was the most capped American with 62 appearances for the Eagles. Since his playing career ended, he's joined the U.S. national team coaching staff as a specialist lineout coach and travels around the country providing lineout clinics.

Winston Stanley

A fantastic finisher, Stanley earned 66 caps for Canada and was part of the 2001 treble-winning Leicester Tigers. He also played professionally for Auckland and Leeds Carnegie. Stanley was a member of Canada's 1997 and 2007 World Cup Sevens teams and was arguably Canada's most evasive player with ball in hand.

Todd Clever

Clever is the current caption of the Eagles and the face of American rugby. Nicknamed Captain America, he's taken his talents all around the globe. He's played professionally for North Harbour in New Zealand, was the first American to play Super Rugby for the Lions, and led Suntory Sungoliath to the 2011 Japanese Top League Championship. He was also a force in the Sevens World Series, combining speed and power.

Honorable Mentions

Whenever you construct a list like the preceding one, you're forced to leave off some worthy candidates. To properly acknowledge their achievements, we've come up with a list of notables who deserve recognition.

Outstanding players from the Eagles who deserve mention include the following:

- ✔ **Mike MacDonald:** America's most capped prop of all time has been playing for the Eagles since 2000, amassing 60 caps. He is currently playing professionally in England for Leeds Carnegie.

- ✔ **Vaea Anitoni:** A speedy wing, Anitoni was the Eagles' all-time leading tryscorer when he retired after 46 tests.

- ✔ **Mike Hercus:** Since making his debut for the United States in 2002, Hercus has become the all-time leading scorer for the Eagles with 361 points.

- ✔ **Fred Paoli:** Perhaps the U.S.'s best all-time prop, Paoli was a no-nonsense captain and natural team leader who earned 20 caps.

- ✔ **Dennis Jablonski:** A standout fullback in defense and attack (and the first in a long line of Eagles from Occidental College), Jabbo was also the first American ever named to a World XV representative team.

On the Canadian ledger, the following players are worthy of an honorable mention:

- ✔ **Scott Stewart:** Canada's all-time standout fullback made 64 appearances for his country including the 1991, 1995, and 1999 Rugby World Cups. He played overseas for Harlequins and Bedford and was also an accomplished sevens player who appeared in two Sevens World Cups. He currently coaches rugby at UCLA in Los Angeles.

- ✔ **Dan Baugh:** Although his career was cut short by injuries, the 30-times-capped and very athletic Baugh played some very tough rugby for Canada and Cardiff.

- ✔ **Dave Lougheed:** This rangy and deceptively fast winger was a veteran of three World Cups and one of Canada's best-ever finishers.

- ✔ **Bob Ross:** Upon his retirement in 2003, Ross was the world's longest serving international. He made his debut in 1989 against Ireland, earned 54 caps, and was Canada's second all-time leading scorer.

- ✔ **Morgan Williams:** The scrumhalf played 56 times for Canada and was part of three World Cup teams. Williams was also a standout in sevens for his country. He played in Europe with Bordeaux, Stade Français, and Saracens.

Chapter 24

The Ten Greatest
North American Women

*I*n this chapter, we recognize the contributions of the ten greatest female players ever to play on North American pitches for the United States and Canada.

Rugby players from Canada and the United States have long been amongst the very best in the world, and the Canadian and American women's national teams have consistently performed at a high level on the international stage, which makes selecting the top ten individuals a daunting task. Our list is given in no particular order and includes greats from the era of the first Women's Rugby World Cup (WRWC), recently retired standouts, and currently active ruggers. For those who didn't crack the uppermost echelon, we've awarded honorable mentions.

Patty Jervey

A top-class player with more than 23 years of experience, Eagle Patty Jervey (see Figure 24-1) competed in five World Cups and retired after the 2006 WRWC as the all-time leader for the United States by a country mile in women's caps (37), points (178), and tries (38). A tenacious defender and powerful attacker, seven of her U.S.A. tries were worth four points!

Figure 24-1:
Patty Jervey
prepares
to make a
tackle.

Jen Crawford

Jen Crawford is the finest female player that North America has ever produced. The former all-time leading Eagles tryscorer, Crawford captained the Eagles to the final of the 1998 Women's World Cup while earning a record 20th cap. Still deeply involved in the club game, she led the Berkeley All-Blues to nine consecutive USA Rugby National Women's Club Championships as both a player and an assistant coach.

Crawford had an instinctive feel for the game and a deadly ability to set up defenders and either sell the dummy or blow straight through them. She was a devastating finisher when the goal line was in sight and led representative sides to national titles in fifteens and sevens.

Gillian Florence

A powerful and aggressive flanker who's amassed 44 caps representing her country — the most ever by a Canadian woman — Florence earned the game MVP in her test debut at the 1994 World Cup. A devastating tackler and hard runner with the ball in hand, she was a key performer on the fourth-place Canadian team at the 1998 Women's Rugby World Cup. Florence was selected to the 2003 All-World Team. She's a graduate of McGill University and was named one of their top 20 athletes of all time. (See Figure 24-2.)

Figure 24-2:
Rugby
Canada's
Gillian
Florence.

Phaidra Knight

A super-fit and versatile player, Knight began her career as a front-rower and has since become a dominant back-rower. She's earned 32 caps and has appeared in three Women's Rugby World Cups. The only American woman named to the 2003 World XV, the athletic forward combines size, power, and quickness plus good technique. Her contribution is huge in attack and on defense. She appeared on MTV's *Made* as a rugby coach in 2010.

Heather Moyse

Heather Moyse made her Canadian women's national team debut in 2004, and since then has consistently shown she's one of the best fullbacks in the game. She was Canada's only member of the All-World team at the 2006 World Cup, and was the leading tryscorer in the tournament with seven. Moyse has been named to the All-Canadian CIS team three times, twice as an undergraduate at the University of Waterloo and once as a graduate at the

University of Toronto. She is also a Canadian Olympian, having represented her country in the two-person bobsleigh event, where she placed fourth at the 2006 Games in Turin and won a gold medal in Vancouver in 2010.

Ellie Karvoski

Ellie played in three World Cups for the United States, and in 2006 and 2010 was named to the All-World team. She scored a hat trick of tries in the U.S.A.'s win over Australia. A gifted athlete — she has also represented the United States in field hockey — she is also one of the country's most talented back-line players. An outstanding scorer from her wing position, Karvoski has been named the MVP at the inter-territorial tournaments in both sevens and fifteens.

Maria Gallo

Maria is originally from Argentina and made her debut for Canada in 1999 against the U.S. She's played both wing and center in earning 50 caps for her adopted country. Gallo was a key member of the Canadian national team that competed in the 2002 and 2006 Women's Rugby World Cup. Also a top sevens performer, she represented Canada in the inaugural Women's Rugby World Cup Sevens in 2009 in Dubai. Maria Gallo is an instructor with the School of Human Kinetics at the University of British Columbia.

Kathy Flores

Playing at number 8, Kathy was an integral part of the 1991 and 1994 Eagles World Cup champion and runner-up teams. Flores then coached the Berkeley All Blues to an unprecedented 11 national women's club titles in 14 years. Kathy was also the longtime coach of the USA Rugby women's national team and was named the IRB's Female Personality of the Year in 2003.

Sarah Ulmer

Sarah Ulmer made her debut for Canada in 2001 against the United States at Saranac Lake (and we remember, because we televised the match!). She went on to earn 33 caps and played in the 2002 and 2006 IRB Women's Rugby World Cups. After playing for Saskatchewan's provincial team between 1994 and 2002, she is currently playing for Saracens in London, England. When not on the pitch, she works as a physiotherapist.

Leslie Cripps

Leslie is the captain of Canada's national senior women's team. Leslie also plays for Saracens in London, England. She's been a part of the Canadian women's national team for more than ten years and has amassed an impressive 40 caps. The front-rower appeared in both the 2002 and 2006 IRB Women's Rugby World Cups. When not on the pitch, the 32-year-old loose-head prop is a school teacher.

Honorable Mentions

As in any summary of all-time greats, certain players didn't quite make the cut for top ten status yet still had distinguished careers and deserve recognition. The four below are indeed worthy of inclusion.

For the U.S. women, this duo stands out:

- **Candi Orsini:** This gifted and ageless center combined speed, agility, and power to wreak havoc from the midfield. Another veteran of the U.S.'s 1991, 1994, and 1998 Rugby Women's World Cup squads, Orsini now serves as an assistant coach with the national team.

- **Diane Schnapp:** She was a stalwart flanker for both the Eagles and the Berkeley All Blues. One of the best players ever at the breakdown, Schnapp was tough as nails in contact situations.

The Canadian women who deserve to be singled out are these two:

- **Sommer Christie:** Christie played for Canada in the 2002 and 2006 World Cups and was part of the first-ever World University Sevens Championship team.

- **Josée Lacasse:** Previously the most capped Canadian woman, Lacasse retired after the 2002 Women's Rugby World Cup — her third WRWC — having earned 29 caps at prop.

Chapter 25

The Ten Best Rugby Moments

*R*ugby fans are particularly passionate about the history of their game and love nothing more than to discuss fantastic moments from the past over a cold beverage. Good-natured debate about the greatest game, best try, and most awesome team is a staple activity in clubhouses around the globe.

In this chapter, we provide our picks of the five greatest moments in the history of the game from around the oval planet and then put forth our selections for the top five moments in the game for North American teams.

Top Five Around the World

In the more than 125 years since the first test match was played between England and Scotland in 1871, rugby has delivered hundreds of great games marked by dramatic finishes and featuring monumental team and individual performances. The process of paring this mountain of history into just five games demonstrated to us yet again why rugby is such an amazing sport. Here's our list of the five best games of all time.

The greatest test ever

On July 15, 2000, Australia hosted New Zealand at Olympic Stadium in Sydney in what we believe was the single best test ever played. The setting befit the occasion, as a world-record rugby crowd of 109,874 filled the stadium to watch the defending World Champion Wallabies face the New Zealand All Blacks with the Bledisloe Cup on the line in the opening match of the Tri Nations. The match started with a flurry as Tana Umaga scored an intercept try off an ill-advised pass by Chris Latham. From the ensuing kickoff the Kiwis controlled the ball, and Jonah Lomu got into the action by putting Pita Alatini in the clear after a break down the touchline. Fullback Christian Cullen was next on the scoresheet, stunning the Aussie crowd with a burst through the Wallaby defense for the third try. Then, after an Andrew Mehrtens penalty, with just nine minutes gone, the scoreline read Australia 0, New Zealand 24. With 70 minutes left to be played, it was shaping up to be the worst beating that the All Blacks had ever inflicted on the Wallabies.

Wallaby Captain John Eales summoned his troops and told them to keep their cool and stay focused on the game plan — the key thing was not to panic. From the next restart, Stephen Larkham broke the line and put Stirling Mortlock into the clear with a perfectly weighted pass. The huge crowd let out a collective sigh of relief as they all wondered, "Can the boys come all the way back?" Over the next 25 minutes, the World Champions did exactly that to level the scores at 24–all at the half.

The Aussies took the lead 27–24 with a penalty in the 58th minute, but the All Blacks answered with a try by Justin Marshall to reclaim the lead 29–27. After the conversion and a Mehrtens penalty, the Kiwis led 34–27. Stirling Mortlock then added a penalty, and the lead was down to 34–30 with only a few minutes remaining. In the 78th minute, Wallaby hooker Jeremy Paul drove over the tryline in the corner and raised his arms in triumph as the all-time record crowd went absolutely nuts, celebrating yet another amazing comeback by their beloved boys — who had moved ahead of their biggest rivals 35–34.

All that remained was to run out the clock. Trailing by one point, the All Blacks had to score on their last possession. After several phases of slowly advancing the ball, reserve scrumhalf Byron Kelleher moved the ball wide to Taine Randell, who drew two defenders and passed over the top to Jonah Lomu. The big man rumbled around the corner, beating Larkham's last-ditch tackle attempt to score the match-winning try!

We've seen the match at least 15 times and it still gives us chills to watch the finish. If you ever want to explain to someone who's unfamiliar with rugby what the game's all about and you're lucky enough to have it on tape, show them this match — they'll be a believer in no time.

The 2003 World Cup final

The 2003 Rugby World Cup final pitted host Australia against the pre-tournament favorites, England. The home nation against the former colony, the best of the north against the best of the Southern Hemisphere, this match had a story line that was longer than the queues waiting to catch a train after the match at Homebush station. The stadium was half full of English and half full of Aussie supporters; white and gold jerseys dominated the jam-packed venue. The match started well for the home side when Lote Tuqiri hauled in a cross-field bomb by Stephen Larkham and the Wallabies took a five-point lead.

England kept their composure as Jonny Wilkinson converted three shots at goal to put England in front 9–5. Then just before halftime, Wilko put Jason Robinson into the clear down the right sideline, and England went into the changing rooms with a well deserved 14–5 halftime lead.

The second half settled into a contest of wills: The Wallabies scratched their way back into the match with two penalty goals, but England still led 14–11 as fulltime approached. On the final possession by the Wallabies in injury time, a penalty gave Elton Flatley his chance to level the scores and force extra time. With ice water coursing through his veins and the rugby world holding its breath, he calmly slotted the goal and the fulltime whistle was blown, leaving the world's two best teams even at 14–all.

In extra time, the teams continued the pattern. England took the lead on a penalty, and then Australia leveled the scores with 30 seconds left in the second of the two ten-minute periods. With just seconds remaining and the commentators speculating about a third ten-minute sudden-death period, England's scrumhalf Matt Dawson somehow broke through the Wallaby defense and got close enough to the line for Jonny Wilkinson to line up a final drop goal attempt. Everyone in the stadium knew what was coming: Jonny stroked the drop and history was made when the ball sailed through the uprights and England became the first Northern Hemisphere nation to ever win the World Cup. All hail Sir Clive Woodward and England!

Barbarians versus New Zealand 1973

Before July 15, 2000, when the subject of greatest games came up the 1973 contest between the Barbarians RFC and the New Zealand All Blacks topped the list. The game matched a Barbarians team chock-full of Welsh legends, including the incomparable Gareth Edwards, JPR Williams, Phil Bennett, and John Dawes, plus Irish icons Willie John McBride, Mike Gibson, and Fergus Slattery, and other notables from Scotland and England. The All Blacks featured the uncompromising Ian Kirkpatrick, Alex Wyllie, Sid Going, and Bryan Williams, who had just shut out England 9–0 and now faced the star-studded Barbarians to finish up their tour.

After the opening kickoff, the teams traded deep kicks, jockeying for field position until All Blacks Brian Williams launched a high kick deep behind the Welsh 22-meter line. Instead of taking the sensible option and kicking for the safety of touch, Phil Bennett counterattacked, beginning an 80-meter movement that would be forever etched in the memories of rugby fans around the world.

Bennett picked up the ball around his own 10-meter line and made three successive sidesteps to elude Alistair Scown, Ian Hurst, and Ian Kirkpatrick. Bennett then passed on to JPR Williams, who nearly had his head ripped off but still managed to offload to John Pullin. Pullin transferred the ball to John Dawes, who sold a dummy, covered more ground, and passed inside to Tom David as he crossed the halfway line. David made a one-handed pass inside to Derek Quinnell, who moved the ball on with another one-handed pass inside. Just then, Gareth Edwards blasted from nowhere to join the line at precisely the right angle and pace to round the corner, evaded Joe Karam's covering tackle, and covered the final 20 meters to dive headfirst into the left-hand corner of the river Taff end to score what is now known as "The Try." The capacity Cardiff Arms Park crowd erupted into a delirious state of rapture, and the Barbarians went on to defeat the mighty All Blacks 23–11.

If you ever get lucky enough to hear Gareth Edwards describe "The Try" in person, you'll see his eyes light up as he relives every step of the movement from more than 30 years ago like it was yesterday, despite the fact that it's the 25,000th time he's told the story. Some things really do improve with age.

The Bulls win the Super 14

Until 2007 first the Super 12 and then the Super 14 (now Super Rugby with 15 teams — refer to Chapter 14 for details) were dominated by sides from New Zealand and Australia. In the early years of the competition, the South African squads occasionally made the postseason but were never able to hoist the trophy. Beginning play as the Bulls franchise in 1998, the former Northern Transvaal were far and away the worst team in the tournament for many years. Their turnaround began in 2004 when they finished sixth, followed by semifinal appearances in 2005 and 2006. In 2007 they started slowly, had a fantastic tour of Australia, and gained significant momentum when they returned to their fortress, Loftus Versfeld in Pretoria. Going into the last match of the season they knew that they had to outscore the Reds by 72 points in order to host a playoff match. So what did they do? They scored 13 tries and won 92–3!

The Bulls semifinal against the six-time and defending champion Crusaders wasn't the prettiest rugby match of all time, but their 27–12 victory earned the desired result — a spot in the final the following week against the Sharks in Durban. The Sharks had topped the Super 14 table and had beaten the Bulls in their meeting back in Week One, so everyone in the Republic of South Africa knew that this would be a walkover.

The match was played in somewhat windy conditions and the Bulls were definitely the second-best team for the first 78 minutes. The Sharks looked as if they'd wrapped up the title late in the contest when Albert van den Berg crashed over from a ruck near the goal line and gave his team a 19–13 lead. Young winger Francois Steyn missed a tough conversion, and the Bulls had one last chance to win with less than two minutes to play. The Sharks twice got possession and kicked it back to the Bulls during the final sequence. The Bulls then held on to it and made ground for phase after phase until finally winger Bryan Habana got around and through the Sharks defense and flew over for the try! Flyhalf Derick Hougaard — the competition's top goal kicker in 2007 — calmly stepped up and slotted the kick to give the Bulls an improbable 20–19 win and their first Super 14 title!

Since that season, the Bulls have proved that their victory was no fluke; they again took top honors in the competition in 2009 and 2010!

1995 World Cup final

The 1995 Rugby World Cup was staged in South Africa and marked the return of the mighty Springboks to the international order after years of isolation because of their government's apartheid policies. The tournament started with a bang for the hosts, when they beat the defending champion Wallabies in the opening match. The Boks eventually faced a heavily favored New Zealand side in the final.

The 1995 World Cup final was not the most exhilarating exhibition of tryscoring rugby ever played — neither team was able to touch down over the more than 100 minutes of play. However, the contest's dramatic ending made up for this: With time running out in the second extra time period, Springbok flyhalf Joel Stransky drop kicked a monster goal that sailed high through the uprights to set the 62,000 spectators into a frenzy of delight.

South Africa had indeed returned to claim the top spot on the world stage, and when Nelson Mandela joined François Pienaar on the podium for the trophy presentation and pumped his fists in the air to celebrate the Boks victory, sport had transcended politics; the Rainbow Nation rejoiced in harmony as one.

Top Five North American Moments

Although the United States and Canadian men's national teams have yet to win the Rugby World Cup, that doesn't mean North American rugby teams have failed to impress around the world. In fact, if you look back in time, both the American and Canadian men's and women's teams have had their fair share of moments over the years.

Women's Rugby World Cup final 1991

The first Women's Rugby World Cup was staged in Cardiff, Wales, in 1991, as the United States, France, the former Soviet Union, Wales, Japan, Sweden, Canada, the Netherlands, Italy, and New Zealand battled it out for the inaugural unofficial women's world championship. The United States beat the Netherlands and the former Soviet Union to qualify for the semifinals, where they faced the New Zealand Black Ferns. The Eagles defeated the New Zealanders and qualified to meet England in the final. The Eagles soared over the Arms Park and defeated England 19–6, much to the delight of the Welsh crowd and the U.S. supporters. Women's rugby had finally arrived as a real sport, and the Eagles were perched on top of the world.

Canada versus France 1994

In June 1994 Canada played host to France in a test match played in Nepean. The highly rated French brought over their first team, which included the likes of Philippe Sella, Emile N'Tamack, Philippe Saint-Andre, Abdelatif Benazzi, and Laurent Cabannes. The upstart Canadians were quietly confident after having defeated Wales at the Arms Park the previous November (read on).

Even though the French scored the only try of the match, flyhalf Gareth Rees carried the Canucks on his back with six penalty goals and the locals came out the winners, 18–16, to take their biggest scalp of all time.

U.S. Olympians versus France 1920 and 1924

In 1920 in Antwerp, and again four years later in 1924 in Paris, the United States defeated France in the Olympic gold medal rugby match. The U.S. team was composed primarily of players from Stanford University and the University of California at Berkeley. In 1924, the Americans beat Romania to advance to face France in the gold medal game.

The match was the first gold medal contest of the games, and a partisan French crowd expected their countrymen to dispose of the Americans with ease. To the shock of the 17,000-plus in attendance at Stade Colomiers, the United States defense totally frustrated the Tricolors attack, and when it was all over the upstart Americans were victorious 17–3 to take the gold. Because rugby was dropped following the 1924 Games, the United States are still technically the two-time defending Olympic gold medal champions.

Wales versus Canada 1993

On November 10, 1993, the Canadian team posted their first-ever win over an International Rugby Board (IRB) founding nation when they defeated Wales at the venerable Cardiff Arms Park. The final score was Wales 24–26 Canada, but what made the victory even sweeter was the fact that Canada scored two tries and managed to keep the Welsh from scoring a try, with all of the points for the Dragons coming from the boot of Neil Jenkins. Canadian Captain Ian Stewart and future skipper Al Charron both scored five-pointers, while Gareth Rees was perfect with his kicks, converting both tries and slotting four penalties of his own.

Canada versus France A 2010

In 2010 the Churchill Cup pool stages were held at Infinity Park in Glendale, Colorado. The six competing teams were the United States, Canada, Russia, Uruguay, France A, and the England Saxons. The pools were set up to eventually have France A and the Saxons meet in the final, but Canada had other ideas. After easily dispatching Uruguay 48–6 in their opener, they next squared off against a heavily favored French team that was loaded with current and former internationals. The Tricolors took an early lead on two penalty goals before Canada responded with a converted try. France went back out in front with a try before halftime and led 16–10 after the first 40 minutes.

The second half saw five more lead changes, the most significant when France was driving in the 70th minute and Canada intercepted and went the distance to pull out to a 33–27 advantage. The Canadians had to hold out a furious French charge at the end but held on to come away with the victory and a first-ever appearance in the Churchill Cup final.

Glossary

advantage: Occurs when a referee allows play to continue even though there has been an infringement. The referee gives the non-offending team the chance to do something positive with the ball. If the team is unable to do so, the referee goes back to the site of the original infraction and restarts play with the appropriate method. The goal of advantage is to minimize stoppages and keep play flowing.

age-grade rugby: The term for all rugby from ages 6–18.

ankle tap: When a defender attempts to stop a ball-carrier by tapping her on the ankle from behind in an attempt to bring her down. This is a last-ditch, desperation tackle.

back row: The third line of the scrum, comprising a number 8 and two flankers. These three are known as back-rowers.

back three: The fullback and the two wingers.

backs: Numbers 9–15; generally faster players.

ball-carrier: The player carrying the ball.

binding: Firmly grasping another player's body from the shoulder to the hips with the whole arm from hand to shoulder.

blindside: The area between the ball and the closest sideline.

blindside flanker: The flanker who binds onto the scrum on the blindside; usually wears number 6, except in South Africa.

blood bin: If a player is bleeding, he must leave the field of play until the wound is covered or dressed. While he is being treated, he is said to be in the blood bin — but it's not an actual place.

bomb: A high kick generally aimed at the opposition fullback in the hope that under pressure she'll drop it and lose possession.

box kick: A high kick aimed to land in front of the opposition winger, usually taken by the scrumhalf.

breakaway: Another name for flankers who wear numbers 6 and 7. They bind on the side of the scrum and break away when the scrum is over. Their primary jobs are to win the ball at rucks and mauls and to make tackles.

breakdown: When play transitions from one phase to another, usually because of a tackle and the resultant struggle for possession.

caps: A term used to denote the number of times an individual has played for his national team in a test match. When someone is said to have 22 caps for the United States, it means that he has played in 22 tests for the Eagles.

centers: The players wearing number 12 (inside center) and number 13 (outside center). They are the heart and soul of a team's attack. Also called the midfielders.

channel: The path a ball takes when coming back through the scrum between the legs of the forwards.

charge down: The blocking of a kick by an opposing player.

chip kick: A short kick, usually directed over the top of the opposition's defensive line, hopefully to be regathered by the kicker or a teammate.

clearing kick: A kick aimed to go over the touchline as a way of relieving pressure and gaining territory.

Colts rugby: The under-19 age group level before adult rugby.

conversion: After a try is scored, the attacking team is given a kick at goal from a spot in line with where the try was touched down. If good, it's worth two points, making a converted try good for seven total.

counter attack: An attacking move in response to an opposition attack when the ball has changed possession.

cross kick: A kick across the field aimed toward the attacking team's openside winger, who plans to run through the defense and regather the ball.

crossbar: The bar joining the two uprights of the goalposts. For a conversion or penalty goal to be successful, it has to go over the crossbar.

cut-out pass: A pass that deliberately misses one or more players and goes to the next player in the attacking line.

dead: Means that the ball is out of play. This occurs when the ball has gone outside the playing area and remained there, or when the referee has blown the whistle to indicate a stoppage, or when a conversion kick is being taken.

dead-ball line: The farthest lines at the back of the in-goal areas at both ends of the field.

decoy: A player who pretends that she is about to receive the ball in an attempt to deceive the opposition's defensive line.

defense: Used by one team to stop another when it is attacking.

dive pass: Passing the ball while diving toward the person for whom the pass is intended.

drawing the man: Making an opponent commit to tackling you just before you pass to a teammate.

drift defense: A defensive system that has the defending players drift sideways across the field.

driving maul: A maul where the opposition is driven back through sheer force and coordination.

driving tackle: When the tackler pushes the ball-carrier backward.

drop goal: When a player kicks the ball over the opposition's crossbar during general play. The ball must hit the ground before being kicked. It is worth three points.

drop kick: A type of kick where the ball hits the ground first; used for a drop goal or to restart play after a score or at the beginning of a half.

drop out: A drop kick used to restart play from a team's 22-meter line.

feed: The placing of the ball into the scrum by the scrumhalf.

fend: When an attacking player uses an arm to push away a defender. The same as a straight-arm in American or Canadian football.

field goal: Another name for a drop goal.

five-eighth: Another name for the flyhalf, used in Australia and New Zealand.

five-meter scrum: A scrum that is set 5 meters from the tryline.

flick pass: A quick pass to a teammate. The player throwing the ball flicks his wrists to quicken the pace of the ball.

flyhalf: The back who wears jersey number 10. The flyhalf is one of the most important players on the team, often dictating the flow of play.

forward pass: An illegal pass that travels forward when released.

foul play: Play deemed by the referee to be illegal. The offending player is penalized or, in serious cases, given a yellow or red card.

free kick: A kick awarded to a team for a minor penalty.

front row: The forwards in the first line of the scrum: the loose-head prop, the hooker, and the tight-head prop. These three players are called front-rowers.

fullback: The back who wears the number 15 jersey, who is the last line of defense.

fulltime: The end of the game.

Garryowen: A high kick, also known as an up and under, designed to be chased and taken. Named after the Irish club renowned for using the tactic.

goal: A successful kick between the goalposts.

goal kicker: The designated player in the team who has the task of kicking conversions and penalty goals.

goal line: The line that has to be reached for a team to score a try. For this reason, the goal line is often called the tryline.

grubber kick: A kick that travels along the ground and bounces unpredictably.

halfback: Another term for scrumhalf.

halfback pass: A fast, accurate pass thrown by the halfback.

halfway line: Marks the middle of the field where the game is started and also restarted after tries or successful penalty goals.

halves: The term used for the scrumhalf and flyhalf.

high tackle: A dangerous tackle that hits the opponent above the line of the shoulders. Punished with either a penalty or a yellow or red card, depending upon the severity of the tackle.

hit and spin: When the ball-carrier commits herself to being tackled and then spins out of the tackle.

Home Nations: England, Ireland, Scotland, Wales.

hooker: The forward in the number 2 jersey, who is a central figure. In the front row of the scrum, he is supported by the two props and hooks the ball backward. In the lineout, he throws the ball in.

hospital pass: A badly timed pass that puts the person catching the ball in great danger because it arrives just before she is about to be smashed by an opponent.

infringement: Occurs when a team is guilty of breaking a law, prompting the referee to blow the whistle or play advantage.

injury time: During a match, the referee stops the clock whenever play is halted for an injured player. After normal time has finished (40 minutes each half), play continues for the amount of time lost for the injury stoppages.

inside center: The back who wears number 12. Also known as the second five-eighth in Australia and New Zealand.

International Rugby Board (IRB): The governing body that controls the world game, runs the World Cup, and determines the laws of the game.

judiciary committee: A group of officials (usually three) who determine whether a player should be suspended and for how long after serious incidents on the field of play.

kickoff: Used to start a game. One team kicks the ball from the center of the halfway line to the opposition.

knock-on: A knock-on occurs when a player loses possession of the ball and it goes forward. Or, when a player hits the ball forward with the hand or arm, or when the ball hits the hand or arm and goes forward, and then the ball touches the ground or another player before the original player can catch it.

lifting: When a player is helped into the air by his teammates, either to secure a lineout or a restart kick.

lineout: How play is restarted when the ball goes into touch or out of bounds. The two sets of forwards line up in a row beside each other, and the team with the ball throws it in. The throw must go straight down the middle of the tunnel formed by the two rows.

lob pass: A high, looping pass, aimed to go over the heads of the opposition.

locks: The two forwards who wear jerseys number 4 and 5. Usually the tallest players in the team, the locks are charged with providing strength in the scrum and winning the ball in the lineouts. Together they form the second row, or the engine room.

loitering: Refers to someone who is standing or jogging in an offside position, preventing the opposing team from playing the ball as they wish.

loop: When a player runs around a teammate to whom she has just passed in the hope of receiving the ball back from her.

loose-head prop: The prop on the left hand side of the scrum, closest to his scrumhalf when his team is putting the ball in the scrum.

loosie: A term used for the three members of the back row: the number 8 and the two flankers. So called because they are supposed to be the first to the loose ball.

man-on-man defense: A form of defense where the tackler takes on the man directly opposite.

mark: A player who catches a kick inside her own 22-meter line while calling "mark" can be awarded a free kick by the referee.

match ball: The high-quality rugby ball used in a match.

maul: A maul occurs when a player carrying the ball is held by one or more opponents, and one or more of the ball-carrier's teammates bind on the ball-carrier. All the players involved are on their feet and moving toward a goal line. Open play has ended.

obstruction: Unfairly getting in the way of an opposing player.

offside: A player is offside if he is in front of a teammate who is carrying the ball or in front of a teammate who last played the ball. Offside means that a player is temporarily out of the game. Such players are liable to be penalized if they take part in the game.

onside: A player is onside if she is behind a teammate who has the ball. An onside player can participate fully in the match.

openside: The area between the ball and the farthest sideline.

openside flanker: The flanker who binds on the openside of the scrum and usually wears number 7.

outside center: The back who wears jersey number 13.

overlap: When a team has more players in an attacking line than the opposition.

pack: The term for the entire group of forwards.

pass: When a player throws the ball to a teammate.

peel: When a forward runs around the front or back of the lineout to take the ball upfield from a catch or tap.

penalty: When the referee rules that a team is guilty of an indiscretion or has contravened the laws of the game, he awards a penalty to the non-offending team.

penalty kick: When a team chooses to kick at goal after it has been awarded a penalty.

penalty try: When the referee believes a team would have scored if not for the opposition's illegal play, she can award the try anyway.

pick-and-go: A forward charge where the ball is placed on the ground at the tackle and another forward quickly picks it up and continues the attack.

pill: Another name for the ball.

props: The two forwards who wear jerseys number 1 (loose-head) and number 3 (tight-head). They support the hooker in the scrums and lift the jumpers in the lineout.

punt kick: The most common form of kick used in a match.

pushover try: A try that happens during a scrum when the pack is able to keep the ball under their feet and push the opposition scrum across the tryline.

quick throw-in: When the ball is thrown in before the lineout forms.

red card: The card shown to a player when the referee is sending him off for the rest of the match.

referee: Person appointed to officiate a match by the organizers. Called "Sir" or "Ma'am," by the players; also known as the whistle-blower.

reserve bench: The name given to the place where the replacements sit during the match.

restart kick: The kick that restarts play at each half and after points have been scored.

ruck: When one or more players from each team, who are on their feet and in contact, close around the ball on the ground. Once a ruck has been formed, players cannot use their hands to get the ball but are allowed to use their feet.

scissors pass: Passing to a teammate who cuts back in the opposite direction in a bid to disorient the opposition.

screw punt: A form of punt where the ball spirals in the air, which increases the distance it travels.

scrum: Players from each team come together in a formation, where eight forwards bind in against eight opposing forwards, with the aim of winning the ball that is thrown in between the front rows of the two packs.

scrumhalf: The player wearing jersey number 9, who puts the ball into the scrum and usually distributes it from scrums, rucks, mauls, and lineouts. Also called a halfback.

scrum machine: An apparatus used at training where teams practice their scrummaging skills.

second row: Another name for the locks.

sevens: An abbreviated form of rugby where just seven players play on a full field for seven minutes a half.

shortened lineout: When the team throwing the ball in decides to have fewer than seven players in the lineout.

shove: When the players in an attacking scrum push in unison.

side: Another name for a team.

sideline: The same as the touchline.

side-on tackle: A tackle used when a ball-carrier is trying to run in between defenders.

side-step: A way to evade a tackler by stepping to one side and then quickly to the other.

sin bin: The referee can send players to the sin bin for ten minutes if they are guilty of foul play, a repeated infringement, or a professional foul. The sin bin is usually a seat on the sideline where the player waits for her time to expire so she can reenter the match.

spiral pass: A pass where the player imparts spin on the ball to improve its trajectory.

squad: A group of players who make up a rugby team. A squad usually is made up of 22 team members.

support: Following the ball-carrier in order to help if he is tackled or needs to pass.

swerve: A form of run where the attacking player attempts to swerve past her opponents.

tackle: Where a player brings an opponent carrying the ball down to the ground.

tackle area: The general area in which a tackle has been made, usually defined as several meters around where the player has been brought to ground.

television match official (TMO): During most televised matches, the TMO can be asked by the referee to assist on in-goal decisions.

throw-in: When the ball is thrown into the lineout.

tight five: The term given to the three front-rowers and the two second-rowers.

tight-head: The prop on the right-hand side of the scrum who packs in on the opposite side of where his scrumhalf puts the ball in. This player is the anchor of the scrum. "Winning a tight-head" happens when the team that didn't put the ball in is able to win possession.

touch judges: These two officials assist the referee during the course of the game. They patrol either sideline and determine the exact position where lineout throws are taken, check whether teams are offside, watch for foul play, and decide whether penalty goals and conversions are successful.

touchline: The two lines situated on either side of the field. A ball is described as going "into touch" when it crosses either of these two lines and goes out of the field of play.

training ball: The type of rugby ball used for training purposes.

Triple Crown: The term used in the Six Nations if one of the Home Nations (England, Scotland, Ireland, or Wales) beats all the others during a season.

try: The grounding of the ball by an attacking player in the opposition's in-goal area. It is worth five points.

tryline: The line marked at either end of the field of play that must be crossed to score a try. Also called the goal line.

up and under: A tactical kick that goes high in the air and tests the catching ability of the opposition as defenders run at her. Also called a Garryowen.

wheel: When a scrum turns more than 90 degrees.

wing: The two attacking players that wear jersey numbers 11 and 14, who play closest to the touchline and are usually the fastest on the team.

Wooden Spoon: The term used in many tournaments to designate the last-place team.

yellow card: A card shown to a player by the referee if that player is considered guilty of foul play, a professional foul, or a repeated infringement. Results in a ten-minute suspension in the sin bin.

Index

• D •

• **G** •

• I •

• M •

• S •

• *T* •

Notes

EDUCATION, HISTORY & REFERENCE

978-0-7645-2498-1   978-0-470-46244-7

Also available:
- Algebra For Dummies
  978-0-470-55964-2
- Art History For Dummies
  978-0-470-09910-0
- Canadian History For Dummies
  978-0-470-83656-9
- Chemistry For Dummies
  978-1-118-00730-3

- French For Dummies
  978-1-118-00464-7
- Math Word Problems For Dummies
  978-0-470-14660-6
- Speed Reading For Dummies
  978-0-470-45744-3
- Statistics For Dummies
  978-0-470-91108-2
- World History For Dummies
  978-0-470-44654-6

FOOD, HOME, & MUSIC

978-0-7645-9904-0   978-0-470-43111-5

Also available:
- 30-Minute Meals For Dummies
  978-0-7645-2589-6
- Bartending For Dummies
  978-0-470-63312-0
- Brain Games For Dummies
  978-0-470-37378-1
- Gluten-Free Cooking For Dummies
  978-0-470-17810-2

- Home Improvement All-in-One Desk Reference For Dummies
  978-0-7645-5680-7
- Home Winemaking For Dummies
  978-0-470-67895-4
- Trumpet For Dummies
  978-0-470-67937-1
- Violin For Dummies
  978-0-470-83838-9
- Wine For Dummies
  978-0-470-04579-4

GARDENING

978-0-470-58161-2   978-0-470-57705-9

Also available:
- Gardening Basics For Dummies
  978-0-470-03749-2
- Organic Gardening For Dummies
  978-0-470-43067-5

- Sustainable Landscaping For Dummies 978-0-470-41149-0
- Vegetable Gardening For Dummies
  978-0-470-49870-5

Available wherever books are sold. For more information or to order direct: U.S. customers visit www.dummies.com or call 1-877-762-2974. U.K. customers visit www.wileyeurope.com or call 0800 243407. Canadian customers visit www.wiley.ca or call 1-800-567-4797.

GREEN/SUSTAINABLE

978-0-470-84098-6   978-0-470-59678-4

Also available:
- Alternative Energy For Dummies 978-0-470-43062-0
- Energy Efficient Homes For Dummies 978-0-470-37602-7

- Green Building & Remodeling For Dummies 978-0-470-17559-0
- Green Cleaning For Dummies 978-0-470-39106-8
- Green Your Home All-in-One For Dummies 978-0-470-40778-3

HEALTH & SELF-HELP

978-0-470-58589-4   978-0-470-445-39-6

Also available:
- Borderline Personality Disorder For Dummies 978-0-470-46653-7
- Breast Cancer For Dummies 978-0-7645-2482-0
- Celiac Disease For Dummies 978-0-470-16036-7
- Cognitive Behavioural Therapy For Dummies 978-0-470-66541-1
- Depression For Dummies 978-0-7645-3900-8

- Emotional Intelligence For Dummies 978-0-470-15732-9
- Healthy Aging For Dummies 978-0-470-14975-1
- Improving Your Memory For Dummies 978-0-7645-5435-3
- Neuro-linguistic Programming For Dummies 978-0-470-66543-5
- Understanding Autism For Dummies 978-0-7645-2547-6

HOBBIES & CRAFTS

978-0-470-28747-7   978-0-470-29112-2

Also available:
- Crochet Patterns For Dummies 97-0-470-04555-8
- Digital Scrapbooking For Dummies 978-0-7645-8419-0
- Home Decorating For Dummies 978-0-7645-4156-8
- Knitting Patterns For Dummies 978-0-470-04556-5

- Oil Painting For Dummies 978-0-470-18230-7
- Quilting For Dummies 978-0-7645-9799-2
- Sewing For Dummies 978-0-470-62320-6
- Word Searches For Dummies 978-0-470-45366-7

HOME & BUSINESS COMPUTER BASICS

978-0-470-49743-2

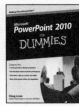

978-0-470-48765-5

Also available:
- Excel 2010 For Dummies
8-0-470-48953-6
- Office 2010 For Dummies
978-0-470-48998-7
- Pay Per Click Search Engine
Marketing For Dummies
978-0-471-75494-7

- PCs For Dummies 978-0-470-46542-4
- Search Engine Optimization For
Dummies 978-0-470-88104-0
- Web Analytics For Dummies
9780-470-09824-0

INTERNET & DIGITAL MEDIA

978-0-470-44417-7

978-0-470-39062-7

Also available:
- Blogging For Dummies
978-1-118-15194-5
- Facebook For Dummies
978-1-118-09562-1

- The Internet For Dummies
978-0-470-56095-2
- Twitter For Dummies
978-0-470-76879-2
- YouTube For Dummies
978-0-470-14925-6

MACINTOSH

978-0-470-87868-2

978-1-118-02205-4

Also available:
- iMac For Dummies
978-0-470-60737-4
- iPad For Dummies
978-1-118-02444-7
- iPod Touch For Dummies
978-1-118-12960-9

- iPod & iTunes For Dummies
978-1-118-13060-5
- MacBook For Dummies
978-0-470-76918-8
- Macs For Seniors For Dummies
978-0-470-43779-7
- Switching to a Mac For Dummies
978-1-118-02446-1

NETWORKING & SECURITY

978-0-470-53405-2

978-0-470-53791-6

Also available:
- Active Directory For Dummies
  978-0-470-28720-0
- Firewalls For Dummies
  978-0-7645-4048-6

- Identity Theft For Dummies
  978-0-470-56521-6
- TCP/IP For Dummies
  978-0-470-45060-4
- Wireless All-in-One For Dummies
  978-0-470-49013-6

PETS

978-0-470-60029-0

978-0-470-06805-2

Also available:
- Birds For Dummies 9780764551390
- Boxers For Dummies 9780764552854
- Cockatiels For Dummies
  9780764553110
- Ferrets For Dummies 9780470127230

- Golden Retrievers For Dummies
  9780764552670
- Horses For Dummies 9780764597978
- Puppies For Dummies
  9780470037171

SPORTS & FITNESS

978-0-471-76871-5

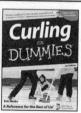

978-0-470-83828-0

Also available:
- Exercise Balls For Dummies
  978-0-7645-5623-4
- Coaching Hockey For Dummies
  978-0-470-83685-9
- Coaching Volleyball For Dummies
  978-0-470-46469-4
- Fitness For Dummies
  978-0-470-76759-7

- Lacrosse For Dummies
  978-0-470-22699-5
- Mixed Martial Arts For Dummies
  978-0-470-39071-9
- Sports Psychology For Dummies
  978-0-470-67659-2
- Wilderness Survival For Dummies
  978-0-470-45306-3
- Yoga with Weights For Dummies
  978-0-471-74937-0

WEB DEVELOPMENT

978-0-470-38541-8

978-0-470-38535-7

Also available:
- Adobe Creative Suite 4 Web Premium
  All-in-One For Dummies
  978-0-470-41407-1
- CSS Web Design For Dummies
  978-0-7645-8425-1
- HTML, XHTML & CSS For Dummies
  978-0-470-91659-9

- Joomla! For Dummies
  978-0-470-59902-0
- Web Design For Dummies
  978-0-471-78117-2
- Wikis For Dummies
  978-0-470-04399-8